THE KING COOKBOOK

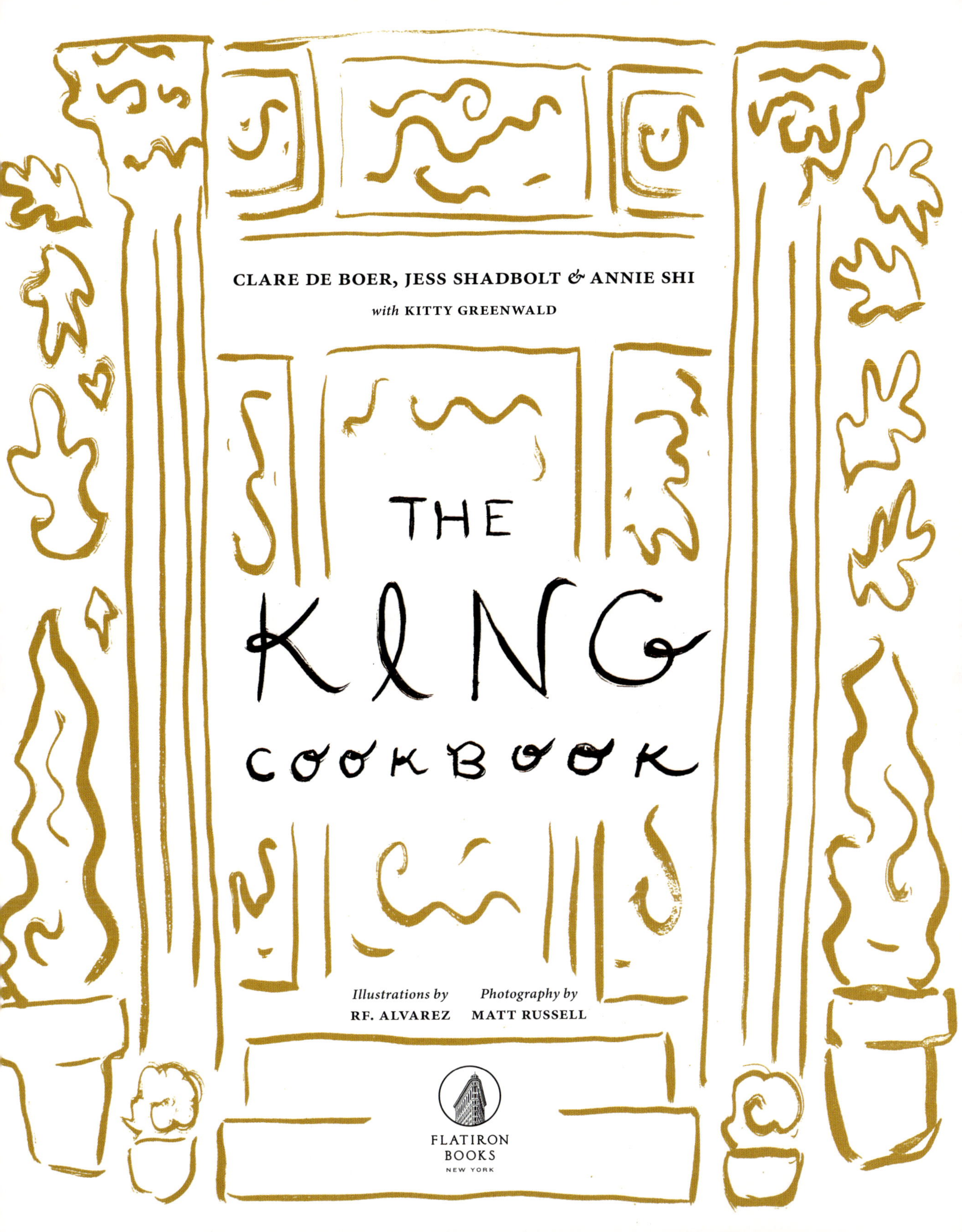

CLARE DE BOER, JESS SHADBOLT & ANNIE SHI
with KITTY GREENWALD

THE KING COOKBOOK

Illustrations by RF. ALVAREZ
Photography by MATT RUSSELL

FLATIRON BOOKS
NEW YORK

 Printed in China. For information, address Flatiron Books, 120 Broadway, New York, NY 10271. EU Representative: Macmillan Publishers Ireland Ltd., 1st Floor, The Liffey Trust Centre, 117–126 Sheriff Street Upper, Dublin 1, DO1 YC43.

www.flatironbooks.com

Designed by Shubhani Sarkar, sarkardesignstudio.com
Photography by Matt Russell
Illustrations by RF. Alvarez

Library of Congress Cataloging-in-Publication Data

Names: De Boer, Clare, author. | Shadbolt, Jessica, author. | Shi, Annie, author.
Title: The King cookbook / Clare de Boer, Jessica Shadbolt, & Annie Shi.
Description: First edition. | New York : Flatiron Books, 2025. | Includes index.
Identifiers: LCCN 2025000737 | ISBN 9781250868701 (paper over board) | ISBN 9781250868718 (ebook)
Subjects: LCSH: King (Restaurant) | Seasonal cooking. | Restaurants—New York (State)—New York. | LCGFT: Cookbooks.
Classification: LCC TX714 .D4225 2025 | DDC 641.59747/1—dc23/eng/20250208
LC record available at https://lccn.loc.gov/2025000737

First Edition: 2025

10 9 8 7 6 5 4 3 2 1

To King

CONTENTS

Welcome to KING

IN 2015, WHEN CLARE, JESS, AND I BEGAN SEARCHING FOR KING'S LOCATION. WHILE LOOKING, we were asked time and again, "What's your concept?" The question confused us. King was never a concept. It was our ideal restaurant, our first, one that celebrated the food and wine of France and Italy. Most important, King was to be an embodiment of how we like to dine—simply but with warmth and generosity.

Between the three of us, no one had ever worked in a New York City restaurant. Perhaps our lack of experience should have rattled us. But now, looking back, I believe our naivete was really a blessing.

The three of us met in London, where Jess and Clare worked at the River Café and I worked in finance (plus four weekends of potato peeling in a restaurant basement). In no time, we were friends who had found our common ground—strong appetites!

At the time, New York's dining scene was much different from that of London. It felt a lot flashier, and a daily-changing menu, our favorite way of dining, was largely unseen. We decided to land in New York, where I grew up, and open our first restaurant there. The three of us quit our jobs and moved across the ocean. There were infinite details to figure out in the lead-up to opening, but the important ones—how our cooking would taste, how our guests would feel—we were clear on.

Our dining room, we said, would be still enough to make space for the energy of service. Music would play quietly, so you'd never strain to hear the table's chatter. The lighting would be flattering but maybe a little too warm for social media. Above all, ours would be the kind of place where you'd end the night hours later than intended, drunk on deliciousness and the pleasure of company. And when you did get up, unsure of where the time had gone, the table would bear evidence to the evening's indulgence: dribbles of olive oil, rings of red wine, perhaps some lazy doodles, and certainly several empty coupes of grappa.

The food, the heart of it all, would be simple but familiar and irresistible. Our menus, written out each morning, would mark the season's subtle shifts—the fava bean at the start of spring, still a little green, would be braised, low and slow, to coax out its flavor. If you came back to dinner a few weeks later, the fava, now at its peak, would be served sott'olio—simply boiled and then held under good olive oil—so that its sweetness would shine.

Our friendship would provide the template for all the relationships forged under our roof, from the cooks to the servers to our guests. Though we lacked experience as restaurateurs, we intuitively knew that these connections would create the atmosphere to which guests would want to return.

Finding 18 King Street in SoHo was mostly luck. We'd spent months walking around the city and knocking on doors. We knew, quite literally, every listing in town. And then over half a year later, by complete coincidence, I walked into a restaurant called Mekong. It lived within a sun-dappled space on the corner of King Street and Sixth Avenue. We fell in love with the bones of the building—with the accordion doors that wrapped around the bar and the windows that hugged the dining room and that, from our soon-to-be terrace, you could see the Empire State Building. This was our spot, and we would call it King.

It goes without saying that the following year was equal parts frantic, joyful, and painful. Building a restaurant without experience is not for the faint of heart! We became plumbers and electricians before we even thought about menus and wine lists. Clare's mom drew the bar on the back of the napkin, Jess laid the floor tiles in the kitchen, and my dad was drafted daily to help with hanging shelving and single-handedly making every table in the dining room. We turned the space around in three months, and before we knew it we had built a restaurant. And then the real work began!

Now, every night at 5:30, King's lights are dimmed, the candles are lit, and soft music comes crooning out of our speakers. For me, it's the most beautiful hour: Our dark green facade soaks in the sun's last rays, while the dining room fills with the aroma of rosemary wafting from the kitchen. Our little but mighty bar, set and ready, twinkles in golden light.

Over the years, we've learned to honor and amplify the cadence of good dinners. As guests filter in, smiling servers greet regulars by name and offer them the evening's menu. Aperitifs arrive in long cool glasses alongside King's signature offering, a grilled carta di musica. Sculptural and dramatic, the paper-thin Sardinian flatbread comes doused in peppery olive oil with fried rosemary. It is our way of giving before there is any taking.

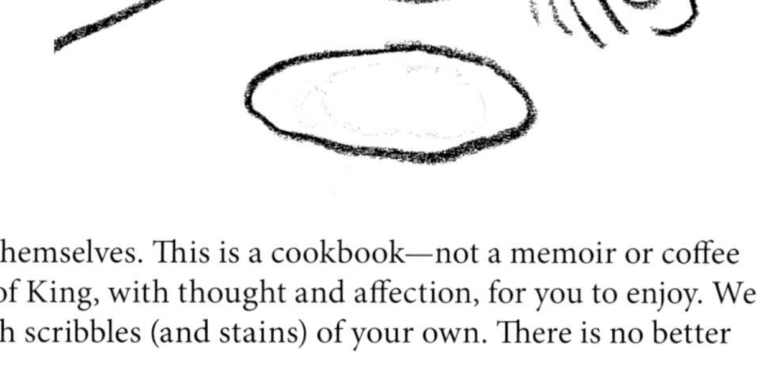

In this cookbook we have tried to bring the spirit of King to your kitchen: in the way our chapters are organized, which is the same way we would teach a new cook in the kitchen; in the drawings that our dear friend Robert has created; and in the tone of the writing and recipes themselves. This is a cookbook—not a memoir or coffee table book. We have distilled the best of King, with thought and affection, for you to enjoy. We hope you will mark up these pages with scribbles (and stains) of your own. There is no better way to eat or cook.

—Annie

How to use this book

THE DAY AT KING BEGINS AT TABLE 25, A LARGE ROUND TABLE IN THE CORNER OF THE DINING room. It's where morning light first peeps in over King Street. Chairs are stacked on every table, from the night before. The only sound is the hum of kitchen exhaust. In this near silence—before the fish arrives or delivery trolleys with artichokes and eggs bump into the basement—the menu is written, every day.

We pull a large sheet of parchment paper from our speed rack in the kitchen and begin to plot the bones of the menu, Sharpies in hand. Every menu has the same framework: nibbles (always panisse, our signature fried ribbons of chickpea batter) first and then three starters (a vegetable, a salad, and a small seafood or meat dish); next there's a single pasta and then three mains (a fish, a beef, and a wild card of pork, bird or rabbit, or lamb). To finish, a few slices and scoops . . .

King's menu is small because our kitchen is small. "This is it," we tell cooks entering for the first time. You can see the kitchen's entirety through a five-foot window in our dining room. At a squeeze, there's just enough room for three cooks, a dishwasher, a pantry shelf, and a few pots hanging by the stove.

Soon a new cook learns that there are no recipes at King and that she will be taught to cook. For the first six months, she will stand to the right of the stove, blanching greens and cooking beans. These staples are the foundations of the kitchen. She stays here until, like us, she loves the two more than anything. After some time, she'll instinctively blanch spinach, rainbow chard, and cima di rape in batches, seasoning their water with just the right amount of salt. And she'll gently simmer pots of beans, perfumed with sage. Long before a roasting tray gets pulled from a shelf, these will be mastered . . .

Next she will learn to make the sauces we rely on day in and day out. Salsa verde and tapenade come first: they require knife skills and a delicate hand. Whipped bottarga, anchoïade, and fonduta follow. Each gets made with ingredients carefully selected to evoke a sunny Mediterranean coastline or an Alpine lodge. Our pantry—with capers, olive oil, lemons, olives, nuts, and more—lets us travel from our corner on King Street across France and Italy.

That cook will soon learn to dress a salad and to grill, roast, and braise all sorts of fish and meat. If there's interest in pasta, to the bench she goes! If butchery is preferred, there are rabbits to break down, quail to spatchcock, and hanger steaks to trim. By the end, King's new cook has become an old cook, capable of re-creating the heartfelt, rustic cooking that defines our small kitchen.

We have mirrored that cook's journey in the pages that follow to teach you as we have taught everyone who has passed through our kitchen over the years. Feel free to follow suit, or to flip through and cherry-pick seasonal recipes that appeal. The collection has been organized to follow the contours of our menus, beginning with nibbles and ending with desserts. To get you started, we've laid out our beloved and most used pantry items and staple sauces. With these—and recipes taken from throughout the book—you will be equipped to make dishes of your own as we would at King. Instructional photography grids are included to show you how we put plates together using components from various chapters. There are also some of our signature stand-alone recipes. Our hope is that this book feels like a flick through the pages of our dog-eared kitchen notebooks.

And since we love nothing more than a party, we've included four celebratory menus, one per season, to offer some ideas for larger feasts. Annie has also offered up some wine pairing tips to make sure that your guests are well watered. For these occasions, we believe that more is certainly the merrier! These celebrations are for you, your family, and friends.

But it all begins with a bean! Let's get some on to soak.

—Jess & Clare

CHAPTER 1

King's pantry

On the shelves of our pantry sit the worker bees of our kitchen: the jars, bottles, tins, and parcels that contain the ingredients we use daily. We think of the pantry as the circulatory system that feeds the heart of our cooking. No recipe begins without one of these provisions from the pantry, and almost every plate is finished with one too—a marinated olive, a pinch of fresh herbs, a grating of bottarga di muggine or salty cheese. Traditionally, pantry items are limited to dry goods, but ours extend to the cheeses, herbs, and cured meats we keep on hand too.

At the top of this list are the items we reach for without thinking: olive oil, salt, and lemons. After that, the rest of our "musts" are listed alphabetically here. All are important and serve a purpose.

Since our pared-back approach to cooking gives little to hide behind, we choose these items as we do all our ingredients—with great care. Where it is especially important, we have specified brands and other significant details. But, as ever, know that flexibility is fine, and if you simply buy the best quality available to you, you're off to the races. A well-stocked pantry can take you anywhere.

OLIVE OIL

Olive oil defines the taste of King. We use three: a Tuscan single-estate fresh press from Capezzana; our own fresh press from friends at Sesti, also in Tuscany; and a Californian Arbequina. The laser-green bottles of fresh press are for salads and for finishing dishes. The nutty, round Arbequina is for cooking.

We receive our Italian oils in November, just after October's olive harvest. Like freshly pressed juices, they are vivid and intense, and we celebrate their arrival with simple dishes—vessels for the oil—like a bowl of chickpeas or plain ravioli. Cooking diminishes their vibrant flavor, so we avoid direct heat, but pouring an oil—not drizzling it—onto warm, steaming food magnifies its flavor. So we pour these oils over meat and fish just off the grill. Or onto a soup pulled off the flame. Everything—*everything*—that leaves our pass gets "finished" with a pour.

Our California cooking oil is less precious but still something we're proud of. It's extra virgin, with a fresh taste and scent. Neither "oily" nor peppery, it adds a clean, rich flavor without getting in the way or tasting greasy. We use it in robust vinaigrettes and sauces, so as not to compete with mustard's pepperiness or a roasted walnut's sweetness.

In this book, we assume olive oil is always on hand in your kitchen. To encourage extra pours and seasoning to taste, we've listed the oil without a specific measurement unless a cup of it or more is required.

SALT

Food should never be "salty." Rather, the primary flavor should be of the ingredient itself, enhanced by salt. We mostly use Maldon, a flaky sea salt, for everything other than blanching water—we think it has the best texture and flavor. Blanching water is seasoned with kosher salt. Before adding anything to a boiling pot, we dip a finger into the water and taste, making sure the water is as salty as the sea. If it's Dead Sea–salty, dilute!

We use coarse sea salt, with large crystals, when baking whole fish or small birds (see pages 247 and 289), encasing them in a shell. When a salt crust is baked, the salt hardens and creates a chamber that gently steams the ingredient through.

In the pages that follow, if a type of salt is not specified, assume we mean Maldon. If you only have kosher, that's fine—but keep in mind that the salinity will be more concentrated, so hold back a bit more at first and taste as you go. Kosher salt can also be used instead of coarse salt for salt-roasting, but it's harder to clean away at the table.

Generally, salt is listed in the ingredient lists without a specific measurement to encourage seasoning as you go. If a large amount is required, as when salt-roasting, we do specify that measurement.

LEMONS

Juiced, zested, peeled, and/or preserved, lemons are among our most reached-for ingredients.

Since lemon juice is most pure when freshly pressed (left to oxidize, its brightness turns acrid), we juice as we go, always straining the juice once it's pressed. We use lemons predominantly in dressings for salads and marinades for warm greens. If acid is needed in any dish, we taste and often add a squeeze of lemon.

The zest holds all the oils and fragrance. We grate it over anything wanting a lift, particularly salads, fresh pastas, and seafood. Be careful not to puncture the white pith, as it is particularly bitter.

ANCHOVIES

Our anchovies come from Agostino Recca in Sicily. Cured for twelve months and packed, heads-on, in salt, these are large, firm, and intensely flavorful. Within their tins, the fillets last indefinitely.

Preparing anchovies is meditative: Stand over the sink and handle one at a time. First, rinse off the salty husk, then remove and discard the head. With cold water running over it, split the anchovy lengthwise and remove the spine, dorsal fin, and guts. Lay each cleaned fillet over an inverted sieve to dry as you press on with the rest of the tin, repeating the exercise until it is empty. To finish, stack all the cleaned anchovies in a container and top off with olive oil. Submerged and covered, these will last for days in the fridge.

At their simplest, cleaned anchovies are a chef's breakfast, set over a wedge of unsalted butter spread onto filone, a classic Italian yeasted bread.

We like to add anchovy fillets, marinated in olive oil, lemon zest, dried chili, and fennel seeds, to plates of antipasti or drape them over grilled fish. When the fish has been pulled straight from the grates, the anchovies will melt slightly from the residual heat. Roughly chopped fillets sneak their way into rabbit, lamb, and beef braises, adding a depth of flavor that even the anchovy-averse are unable to detect (but always unwittingly appreciate).

BEANS AND BEAN WATER

We consider ourselves *mangia fagiolis*, bean eaters, like the Tuscans. With each day's menu, we do a bean check: Have we used a bean in every dish? Is the menu *too* beany? Most days we use two or three varieties. Sometimes they get dressed with acid and herbs, always with olive oil. Then they are either left whole or smashed.

Dried borlotti, cannellini, and chickpeas are year-round staples. Fresh cannellini and borlotti are highlights of summer. Shelling them is a social activity: we gather and turn mountains of them into bowls of shucked beans.

Bean water is as precious as the beans themselves—we never throw it out. Pouring it into braises, stockpots, and soups, we treat it like liquid gold. And if there is any left, we freeze it just as we do our stocks.

BOTTARGA DI MUGGINE

There is a variety of bottargas, a delicacy of dried gray mullet roe made along the Mediterranean coastline. But for us, there is only the Sardinian bottarga di muggine. It is rich and briny and tastes of salty sea air. We are completely addicted. Once it has been peeled, we shower it over everything using a cheese grater: carta di musica, grilled seafood, blistered greens, pasta, salads . . .

Any nubbins that don't get past the grater are reserved for sauces. We make three of these: a vinaigrette (page 243) for puntarelle, blanched agretti, or broccolini; a butter (page 23) for asparagus or grilled fish; and a velvety whipped sauce (page 34) that is often the base for our winter-leaf salads or a dressing for raw fennel and Sungold tomatoes (page 46).

Peeled bottarga di muggine (wrapped carefully so it doesn't absorb odors) lasts for weeks in the fridge.

CAPERS

We prefer small, tender salt-cured capers. These are packed in salt, just like our anchovies, and their brine preserves both flavor and shape far better than a liquid cure. To prepare them, shake off the salt crust and gently run them under cold water in a sieve for 5 to 10 minutes, dissolving the salt until the capers taste briny but not eyewateringly so. Once cleaned and dried, they hold under oil for a week in the fridge.

However, brined or oil-preserved capers are more readily available, and these can be substituted as needed. They will need to be drained and briefly rinsed before use.

We mostly roast capers directly in a sauté pan, along with white meat or fish, heating them until the buds burst open. Or we chop them up, for brightness, and add them raw to salads and sauces.

Always, when it comes to capers, it's best to leave diners wanting another one or two than to overuse.

CRÈME FRAÎCHE AND CHEESE

In our kitchen, we always have one hard cheese (almost always Parmesan) and one soft one (usually ricotta or ricotta salata). Hard cheeses are most flavorful just after they've been cut from the wheel. With fresh cheeses, the fresher the better!

Parmesan's robust flavor—corresponding to its age—stands up to hearty winter dishes and ragùs. Beyond grating it over pasta, we use it in fonduta, an Alpine sauce made with crème fraîche, egg yolk, and lots of Parmesan (see page 28), which we ladle onto boiled vegetables, polenta, and crespelle (see page 140).

Soft cheeses are more delicate and versatile. We stuff fresh ricotta into filled pastas and spread it over carta di musica. Sweet and creamy, it's luxurious without being heavy. We like soft, chalky goat cheeses for French-style salads (see page 101) and cheese plates.

Ricotta salata has a crumbly texture that's ideal for shaving over tender leaves, herbs, and other delicate flavors. We buy it in large wedges and, using a chef's knife, shave shards—large, thin, and architectural—right off the block.

CURED MEATS

Beyond serving cured meats as part of an antipasto plate, we use them to add savory richness. Prosciutto brings a gentle nuttiness, speck a smokiness, and lardo an elegant fatty flavor. We drape thin slices over roasted meats (Pork Chops Roasted with Cherries, Thyme, and Prosciutto, page 220) and polenta to elevate them, turning the simple into something far more sumptuous. We also wrap and roll lean cuts of meat—like loin of rabbit—in slices of prosciutto (see page 270) for extra flavor and a bit of snap.

Any leftover butts should be added to a pot of beans (e.g., Cassoulet, page 296) or reduced with some cream and sage for a pasta sauce (see page 161). If you have extra lardo, whiz it up and spread it over toast or a pork belly that will gently roast (see page 215).

FRESH CHILIES

We subscribe to the Italian philosophy: You needn't make food "heat-y" thrice. Meaning, choose among garlic, black pepper, and fresh chilies. Although we sometimes use two of these (for contrasting levels of heat), we *never* use all three.

Holland chilies, a less-hot relative of the Calabrian chili, are pillar-box red and measure (with their pointy tips) 4 to 6 inches in length. Their mild sweetness is slightly smoky, and their heat won't blow your socks off. This is our chili of choice.

After they've blistered on the grill, we peel off their charred skins and seed them, leaving only their hat-like stems in place. Save the skins and seeds to make yourself a Rizzo cocktail (page 60).

Our cleaned Hollands are served bare or marinated in oil with some acid and soft herbs. We drape them over everything. Other times, we make a sauce by whizzing them with almonds and a handful of grated cheese (for pastas) or acid (for anything grilled) in a blender.

In the summer, we also use Jimmy Nardellos. They are a little larger and sweeter, with a thicker skin. If you have the patience, grill, peel, and seed these and stuff with ricotta.

GARLIC

Always remove the clove's embedded green root and stem from garlic before using. These add an acrid taste. Frequently we'll crush cloves with Maldon salt—using the flat side of a chef's knife—to form a raw paste that slips into sauces and marinades.

When recipes call for cooked garlic, chop it fine and gently warm in olive oil, taking care not to burn any tiny pieces. Once it's turned golden, it's gone too far.

HERBS

Hard herbs—sage, rosemary, thyme, bay—are strong enough to withstand long, slow cooking, since their astringency diminishes with time and heat. When it comes to bay leaves, we only use fresh, which lend a floral rather than dusty flavor. We sometimes fry hard herbs to intensify their flavor—fried rosemary is flaked over our house bread, carta di musica. Except for resting cuts of meat over a bundle of hard herbs, we seldom use these branches raw. We sprinkle them over salads and pastas or use them to marinate grilled vegetables.

Soft herbs—marjoram, parsley, fennel sprigs, basil, mint, tarragon—go into salads, warm beans, potatoes. . . . They transform everything. We crush them, along with salt and lemon juice, in our mortar and pestle to make Salmoriglio (page 186), a green, herby oil from Italy.

The only dried herb we use is wild oregano from the hillsides of Sicily. It comes in a glamorous bouquet that we roll between our palms to make oregano rain. It's quite twiggy, so it pairs best with wet things—like olive oil and pan juices—to avoid a scratched mouth. With its delicate floral flavor, dried oregano is ideal for seafood, vegetables, and, in particular, tomatoes.

Throughout the book, you will sometimes see us refer to small or large handfuls of herbs when a precise quantity wouldn't define the outcome. For guidance, a small handful is 5 to 7 herb sprigs, and a large handful is more of a bunch.

KITCHEN WINE

We cook with wine that we would like to drink. Occasionally it happens simultaneously.

Since cooking concentrates flavor, its quality is important. Anything too unbalanced—too acidic or too tannic—will reduce poorly. In general, we find that Soave, a dry white wine from the Veneto region in Italy, cooks down beautifully and provides lift to dishes while rounding them out, especially when it comes to sauces and braises. For reds, we prefer Sangiovese or Montepulciano: both have body and acidity in equal measure.

Many of our dishes hail from specific regions of France or Italy. In these instances, we cook with wines from the region. That old adage, what grows together goes together, holds true.

In spring, when we look to Provence for inspiration, we often use our own King rosé, which comes from Corbieres in the South of France, in any recipe that calls for wine. Made from grenache gris grapes, our rosé is always a perfect balance of lush fruit and salty minerality.

NUTS

Walnuts, pine nuts, hazelnuts, and almonds are used in both our sweet and savory dishes. We buy all nuts whole and raw and roast them ourselves if they're heading to a salad. We leave them raw for many of our sauces, including Salsa Mandorla (page 31) and Salsa di Noci with Pepperoncini (page 32), using the nuts' high fat content and mellow flavor to impart richness and texture without turning the result roast-y.

Blitzing nuts in a food processor releases their natural oils, making them ideal for emulsifying with olive oil, herbs, and chilies.

OLIVES

Soft-skinned fruity Taggiasca olives from Liguria are our favorites. Their inky pop and high flesh-to-pit ratio means they are both an excellent table olive and a saucepan ingredient. When our cooking goes to Provence, we prefer the more mellow, nutty flavor of a Niçoise olive. When the Niçoise is combined with garlic, tomato, and anchovy, it creates the quintessential flavor that lies at the heart of the Provençal kitchen.

POLENTA

Patience and greed are both required when making polenta. We use a coarse grind (Moretti Bramata is our preferred brand), which requires a long cook and produces a creamy pot.

Our polenta cooks in unsalted water for about an hour or so, the exact timing depending on the size of the batch. We season it at the end with handfuls of grated Parmesan and butter, and we know that it is ready when second tastes are irresistible.

We also do as the Venetians do and make a lighter pot, finished with a dash of white wine, dried chili, and fennel seeds, for grilled scallops or clams.

Left to cool, a pan of soft-cooked polenta firms and sets. We cut out wedges for the grill or fryer. Grilled wedges with quail (see page 281) or Ligurian Olive Sauce (see page 30) are particularly delicious, but we use these often, because their versatility never fails.

PRESERVED TOMATOES

For nine months of the year, when we are without fresh tomatoes, we rely on canned tomatoes. Like many, we favor the San Marzano. Harvested and immediately preserved whole, they are intensely tomatoey, low in acid, and, thanks to their thick skin and low seed ratio, great for slow-cooking.

A slow-cooked tomato sauce, seasoned only with slivered garlic, olive oil, and salt (see page 27), should be patiently reduced for hours. It can be added to the base of stews, braises, and soups for extra depth and acidity. We also take great comfort in a simple bowl of fresh tagliarini tossed with a slow-cooked tomato sauce.

RED WINE VINEGAR

Like table wine, red wine vinegar ranges greatly in quality. There are scorchingly acidic vinegars with minimal flavor and balanced ones that transform when heated. Ours is the latter.

It comes from the Volpaia Estate in Tuscany and has a nuanced flavor that's no sharper than that of a lemon. We use it as a marinade for rabbit (see page 268), and brush more on as it grills, accentuating the meat's sweetness. We roast Treviso radicchio (see page 198) in it, adding splashes as if the vinegar were wine. While vinegar is optional in many sauces, our Salsa Verde, Walnut Aillade, and Mustard Vinaigrette (see pages 33, 269, and 29) rely upon it.

CHAPTER 2

Foundational Recipes

THIS CHAPTER HOLDS OUR RECIPES FOR SAUCES, VINAIGRETTES, CONDIMENTS, LEGUMES, preserves, pastries, and purees. We lean on them daily.

We've placed this collection up front so you can pull from it as we do: this is our arsenal. With these recipes, a simply seared beef steak can turn into a Tuscan feast—just add a spoonful of cooked ceci (chickpeas; page 15) and a scattering of grilled chilies (page 36). Or, if you prefer, it can become an Alpine meal if you serve bubbling polenta (page 21) alongside the sliced steak.

Our hope is that you come to use these recipes (as well as their relatives scattered throughout this book) whenever you're creating a dish of your own, spinning the flavor wheel to go in whatever direction you fancy. If the pantry ingredients in the previous chapter are your building blocks, these recipes are your paints and plasters—adding color, stature, and finesse.

We've grouped them according to function. To begin, we have our greens, beans, and polenta. These will turn any meal into more, but just as they are, they also hold their own and make a fine dinner with some bread or a salad. Then come sauces, our keys to dressing up any plate. At the end, we've included our recipes for preserves, chicken stock, tomato sauce, and pastry. All these *can* be bought, of course, but they are best when they come from your kitchen.

A NOTE ON BLANCHING GREENS

Blanching greens was the first lesson Clare and Jess were each taught in the kitchen at the River Café, and to this day, the technique remains integral to our cooking both at the restaurant and in our homes. Here we endeavor to pass on the lessons learned: How to season the water correctly—salty, but not overpoweringly so. How not to overcrowd the pot, so there is plenty of room for the greens to bob and boil. How we add a couple of peeled garlic cloves when cooking cavolo nero but not for the other varieties. How to occasionally stir the greens to ensure they cook evenly. When to pull them from the water—just as the stems have softened and there is no bite. How to drain them in a colander, turning the bundles every so often to let the steam escape and prevent them from overcooking as they cool. And, finally, how to gently press them to release all the water so that they will be thirsty for the olive oil that will inevitably dress them.

Greens and some beans. We love nothing more.

Blanched Greens—
a Recipe of Sorts

Serves 4

Salt
3 bunches (about 1½ pounds) spinach,
Swiss or rainbow chard,
dandelion greens, or similar
Olive oil

Fill a large pot with cold water and season with a large pinch of salt. Bring the water to a boil and taste; it should be seawater-salty.

While the water comes to a boil, prepare the greens by trimming off any tough or wilted stems.

Add the greens to the boiling water and, using a pair of tongs, gently stir them so that they are submerged in the water. If necessary, top up the pot to make sure they remain completely covered as they cook.

The greens are cooked when the stems are soft and have no bite—very much the Italian way, in contrast to the flash-blanching of the French. Spinach will cook in a moment (3 minutes), while the more robust stems of chard, kale, or dandelion greens will take a little longer (7 to 10 minutes).

Using a slotted spoon, remove the greens from the water, transfer to a colander, and allow to drain and cool. (If you are scaling up, keep the water boiling and continue cooking in batches.) Turn the greens every now and then as they cool to let the steam escape.

When the greens are cool enough to handle, gently press out any residual water. At this point, they can be covered and refrigerated for up to 2 days and then easily rewarmed with some olive oil and a splash of cold water in a saucepan when ready to serve.

Or, if using them immediately, add the drained greens to a saucepan along with a tablespoon of olive oil. Warm over gentle heat and taste, adding more salt if needed.

Serve with a wedge of lemon and finish with more olive oil.

Cavolo Nero Puree

(and Cima Puree)

A puree that is as much about greens as it is about olive oil. We use our fresh-press olive oil here and we recommend that you use a similarly good bottle.

It's important to squeeze all the water from boiled leaves before dressing them. It primes them to fully absorb the oil's flavor.

To turn the cavolo nero puree into a cima puree, just swap in broccoli rabe (*cima* in Italian) for the kale.

Makes 3 cups

Salt
2 garlic cloves
2 bunches (about 1 pound) cavolo nero
or lacinato kale, stems removed
Olive oil (at least 1½ cups)

Fill a large pot with salted water. Add the garlic and bring the water to a rumbling boil over high heat. Add the cavolo nero and boil until its leaves can be easily squashed against the side of the pot, 10 to 15 minutes. Transfer the leaves to a colander to drain; retain the poached garlic and at least ¼ cup of the blanching water. (If using broccoli instead of cavolo nero [see headnote], shave a few minutes from the cook time—but check that the stems have absolutely no bite before turning off the heat.)

Thoroughly squeeze the leaves dry to wring out any remaining water. Roughly chop them and then add them and the poached garlic to a food processor. Run the blade until a smooth puree forms. With the blade still running, gradually blend in 2 tablespoons of the reserved blanching water to loosen the puree slightly. Then, with the processor running, slowly pour in the olive oil, adding 1½ to 2 cups, or enough so a glossy puree forms. Turn off the machine, taste, and season with salt. Blitz in more splashes of the reserved water and/or additional olive oil if necessary.

If you're not using it straightaway, cover the puree with a thin film of olive oil to prevent oxidation. Sealed and held in the fridge, it keeps for 1 to 2 days.

Erbette Saltate

Erbette saltate translates to "braised greens." This creamy contorno goes well with almost everything. On its own, topped with a grilled chili (page 36), it's also perfect.

Serves 4 to 6 generously

Salt
6 garlic cloves
4 bunches (about 2 pounds) cavolo nero, broccoli rabe, or dandelion greens, or a mix of all three, stems removed
2 generous pinches crumbled dried red chilies
Olive oil

Bring a large pot of salted water with 2 of the garlic cloves to a boil over high heat. When the water is at a rumble, add the greens and cook until the leaves are completely soft, about 15 minutes (yes, that long!). Throughout, press them down to submerge them as often as necessary. When the thickest parts of the stems are soft enough to be squashed against the side of the pot, drain, transfer to a colander, and let the excess water steam off; discard the garlic cloves.

When the greens are cool enough to handle, wring out their water, and then wring again. Once they are balled up and bone-dry, transfer to a cutting board and blot up any remaining moisture. Finely chop them and then run the knife through them once or twice more.

Thinly slice the remaining 4 garlic cloves. Clean the pot you used to boil the greens and place it over low heat. Add ¾ cup olive oil, the sliced garlic, chili, and a pinch of salt and warm until the garlic softens and sizzles but doesn't turn golden, less than a minute. Stir in the chopped greens and gently braise them until they absorb the oil's flavor, about 5 minutes.

As they finish cooking, taste the greens for salt and adjust as needed. Off the heat, drizzle generously with additional olive oil.

Dried Borlotti, Cocos Blancs, Flageolets, or Chickpeas

When cooking dried beans, we choose the freshest possible and simmer them over low, even heat. Only a few bubbles at a time should break the water's surface. As they cook, skim off any foam that rises, and top the pot off with more water if needed. But there should never be more than 2 inches of liquid, and never less than a half-inch, covering the beans.

This recipe makes a pot of plump beans that burst apart when lightly crushed with the back of a spoon. To get flageolets and borlotti creamy and puffed, we use both the stovetop and the oven. We add a tomato (fresh if possible) to their cooking liquor for acidity and extra body.

Once the beans are cooked, we cool them in the liquor to keep them from drying out. We make our bean water as flavorful as the beans themselves. When the pot has fully cooled, we use the beans straightaway or leave them, in their liquid in the fridge, for 3 to 4 days (they're actually best after a day or two). The bean water is never discarded it's essential for loosening purees and enriching soups. If we don't use it right away, we store it like a chicken stock in the fridge or freezer.

Dried beans are best soaked in cold water for at least 8 hours. To soak them, pour the beans into a wide pot and cover them with twice their volume of cool water. Soak the beans overnight in the fridge if possible, but if not, on the countertop. Do not soak dried beans for more than 2 days—as a rule, it's always best to cook the beans for longer than to oversoak. If the soaking water fizzes, signaling fermentation, the flavor starts going off.

Makes 4 cups

2 cups dried borlotti beans, coco beans, flageolets, or chickpeas, soaked in cool water for at least 8 hours
A few sprigs of sage
1 head garlic, halved across its equator
1 fresh red chili
Olive oil
1 large tomato, fresh or canned, sliced in half; omit if cooking chickpeas
Salt

Drain the beans in a colander and rinse them with cold water. Place them in a wide heavy pot and cover with 2 inches of cold water. Add the sage sprigs, split garlic, chili, and a generous glug of olive oil, enough to cover much of the water's surface in a thin film. If cooking borlotti, flageolets, or cocos blancs, add the tomato.

TOP WITH A *CARTOUCHE*, A CHEF-Y TERM FOR A PAPER LID: To make one, scrunch up a piece of parchment paper that is wide enough to cover your pot's contents. Then unscrunch it and lay it over the liquid. The cartouche will keep too much of the water from evaporating and allow the beans to cook more evenly. (In general, using a cartouche allows everything to stay moist

(Continued)

and sealed while allowing some evaporation.) Or, if you don't have parchment paper, simply cover the pot with a lid. Bring the water to a simmer over medium heat, skimming away any scum that rises. Once the water is mostly clear, reduce the heat to medium-low and gently simmer, slow and steady, topping the pot up with extra splashes of water as needed, until the beans are cooked through.

For borlotti, flageolets, and chickpeas, you'll likely need 2 to 3 hours of simmering (older dried beans will take longer). For cocos blancs, 1½ to 2 hours should do. In all cases, as the beans finish cooking, add smaller splashes of water as needed. When done, the beans should be submerged by about ½ inch of liquid and individual beans should taste creamy and yield to the slightest pressure. For flageolets, transfer the pot to a 500-degree oven for an additional 10 minutes to finish plumping. Irrespective of the bean, taste at least three beans from different parts of the pot to ensure they are all cooked. If any still have a bite, keep simmering (or roasting) until samples pass the test.

Remove the pot from the heat and generously season the bean water with salt to taste. Let the beans rest in their liquor until they have absorbed the seasoning and cooled to room temperature, at least 30 minutes. Remove the spent garlic, sage, and chili; if you will be making a puree, save the garlic. Taste the beans after they've rested and cooled to ensure they're properly seasoned.

Smashed Beans

When dried beans are slightly overcooked or when we're after a soft texture, we drain the cooked beans (always holding on to their liquor) and blitz them with plenty of olive oil to make a smooth, creamy puree. For a coarser smash, we use a hand whisk to crush the beans.

Keep the reserved bean water on hand to adjust the consistency as needed—smashed beans will stiffen as they sit.

Makes 2 cups

2 cups cooked beans (see page 15),
held in at least 2 cups of their cooking liquor
Olive oil
Salt

Warm the beans in their cooking liquor over medium heat until they are heated through, about 10 to 15 minutes.

Turn off the heat and, using a slotted spoon, transfer the beans to a food processor (keep the pot with the cooking liquor nearby). Run the blade until a rough puree forms, 1 to 2 minutes. With the blade still running, drizzle in ¾ cup olive oil and continue whizzing until very smooth. If the puree is too thick or lacking shine, blitz in splashes of the reserved cooking water, a few tablespoons at a time. Taste for seasoning and add salt and/or olive oil as needed.

Serve the smashed beans warm. Or, to serve later, reserve a cup or two of the bean cooking water to loosen the smash over low heat right before serving.

Baked Fresh Borlotti Beans

In July, we fill our bags with fresh borlotti beans from the Union Square Greenmarket, New York's most vibrant farmers' market. Shelling them takes place at our back door on King Street.

They require no soaking and cook much faster than dried beans. We almost always bake them, with a split fresh tomato to further celebrate the summer bounty, to ensure they cook evenly.

Makes 4 cups

3 cups shelled fresh borlotti beans
A sprig of sage
1 head garlic, halved across its equator
1 fresh red chili
2 medium tomatoes, sliced in half
Olive oil
Salt

Preheat the oven to 450 degrees. Place the beans in a large deep baking dish and cover with 2 inches of cool water. Add the sage, split garlic, chili, tomatoes, and about ¼ cup olive oil. Cover the dish with aluminum foil, pinching it shut at the edges.

Bake the beans in the oven for 1 hour.

Remove the foil and check that the beans have softened at their centers; taste a few from different parts of the dish to be sure. Season with salt and another glug of olive oil, about ¼ cup. Return the beans to the oven and bake, uncovered, until the liquid has reduced and just skims the top of the beans, about 10 minutes. Remove from the oven and let the beans cool slightly before serving.

Or, if cooking the beans in advance, hold them in their cooking liquor and, once cooled, store them in the fridge for 2 to 3 days. To reheat, gently warm on the stovetop or in the oven. If the beans look thirsty, add a splash of water.

Lentils

Castelluccio lentils from Umbria in Italy are round and tiny, and they cook brilliantly and evenly. Their flavor is distinctively earthy. As they don't call for a soak, or a low-and-slow simmer, they are a staple in our kitchen.

Lentils are susceptible to overcooking. We undercook ours slightly and then let them rest in their hot cooking liquor so they end up just right.

Makes 6 cups

2 cups lentils, preferably Castelluccio
A sprig of sage
1 head garlic, halved across its equator
1 fresh red chili
1 medium fresh or canned tomato, halved if fresh
Olive oil
Salt

Place the lentils in a colander and rinse under cold running water. Tip the rinsed lentils into a medium pot and cover with 2 inches of cool water. Add the sage, garlic, chili, and tomato and drizzle in 2 to 3 tablespoons olive oil, enough to create a thin film across the water's surface.

Bring the lentils to a simmer over medium heat and cook until just tender and still ever so slightly toothsome at the center, 12 to 15 minutes. Season with salt, but keep in mind that since the lentils will continue to absorb the seasoned cooking liquor, you do not want to oversalt.

After the lentils have rested and fully softened, about 20 minutes, taste and adjust the seasoning with salt as needed. Serve the lentils right away, drained of their liquid and finished with oil. Or, alternatively, cool and store them covered in their liquor in the fridge for up to 3 days; reheat gently before serving.

Polenta

Serves 8

10½ cups water, plus more as needed
3½ cups coarse polenta

FOR SOFT POLENTA

4 tablespoons unsalted butter, or more to taste
½ cup finely grated Parmesan cheese, or more to taste
Salt (optional)

FOR SET POLENTA

½ teaspoon crushed fennel seeds
¼ teaspoon crushed red chili flakes
½ cup dry white wine
Olive oil
Salt

Bring the water to a boil in a large, roomy pot. Reduce the heat to low and stream in the polenta, whisking to break up any lumps. Then keep whisking until the polenta begins to thicken, about 5 minutes.

Cook the polenta slowly for about 1 hour and 15 minutes, stirring occasionally; once it becomes porridge-like in consistency, you will need to stir and scrape down the pot's sides every 5 minutes to prevent sticking. Add splashes of water as needed to loosen the polenta if it gets too thick (it should end up thick but pourable). The polenta is cooked when the grains are soft and not at all gritty. Remove the pot from the heat.

AT THIS POINT, YOU CAN GO IN TWO DIRECTIONS: Soft or set polenta is a versatile side dish.

For soft, lava-like polenta, add the butter and Parmesan to the steaming pot as soon as you've removed it from the heat. This recipe's measurements are a guide: We add enough butter and Parmesan so a second taste is compulsory. A little salt may be needed, but that depends on the saltiness of your butter and cheese. Serve immediately.

For set polenta, add the spices, wine, and a tablespoon or two of olive oil, as well as a good pinch of salt. Stir to combine, taste, and add more salt as needed.

Pour the polenta into a 13-by-18-inch pan (half sheet pan) smeared with olive oil. We like our set polenta about 1½ inches thick, so choose a pan that is deep and large enough to give a similar result. Allow the polenta to fully cool, at least 1 hour, then cover with plastic wrap and chill in the fridge until fully firm, at least 12 hours. Set polenta holds for 3 to 4 days in the refrigerator.

To finish, slice the polenta into any size or shape you desire. Set up a scorchingly hot fire in a grill or place a large heavy frying or grill pan over high heat. If using a pan, add enough olive oil to generously slick the pan's bottom, at least ¼ cup. Lift the pieces out of the pan and season each with salt and a drizzle of olive oil. Lay the slices on the grill grate or in the pan and sear on both sides until grill marks set in, 2 to 3 minutes per side. If searing a large number of wedges, do not overcrowd them, or flipping will be difficult. And, finally, only flip once the polenta gives the nod; if it sticks or offers any resistance at all, give it more time.

Aioli

We steer away from thick, gloopy aiolis, favoring a silkier wobble. To master the technique, you may want to develop aioli-making confidence by starting with a bowl and whisk rather than a blender—that way offers more control. Before beating in oil, place the bowl on a damp cloth to hold it in place. Once you master the pace required, go ahead and graduate to a blender.

Either way, when adding the oil to the yolks, slow and steady wins this race. If you're too heavy-handed, and your aioli breaks, begin again with a clean bowl and slowly drizzle the "mistake" into a fresh yolk, whisking it in as if it were the oil. Once incorporated, continue on with fresh oil—no one needs to be the wiser.

Makes 2 cups

½ garlic clove
Salt
2 large egg yolks
Juice of 2 lemons, or more to taste
Olive oil (at least 1½ cups)

Using the side of a knife, smush the garlic with a pinch of salt on your cutting board to form a paste.

Add the egg yolks to a blender, along with the garlic paste, a good pinch of salt, and the lemon juice. Run the blade for a moment before starting to slowly add the oil, drop by drop. Once you've incorporated ½ cup oil, the aioli should be stable. Stop the blade, taste, and season with salt and/or more lemon juice if necessary.

With the blade running, very slowly blend in another 1 cup oil. Toward the end, intersperse the additions of oil with flicks of tepid water, about ¼ cup in total, to give the aioli a silky texture. Adding all the water at once, at the end, could break the emulsion. Season to taste with lemon juice and/or salt again if needed, cover, and refrigerate.

Anchoïade

You could say this is Provence's answer to Bagna Cauda (see page 24). It is an emulsified sauce made with oil rather than butter, and it is thick, meant as a dip to be served with crudités. We also use this as a salad dressing (see page 91) or spread it onto Carta di Musica (see page 49).

Makes 2 cups

20 anchovy fillets, rinsed and roughly chopped
1 tablespoon chopped thyme leaves
1 teaspoon Dijon mustard
Juice of ½ lemon, plus more to taste
½ garlic clove
Olive oil (at least 1½ cups)
Salt

Add the anchovies, thyme, mustard, lemon juice, and garlic to a food processor. Pulse for a moment or so, until a relatively rough paste forms. With the blade running, drizzle in a thin stream of olive oil, about 1½ cups, until incorporated.

Once the anchoïade is emulsified, blitz in 1 to 2 tablespoons tepid water, or as needed, so it is pourable. Season with salt and more lemon juice to taste.

Bottarga Butter

This is the richest but also the least intense of our bottarga sauces. Dollops land on top of grilled white fish, blanched asparagus, and toast, topped with a grilled chili or two (see page 36).

Makes 1 cup

One 5-ounce stick bottarga di muggine, thin skin peeled away
½ pound (2 sticks) unsalted butter, cubed, at room temperature
1 lemon, halved
Salt

Finely grate the bottarga di muggine and add it to a food processor. Add the butter and pulse a couple of times, bringing the two together. Add the juice of one lemon half and a pinch of salt and whiz until completely smooth. Taste and add more salt and/or lemon juice if needed.

Sealed in a container, this keeps in the fridge for about 1 week.

Bagna Cauda

We borrowed this approach to the classic Italian sauce from the River Café.

Most bagna caudas are served broken—puddles of butter with melted anchovies sunk to the bottom. This one is miraculous and emulsified, unlike any other. It is burgundy-tinted, thick, and pourable like a hollandaise. Beating in the butter can be a challenge—the key is to keep the temperature stable and to stick with it. The pan should never get too hot or too cold.

Ladle bagna cauda over boiled vegetables, as is classic, or eat with steak, as we do at King.

Makes 2 cups

16 garlic cloves
2 cups Sangiovese or similar robust red wine
¾ cup anchovy fillets (approximately 40), rinsed
½ pound (2 sticks) unsalted butter, cut into ½-inch dice and chilled
Salt and freshly ground black pepper

Combine the garlic and wine in a medium heavy saucepan, bring to a simmer, and cook over medium heat until the garlic is soft enough to be crushed with a spoon and the wine has boiled down to about ½ cup, about 35 minutes. The wine should have a slightly syrupy consistency.

Add the anchovies and continue heating the reduced wine until they have mostly melted into it, about 2 minutes. Using the back of a spoon or an immersion blender, mash the garlic with the wine and anchovies until you have a strange thick, smelly, purple paste.

NOW COMES THE CHALLENGE: Reduce the heat to low and, knob by knob, add the butter to the sauce while whisking constantly. Don't add the next bit of butter until the previous one has been absorbed and emulsified. To keep the sauce stable and prevent it from breaking, the temperature must be consistently low so the sauce is just lukewarm; control the temperature by pulling the pan on and off the heat. If it gets too warm, add another piece of butter or two or whisk off the heat to cool the pan, or do a combination of the two if necessary. Continue moving the pan, whisking, and adding the butter until it has all been absorbed and the sauce is emulsified; with each addition of butter, the sauce should become creamier. All in, this will take at least 15 minutes of undivided attention and constant whisking; do not try to rush it. Just before removing the sauce from the heat, season with salt and pepper.

Keep the bagna cauda warm in a bain-marie over low heat until ready to use; the water below the pan of sauce should never boil, or it will break.

Boiled-Lemon and Caper Sauce

Boiling lemons has a mellowing effect on their flavor. We like their delicate acidity and toss chopped pieces with warm chickpeas (see page 15) or into pasta with Boiled Lemons, Almonds, and Bottarga (page 146). Dressed with capers and parsley, the chopped lemon becomes a sauce that does especially well with grilled fish.

Makes 2 cups

8 lemons, rinsed
2 garlic cloves
2 fresh bay leaves
Salt
½ cup salt-packed capers, rinsed
Olive oil
Pinch of dried red chili
Pinch of crushed fennel seeds
½ cup parsley leaves (optional)

Place the lemons in a medium pot along with the garlic, bay, a good pinch of salt, and enough water to completely cover. Top with a cartouche (see page 15) and put a small plate on top of the paper to prevent the lemons from bobbing up. Bring the water to a boil and poach until the lemons completely soften and are easily pierced right through with a sharp knife, about 1½ hours.

Drain the lemons and discard the aromatics. Once they are cool enough to handle, slice the lemons lengthwise in half. Be careful! The insides are hot and juice will likely spurt out; go carefully, and cut away from your body. Use a small spoon to scoop out and discard the pulp and flesh from each lemon half, leaving the peel intact.

Lay the lemon halves peel side down on a cutting board. Press each one flat and, using a sharp knife, cut away the white pith and discard. Slice the peel into bits roughly the size of chickpeas.

Transfer the lemons to a bowl and stir in the capers. Cover with 6 tablespoons olive oil, or enough to submerge. Add the dried chili and fennel seeds. If making boiled lemons and chickpeas (see page 15) or using this in the almond, lemon, and parsley pesto (see page 146), stop now. Otherwise, finish by tossing in the parsley.

Dragoncella

The word *dragoncella* translates as "dragon's tongue," referring to the shape of a tarragon leaf. This sauce is delicious with poached ox tongue (see page 212) and boiled vegetables.

Makes 2 cups

¼ garlic clove
Salt
2 anchovy fillets, rinsed
10 salt-packed capers, rinsed
2 teaspoons Dijon mustard
1 teaspoon red wine vinegar, plus more to taste
1½ cups tarragon leaves, finely chopped
Olive oil
Six 9-minute boiled eggs

Use the flat side of a chef's knife to smush the garlic with a pinch of salt on a cutting board to form a paste. Finely chop the anchovies and capers into the paste. Transfer the resulting smush to a bowl, along with the mustard and red wine vinegar. Add the tarragon and 3 tablespoons olive oil.

Peel the eggs and separate the yolks from the whites. Roughly chop the whites and add them to the bowl of seasonings. Crumble in the yolks and gently fold everything together, along with an additional 4 to 6 tablespoons olive oil; do not overwork the yolks, or they'll turn to yellow dust. Season with salt to taste and another splash of the vinegar for sharpness.

French Tapenade

At King, we make both an Italian-style tapenade (page 30) and this French version, smooth and intense and flavored with a dash of Cognac and thyme. Niçoise olives are traditional, but a coastal Italian olive, such as Taggiasca, could also be used.

Makes 2 cups

2 cups Niçoise olives, pitted
1 tablespoon salt-packed capers, rinsed
½ garlic clove
Salt
1 tablespoon finely chopped thyme leaves
1 tablespoon brandy, preferably Cognac
Olive oil

Finely chop the olives and capers together on a cutting board to form a relatively smooth paste. Transfer to a small bowl.

Put the garlic on the cutting board and sprinkle with salt. Using the side of a chef's knife, smush the two together to form a paste. Add the garlic, thyme, brandy, and ⅓ cup olive oil to the olives and capers; taste and add more oil as needed to round out the flavors or loosen the tapenade. Taste and add salt if necessary.

Fresh or Preserved Tomato Sauce

At King, a vast pot of slow-cooked tomato sauce, fresh or preserved, seasoned with only thinly sliced garlic and a handful of basil leaves, will patiently reduce for hours as its sweetness gradually intensifies.

We add flicks of this sauce to the base of braises and to pots of steaming clams for depth. And it dresses bowls of pasta year-round.

Serves 6 to 8

Salt
8 pounds fresh tomatoes
or six 28-ounce cans peeled whole tomatoes, preferably San Marzano

Olive oil
2 garlic cloves, thinly slivered
A handful of basil leaves
Freshly ground black pepper

If using fresh tomatoes, bring a large pot of salted water to a boil over high heat. As it comes up, lightly score the tomatoes at their tops and bottoms with a cross mark. Set up a large ice bath beside the stove.

Working in batches, slip the tomatoes into the boiling water and blanch until their skins start to peel away at the cross marks, 1 to 2 minutes. With a slotted spoon, transfer the tomatoes to the ice bath. Keep the blanching water warm; some of it will be used later.

Once they are cool enough to handle, peel away and discard the tomatoes' skins and place them in a large bowl. With your hands, mush the blanched tomatoes, breaking them into large chunks.

If using canned tomatoes, drain them, reserving a cup of the liquid for later on, and transfer to a large bowl. Smush them with your fingers, breaking the tomatoes into large irregular pieces.

Set a wide heavy pot over medium heat. Pour in 3 tablespoons olive oil, stir in the slivered garlic, basil, a pinch of salt, and a little pepper, and gently fry until the garlic blooms, 1 to 2 minutes (don't let it brown!). Stir in the tomatoes, plus any accumulated juices in the bowl, and gently simmer over low heat until the sauce is sharp and sweet and the juices have thickened, about 1 hour. It's important not to overcook the sauce, or it will turn jammy. Instead, the flavors should concentrate while the sauce stays loose and bright, the color of a British mailbox.

If you accidentally reduce the sauce too far, loosen it with a small ladleful or two of the reserved blanching water or the canned tomatoes' liquid. Season with olive oil and more salt to taste.

Fonduta

We ladle this rich sauce, a cheesy custard of sorts, over soft polenta or toss it with pasta or a head of boiled romanesco. Any strong cheese can be swapped in for the Parmesan for a punchier variation.

Treat the fonduta-making process as you would that for a crème anglaise: Gently heat the sauce in a bain-marie and pay close attention to provent the egg yolks from curdling.

Makes 3 cups

½ garlic clove
Salt
1 cup crème fraîche
1 cup heavy cream
2 large egg yolks
1½ cups grated Parmesan cheese

Using the side of a chef's knife, smush the garlic with a pinch of salt on a cutting board to form a paste. Transfer to a medium heatproof bowl and whisk in the crème fraîche, cream, and yolks.

Set up a bain-marie by filling a medium pot with 4 inches of water. Bring the water to a simmer over high heat and then reduce the heat to medium. Place the bowl with the egg mixture over the pot, making sure the bottom does not touch the water. As the mixture warms, whisk it constantly, taking care that the bottom doesn't scorch and the eggs don't overheat. Every now and then, scrape down the bowl's sides. If wisps of steam escape the bowl, or if things look at all granular, remove the fonduta from the heat and stir to cool; once the temperature settles, set the fonduta back over the pot of water and continue on. After about 20 minutes, the fonduta should be a soft yellow color and thick enough to coat the back of a spoon. Remove the bowl from the heat and whisk in the Parmesan. Once the cheese melts, season with salt to taste.

Ideally, use immediately, or fonduta holds in a warm bain-marie for up to an hour. Do not reheat over high heat or it may curdle.

Horseradish Cream

The hotter the root, the better! At King, we add horseradish cream to grilled mackerel (see page 231) and poached ox tongue (see page 212). At home, no leftover-beef sandwich is complete without a smear on both slices of bread.

Makes 2 cups

1 horseradish root, about 10 inches long, peeled
2 cups crème fraîche, plus more if needed
2 tablespoons red wine vinegar, or more to taste
Salt
Olive oil

Using the finest holes of a box grater or a Microplane, grate the horseradish into a medium bowl, stopping once you have 2 cups' worth. Add the crème fraîche, red wine vinegar, and a pinch of salt, then mix in a tablespoon of olive oil, taste, and adjust with more salt, oil, and/or vinegar. We like this thick, so it stands proud. But if you find yourself with a blazer, simply add more crème fraîche to cool things down.

Mustard Vinaigrette

We like this vinaigrette on the fiery side.

Makes 2 cups

5 tablespoons Dijon mustard
1½ tablespoons red wine vinegar, plus more to taste
¼ cup finely chopped thyme leaves
Salt
Olive oil (about 1 cup)

Add the mustard, vinegar, thyme, and salt to a blender or food processor. Run the blade to combine and then, very slowly, stream in 1 cup olive oil until fully incorporated. Season with salt and more vinegar to taste. The vinaigrette keeps, sealed in the fridge, for 2 to 3 days.

Liguria Olive Sauce

(Tapenade)

Our Italian tapenade is a lovely, rich, summery sauce that complements grilled meats and fish.

Makes 2 cups

Olive oil (at least 2 cups)
1 garlic clove, halved lengthwise
Pinch of ground dried red chili
6 cherry tomatoes
2 teaspoons roughly chopped thyme leaves
4 anchovy fillets, rinsed and roughly chopped
1 teaspoon salt-packed capers, rinsed and finely chopped
1 cup Taggiasca olives, pitted and finely chopped
1 tablespoon crème fraîche

Combine 2 cups olive oil, the garlic, and chili in a small pot, add the tomatoes, and warm over low heat to confit the garlic and tomatoes, cooking until both are soft, about 15 minutes.

Remove the pot from the heat and add the thyme, anchovies, and capers. Swirl everything together to melt the anchovies into the warm oil, about 3 minutes. Using the back of a spoon, smush the garlic, tomatoes, and whatever is left of the anchovies into the oil. Add the olives and return the sauce to low heat, stirring until the flavors meld, 2 to 3 minutes. Turn off the heat and stir in the crème fraîche, marbling it through so as not to fully combine—we like this streaked. Season with salt and more olive oil to taste.

Salsa Mandorla

A mild but fragrant almond and garlic sauce, this salsa is as intriguing with boiled vegetables as it is with charred or steamed fish.

Using stale bread, rather than fresh, is essential, or this will become gluey. Occasionally we speed up the bread's aging process by placing it in a warmed low oven, so the moisture evaporates but the crumb doesn't color.

Makes 2 cups

1 cup walnut-sized pieces stale white bread (crust removed)
¼ cup whole milk, plus more if needed
½ cup blanched almonds
½ garlic clove
Salt
Olive oil
½ lemon

Add the dried bread to a large bowl, along with the milk, and set aside to soak.

Place the almonds in a mortar and add the garlic and a pinch of salt. With the pestle, bash the nuts to a rough paste. (Depending on the mortar's size, this may need to be done in batches.) Transfer the nuts to a food processor.

Once the bread has absorbed the milk, squeeze it dry and reserve the milk in the bowl to use later. Place the bread pieces on a cutting board and run a knife through them a couple of times, chopping them up. Add the bread to the food processor.

Blitz the bread and nuts together until a thick paste forms. With the blade running, stream in 2 tablespoons of the reserved milk, followed by 2 tablespoons olive oil. Add a squeeze of lemon juice and blend again. Add another 2 tablespoons milk, followed by an equal amount of olive oil, and blitz until the sauce becomes creamy and is mostly smooth (some small lumps are okay). If more milk is needed but you've run out of the soaking milk, just add a splash from the fridge.

Taste the sauce and season with more lemon juice and some salt. It should be rather mellow, with a balance of sweet and savory notes. Use this sauce on the day it is made; if not using it immediately, hold in a sealable container, topped off with a thin film of olive oil to prevent oxidation.

Salsa di Noci
with Pepperoncini

Add a handful of cheese to this recipe, and it becomes a pasta sauce. Or, with 1 to 2 tablespoons of red wine vinegar (and no cheese), it's a vibrant accompaniment for anything grilled.

Makes 2 cups

½ garlic clove
Salt
2 tablespoons roughly chopped marjoram leaves
4 Grilled Holland Chilies (page 36), roughly chopped
2 cups blanched almonds, roughly chopped
1 to 2 tablespoon red wine vinegar (optional)
Olive oil (at least 1½ cups)
A handful of grated Parmesan cheese (optional)

Using a mortar and pestle, smash the garlic together with 2 teaspoons salt and the marjoram. Once a paste forms, transfer it to a food processor and add the grilled chilies and chopped almonds. Pulse to combine. If using, blend in the red wine vinegar (see the headnote).

With the blade running, slowly pour in about 1½ cups olive oil, just enough to form a thick sauce. Whiz in about ¼ cup water, adding it slowly and stopping once the sauce looks silky. If adding cheese (again, see the headnote), blend it in now. Season with salt and more oil to taste.

Salsa Siciliana

A Sicilian compote that embraces the region's sweet-and-sour leanings, this is excellent with poultry and oily fish—we drop spoonfuls onto grilled mackerel, sardines, or quail.

Makes 2 cups

⅔ cup sultanas or golden raisins
A generous pinch of saffron threads
1⅓ cups pine nuts
⅓ cup mint leaves
Salt
Olive oil
1½ teaspoons red wine vinegar, plus more if desired

Put the sultanas in a small saucepan, along with the saffron, and add enough water to barely cover, about 1 cup. Bring to a simmer over low heat, then turn off the heat. Let the sultanas stand until they plump and pick up the saffron's stain, about 10 minutes.

Using a slotted spoon, transfer the sultanas to a food processor; keep the saffron water nearby. Add the pine nuts, mint, a pinch of salt, and about 3 tablespoons olive oil to the processor and pulse, to roughly chop. Now, blitz in the vinegar and enough of the reserved saffron water to make a sauce that resembles chunky, wet sand. Season with salt and more vinegar to taste, if desired.

Salsa Verde

This recipe is merely a guide to one of the world's most famous green sauces. Do not feel bound by the selection of herbs—any mix of parsley, marjoram, fennel fronds, basil, mint, and/or dill will do. Chop everything fine, then chop again.

Tinker with it according to what you're serving. For steaks, we add oomph with a dash more mustard. We add more anchovy and capers if this will be paired with grilled fish. And we always add extra tarragon when it is intended for birds.

Makes 2 cups

4 anchovy fillets, rinsed
1 tablespoon salt-packed capers, rinsed
1 tablespoon Dijon mustard, or more to taste
2 tablespoons red wine vinegar, or more to taste
Salt and freshly ground black pepper
A sliver of garlic
2½ cups soft herb leaves (preferably marjoram, fennel fronds, parsley, and/or tarragon)
Olive oil

Finely chop the anchovies and capers together on a cutting board to form a paste. Transfer to a bowl along with the mustard, vinegar, and a small pinch each of salt and pepper. Stir until a paste forms.

Smush the garlic with a pinch of salt on the cutting board, using the side of a chef's knife, to make a paste. Add it to the anchovy-caper paste.

Working in batches, roll the soft herb leaves into cigar shapes and finely slice crosswise with a sharp knife. Then run the knife over the herbs to chop them up more finely still. (Rolling up the herb leaves first prevents bruising and dulling their color.) Add the sliced herbs to the bowl with the anchovies. Immediately pour over enough oil to cover, about ¾ cup. Stir to combine and taste; the sauce should be fragrant and bright. Add more seasoning as needed.

Use this sauce the day it is made.

Whipped Bottarga
with Lemon Juice

This is a rich and briny sauce that is firmer than an aioli but still irresistibly smooth. Raw fennel, tomatoes, carte di musica, toast . . . are all delicious dipped or slathered in this sauce.

Makes 2 cups

One 5-ounce stick bottarga di muggine, membrane peeled away
3 tablespoons lemon juice, plus more if necessary
Salt
Olive oil
Freshly ground black pepper

Crumble the peeled bottarga di muggine into a food processor and whiz until it breaks down like golden sand. Add the lemon juice and a pinch of salt and whiz again. With the blade running, very slowly dribble in ½ cup olive oil, then slowly trickle in ¼ cup tepid water. With the blade still running, finish the sauce by drizzling in another ¼ cup olive oil, adding it just as slowly as before. If the sauce seems too thick, whiz in flicks of tepid water until it has the consistency of mayonnaise and is a corn-yellow color. Season with salt, pepper, and/or more lemon juice if needed.

Whipped Bottarga
with Tomato Juice

When we make this in summer, we use fresh tomato juice instead of lemon. And we save the flesh of our pinched tomatoes, adding them to whatever this sauce ultimately dresses. Our preferred tomatoes are Sungolds, but any small sweet heirloom cherry tomato works.

This is lovely on top of our Carta di Musica with Whipped Bottarga, Sungolds, and Wild Oregano (page 46) or paired with Poached Striped Bass (page 243). And, of course, the sauce does well tossed with spaghetti and finished with freshly torn cherry tomatoes.

A large handful of Sungold tomatoes, halved

Set a sieve over a small bowl and squeeze the tomatoes over it, pinching them with your fingers to extract their juices, catching the seeds and pulp in the sieve. Stop once you have 3 or so tablespoons of juice.

Make the whipped bottarga sauce as detailed in the recipe above, but swap in the tomato juice for the lemon.

King's Chicken Stock

Use whatever chicken pieces make sense for you—the leftover scraps from a Sunday roast, fresh chicken carcasses, or a combination of both. At home, we will often freeze chicken bones as they come until we have enough for a big pot.

Makes 2½ to 3 quarts

4 to 5 pounds chicken pieces
2 medium carrots, roughly chopped
1 large onion, halved
4 large celery ribs, from the outside of a bunch, roughly chopped
1 head garlic, halved across the equator
2 leeks, split lengthwise, rinsed, and roughly chopped (optional)
5 whole black peppercorns
2 fresh bay leaves
A small handful of parsley stems
A small handful of thyme branches
A sprig or two of sage
A sprig or two of rosemary
Salt

Set a large stockpot on the stove, add the chicken bones or carcass, and cover with 5 inches of cold water. Slowly bring the water to a simmer over low heat; as it comes up, skim away any foam. Simmer for about 20 minutes, skimming throughout.

Add the carrots, onion, celery, garlic, leeks, if using, peppercorns, and all the herbs to the pot. Submerge the contents by adding enough cold water to cover them by at least 3 inches, bring to a simmer, and simmer gently over medium to medium-low heat until the liquid reduces by half, about 3 hours. Throughout, skim as needed and take care that the stock does not boil (this will keep it clear). If the vegetables or bones poke through the surface, top up with boiling water as needed to keep everything *just* covered.

Remove the pot from the heat and strain the stock through a sieve into a second large pot. Discard the bones, herbs, and aromatics. Season the stock gently with salt; more can be added later, depending on where the stock will be going. Let cool to room temperature.

The stock can be stored in the fridge for up to 5 days. Alternatively, freeze quarts of it for a gift that keeps on giving.

Grilled Holland Chilies

Hollands are preferred here, but any chili that is not too hot will work.

Makes 10 grilled chilies

10 Holland chilies
Olive oil

Set up a scorchingly hot fire in a grill. Lay the chilies on the grate to char and, using tongs, turn each as it blisters, about 2 minutes on each side; they should be charred all over. Or, to use a gas stovetop, blister the chilies directly over a medium-high flame, working in batches. For either scenario, transfer the chilies to a bowl as they char and tightly cover the bowl with plastic wrap, resealing the plastic after each addition. Let the chilies steam in the bowl until they soften and resemble deflated balloons.

Once the chilies are cool enough to handle, peel away and discard the charred skin (it should come away easily). You'll feel how spicy the chilies are by the tingle on your fingertips; if you're peeling a lot, find rubber gloves before you do this (trust us!). Wash your hands thoroughly afterward, being careful not to touch your eyes.

Using a sharp knife, split the chilies open lengthwise, leaving their stems intact. Remove and discard the seeds.

To serve, drape whole chilies over anything from fresh ricotta to carta di musica (page 52) to grilled hanger steak (page 207). Or, if you like, chop them quite fine, cover with olive oil, and season with salt, then drizzle this condiment over everything as desired.

The grilled chilies keep for a week in the fridge under oil in a sealed container.

Quince Preserves

Our quince preserves are slightly looser and more jam-like than Spanish membrillo. But their heady flavor and ocher color are related. We ripple them through Fior di Latte Ice Cream (page 342), mix them into pasta fillings (see page 163), dollop roasted quail (see page 281) with them, and splodge them over the savory carta di musica (see starting on page 50).

In the restaurant, to strike the right balance between the sharpness of the quince and the sweetness of the sugar, we weigh the quinces and divide that weight in half to determine the quantity of sugar to add. Do the same, or follow this recipe, but note that that will never be as precise as using a scale.

Makes 4 cups

2 pounds quinces (about 4 large)
1 cup granulated sugar (see method)
2 tablespoons lemon juice

Salt

SPECIAL EQUIPMENT:
A ricer or food mill

Wash any fluff off the quinces and roughly chop each one into eighths. Place all the fruit (including seeds and stems) in a medium wide pot and add just enough cold water to cover. Bring the water to a simmer over medium-high heat and cook until the fruit is squashable with the back of a spoon, about 40 minutes.

Drain in a colander over a bowl, reserving the cooking liquid. Place the tender fruit in a ricer or food mill set over a medium bowl and pass it through the ricer into the bowl below.

If you have a scale, weigh the quince puree and divide that amount in half—that is the weight of sugar you should add (see headnote). If you don't have a scale, use the amount specified in the ingredient list.

Add the sugar to a large heavy pot and then scrape in the quince puree, taking care to get every drop. Stir the two together, then cook over medium heat, stirring occasionally with a wooden spoon, until the sugar dissolves, about 15 minutes. You'll notice the color change from pale yellow to pink during this first stage. As the puree continues to cook and darken, stir with increasing frequency so the puree doesn't stick to the pot's bottom. As the puree progresses toward an amber color, about 15 more minutes of simmering, stand by and stir often. When the preserves are the color of deep rust and have thickened significantly but are still spreadable, about 40 minutes in total, they are done; if necessary, stir in splashes of water during this last phase to prevent burning.

Taste and add the lemon juice and a generous pinch of salt, about 1 teaspoon. Remove from the heat and scrape the preserves into a heatproof container. Let cool to room temperature before using.

Sealed and stored in the fridge, this keeps for infinity.

Rough Puff Pastry

This pastry is simpler to make than a classic French puff but it achieves the same layers.

It's important to roll, fold, and chill the dough three times, as each set of folds means more layers in the making. Then the pastry must rest for 24 hours before using.

We use this for both savory tarts (Pissaladière, page 77), and Leek and Chèvre Tart, page 79) and our Tarte Tatin (page 317).

Makes 1 pound

½ pound (2 sticks)
plus 2 tablespoons cold unsalted butter
1½ cups all-purpose flour,
plus more for dusting

Kosher salt
½ cup ice water

Grate the cold butter into a medium bowl, using the large holes of a box grater. Chill in the fridge for about 1 hour.

Sift the flour and ¾ teaspoon salt into a large bowl. Remove the butter from the fridge and rub it into the flour using your fingertips. Once the mixture resembles chunky breadcrumbs, add a few flicks (or tablespoons) of the ice water and rub it into the flour, then add a few more flicks, rubbing again. Bring it all together until a shaggy dough forms—you may not need to use all the water. Form the dough into a disk and wrap it tightly in a cloth or plastic wrap. Chill in the fridge for 30 minutes.

Lightly flour a work surface. Roll the dough out into a rectangle approximately 11 by 16 inches.

Brush away excess flour with a pastry brush. With the long side of the dough facing you, fold the left third of the rectangle over the center of the dough. Brush away excess flour again and then fold the right third over the center, on top of the first fold, aligning the edges. Brush away any excess flour once more and wrap the dough in the cloth or plastic wrap. Chill for 30 minutes.

Unwrap the folded dough and place it on a lightly floured work surface with its cross sections toward you. Roll out the dough to an 11-by-16-inch rectangle again. Now, just as before, square off the edges and fold the sides over. Chill for another 30 minutes.

Repeat the entire rolling and folding process for a third and final time. Wrap and chill the dough for at least 24 hours before using. This dough freezes well, wrapped in plastic wrap. In the fridge, it will keep for up to 3 days.

Short-Crust Pastry

Our go-to short-crust pastry. This yields enough pastry for two tart shells. You can use one right away and the other will keep wrapped in the fridge for a couple of days or freezes very well.

Makes two 12-inch tart shells

2¾ cups (350 grams) all-purpose flour
¾ cup (100 grams) powdered sugar
Salt
½ pound (2 sticks/225 grams) unsalted butter, cut into 1-inch cubes and chilled
3 large egg yolks

Combine the flour, powdered sugar, and a pinch of salt in a food processor and pulse for a few seconds to combine. Add the cubed butter and pulse repeatedly, cutting the pieces into the flour until irregular pea-sized bits form, about 1 minute.

One at a time, add the yolks to the processor, blitzing each one in before adding the next. Stop blitzing once a dry, crumbly dough that's mostly uniform comes together. Turn the dough out onto a sheet of plastic wrap, divide it in half, and pat each half into a log. Wrap each one in plastic wrap and chill in the fridge until firm to the poke, at least 30 minutes.

Once the dough is firm, grate one log directly into a 10-inch tart pan, using the largest holes of a box grater. Then, working from the edges in, press the dough together, forming a ¼-inch-thick pastry shell. Pay extra attention to the corners, as they can typically build up and get too dense.

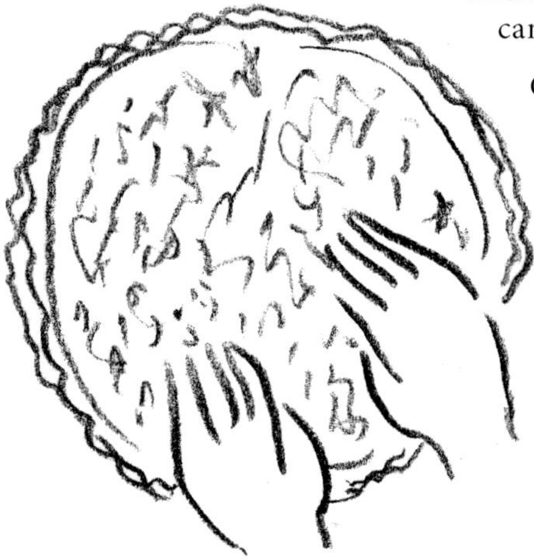

Chill the tart shell in the fridge until cold to the touch, about 20 minutes, before using. The prepared shell holds, covered, for a day in the fridge. Freeze the extra log if you're not making a second tart—it will keep until infinity. When ready to use, thaw it in the fridge.

CHAPTER 3

Carta di Musica with Whipped Bottarga, Sungolds, and Wild Oregano (page 46)

Carta di Musica with Cima di Rapa, Ricotta Salata, and Olives (page 47)

Carta di Musica with Quince, Ricotta, Radicchio, and Walnuts (page 50)

Carta di Musica with Favas, Mint, and Pecorino (page 51)

Carta di Musica with Torn Figs, Mint, and Fresh Ricotta (page 48)

Carta di Musica with Anchoïade, Tomato, and Thyme (page 49)

Carta di Musica with Crème Fraîche, Chili, and Soft Herbs (page 52)

Carta di Musica with Chocolate and Olive Oil (page 52)

THEY SAY THIS SARDINIAN FLATBREAD IS AS THIN AS A SHEET OF MUSIC, HENCE THE name *carta di musica.* On the rugged island that inspires so much of our cooking, large circles of durum wheat dough are puffed in wood-fired ovens, separated into two sheets, then crisped on the floor of the hearth.

The ancient recipe was conceived for shepherds wandering far from home and in need of food that would go the distance. Up in the hills, they'd eat them softened in water and wine. At King, though we have made our own on occasion, we think the job is best left to deft Sardinian hands. We buy them from the source and grill them until they char and soften enough to curl up into shapes that hold the olive oil, fried rosemary, and salt. It's a gift to every table, at the start of the meal, to get the appetite going without filling bellies. The smell of a smoking carta di musica is synonymous with King.

As our customers begin their meals with a King Carta (page 45), our cooks begin each service with a snack of grilled carta spread with whatever treasures they find on the line: a smear of bottarga butter, a handful of chopped cress with some anchovy and egg. When we opened for lunch, we put these topped carte on the menu—they were too good not to share. We've included our most beloved ones here. But, really, you should use these recipes as an inspiration; once grilled and smoky, they're for endless toppings.

Make them your own with whatever lovely things you have lying around. Eat them warm as a nibble, light starter, meal for one, or for dessert, perhaps, smeared with chocolate.

The King Carta di Musica

This is the carta that starts every meal at King. It arrives twisted up like a Frank Gehry concert hall. While the exact shape does not really matter, it should sit proud and contorted on the plate. After a few trials, the feel for twisting the carta into an abstract sculpture will come.

Serves 2 to 4

1 to 2 cups sunflower oil, plus more as needed
5 rosemary branches
Salt
1 carta di musica
Olive oil

Pour 2 inches of sunflower oil into a small heavy pot set over medium-low heat. When the oil is hot but not smoking, 3 to 5 minutes, lay in the rosemary branches. As the needles fry, turn the branches so they crisp evenly; rosemary burns quickly, so take care it doesn't get too dark. When the branches are fried and dark green but not at all brown, 1 minute or so, remove the rosemary from the pot and blot it dry with paper towels.

Once the rosemary is cool enough to handle, working over a small bowl, strip the needles from their branches. Discard the branches and add a few pinches of salt to the bowl of needles: The ratio should be about 1 part salt to 2 parts rosemary. Crush the two together, using your fingertips, until a coarse sprinkle forms—you don't want rosemary dust! Once cool, the rosemary salt holds in an airtight container at room temperature for up to a day.

Holding it with tongs, warm the carta over a medium-high flame on a grill or a gas stovetop. Once the edges catch and color and the surface turns golden, 30 seconds or so, slide your tongs to the carta's center and quickly pinch and twist the carta up and around to form a cone: Work with speed and conviction, hoping for the best, then move the carta off the flame.

Stand the twisted carta on a serving plate and douse it generously with olive oil. Sprinkle rosemary salt on top and into the nooks and crannies and eat immediately. If warm olive oil doesn't dribble down your chin, you've likely not used enough.

Carta di Musica
with Whipped Bottarga, Sungolds, and Wild Oregano

1½ cups Sungold tomatoes
Olive oil
Salt
A few pinches of dried wild oregano
½ lemon
1 carta di musica
½ cup Whipped Bottarga made with tomato juice (page 34)
¾ cup purslane (optional)
2 tablespoons marjoram leaves
Freshly ground black pepper

Halve the Sungolds across their equators. Set a sieve over a small bowl and pinch each tomato, squeezing its pulp and seeds into the sieve. Press on the captured seeds to extract as much juice as possible. Then remove the sieve and discard the seeds; add the pinched tomatoes to the tomato juice.

Season the tomatoes with ½ tablespoon olive oil, a little salt, a pinch or two of the oregano, and a squeeze of lemon juice. Toss, taste, and mix in more salt, oil, and/or oregano as needed until the tomatoes are juicy and delicious.

To finish the carta, use tongs to flip-flop it over a medium flame (on a grill or a gas stovetop) until both sides crisp and singe in spots, less than a minute per side. Once it smokes a bit, turns nutty brown, and smells toasted, lay the crisped carta on a serving board, where it will continue to color slightly.

Season the cracker with a pinch of salt and spread out a thin drizzle of olive oil (take care not to break the carta). Splodge the whipped bottarga across the carta and spread it out evenly using the back of a spoon. Scatter the pinched tomatoes across the carta (and the purslane, if using) and drizzle over some of the tomato juices from the bowl. Finish with the marjoram leaves, a pinch or two of the wild oregano and ground pepper, and a final drizzle of olive oil. Serve immediately.

Carta di Musica

with Cima Di Rapa, Ricotta Salata, and Olives

1 carta di musica
Salt
Olive oil
½ cup Cima Puree (page 13), warmed
⅓ cup Taggiasca olives, halved or quartered and pitted
1 lemon
A 4-ounce wedge of ricotta salata

To cook the carta, use tongs to flip-flop the cracker over a medium, open flame (on a grill or a gas stovetop) until both sides crisp and singe in spots, less than a minute per side. Once it smokes a bit, turns nutty brown, and smells toasted, lay the crisped carta on a serving board, where it will continue to color slightly.

Season the carta with a pinch of salt and spread out a thin drizzle of olive oil (take care not to break the cracker). Dollop the cima puree all around and smudge it across in an even layer. Sprinkle the olives around. Finely grate over the zest of the lemon.

Finish by lightly covering the whole carta with broad shards of the ricotta salata, shaving thin pieces directly off the wedge (save whatever you do not use for later). We like our shards slightly thicker and less uniform than what a vegetable peeler produces, so we use a chef's knife here, but a peeler also does the trick. Drizzle a little more olive oil over the carta and serve immediately.

Carta di Musica
with Torn Figs, Mint, and Fresh Ricotta

6 ripe Black Mission or Tiger Stripe figs, torn into quarters
Olive oil
Finely grated zest of 1 lemon, lemon reserved and halved
Salt and freshly ground black pepper
8 to 10 mint leaves, torn into pieces
1 carta di musica
¾ cup fresh ricotta
¾ cup arugula

Put the figs in a medium bowl and add a drizzle of olive oil, a squeeze of lemon juice, and salt and pepper to taste. Add the mint, saving a couple of leaves for finishing, and toss together. Allow the figs to macerate while the carta grills, just a few minutes.

To cook the carta, use tongs to flip-flop it over a medium open flame (on a grill or on a gas stovetop) until both sides crisp and singe in spots, less than a minute per side. Once it smokes a bit, turns nutty brown, and smells toasted, lay the crisped carta on a serving board, where it will continue to color slightly.

Season the carta with a pinch of salt and spread out a thin drizzle of olive oil (take care not to break the cracker). Dollop the ricotta all around and then smudge it out with the back of a spoon to cover the surface in a more or less even ¼-inch-thick coating.

Arrange the figs all around and drizzle over a spoonful or two of their juices. Scatter arugula leaves. Season with salt, pepper, and a showering of the lemon zest. Sprinkle over the remaining mint and finish with a final drizzle of olive oil. Serve immediately.

Carta di Musica

with Anchoïade, Tomato, and Thyme

1 large heirloom tomato
Salt
1 tablespoon red wine vinegar
1 carta di musica
Olive oil
6 tablespoons Anchoïade (page 23)
½ teaspoon thyme leaves
Freshly ground black pepper

Cut out the hard core from the tomato and slice it into very thin, translucent rounds; ⅛ inch or less is ideal. Arrange the slices on a cutting board and season with salt and the red wine vinegar. Let the tomatoes marinate while you prepare the carta; if they sit too long, they'll lose all their bite.

To cook the carta, use tongs to flip-flop it over a medium open flame (on a grill or a gas stovetop) until both sides crisp and singe in spots, less than a minute per side. Once it smokes a bit, turns nutty brown, and smells toasted, lay the crisped carta on a serving board, where it will continue to color slightly.

Season the carta with a pinch of salt and spread out a thin drizzle of olive oil (take care not to break the cracker). Smudge the anchoïade across the carta, thinly covering its surface. Shingle the marinated tomatoes over the top, covering the carta in a single even layer. Season with the thyme, a pinch of salt, some pepper, and a final drizzle of olive oil. Serve immediately.

Carta di Musica

with Quince, Ricotta, Radicchio, and Walnuts

¼ cup walnuts
Olive oil
Salt
A handful of winter leaves like radicchio, Treviso radicchio, or similar
Lemon juice
½ tablespoon roughly chopped marjoram leaves
1 carta di musica
¾ cup fresh ricotta
2 tablespoons Quince Preserves (page 38) or a store-bought membrillo
Freshly ground black pepper

Preheat the oven to 450 degrees. Add the walnuts to a small bowl and toss them with a tablespoon of olive oil and some salt. Spread the nuts out on a baking sheet and toast in the oven until golden brown, 5 to 7 minutes. Remove from the oven and let cool. The toasted nuts keep for a couple of days in an airtight container.

Place the radicchio leaves in a bowl and season them with a squeeze of lemon juice, a pinch of salt, the marjoram, and a thin drizzle of olive oil; toss to coat.

To cook the carta, use tongs to flip-flop it over a medium open flame (on a grill or a gas stovetop) until both sides crisp and singe in spots, less than a minute per side. Once it smokes a bit, turns nutty brown, and smells toasted, lay the crisped carta on a serving board, where it will continue to color.

Season the carta with a pinch of salt and spread out a thin drizzle of olive oil (take care not to break the cracker). Dollop the ricotta all around and then smudge it out with the back of a spoon, covering the carta with a ¼-inch-thick coating. Drizzle the quince preserves over the ricotta and top with the dressed radicchio and the walnuts. Finish with salt, pepper, and a drizzle of olive oil. Serve immediately.

Carta di Musica
with Favas, Mint, and Pecorino

2 cups shelled raw favas
(see page 176 for instructions)
1 cup coarsely grated pecorino cheese
¼ garlic clove, thinly sliced
6 to 10 mint leaves
Olive oil
Salt

1 carta di musica
Salt
Olive oil
1 cup Favas Sott'olio (page 176)
5 to 7 mint leaves
Freshly ground black pepper

Prepare the fava puree by combining the beans, pecorino, garlic, mint, ⅔ cup olive oil, and a pinch of salt in a blender or food processor. Blitz until a coarse paste forms, about 30 seconds, stopping to scrape down the sides as needed. Taste and add more salt and/or olive oil as needed so the puree is delicious and spreadable.

To cook the carta, use tongs to flip-flop it over a medium open flame (on a grill or a gas stovetop) until both sides crisp and singe in spots, less than a minute per side. Once it smokes a bit, turns nutty brown, and smells toasted, lay the crisped carta on a serving board, where it will continue to color.

Season the carta with a pinch of salt and spread out a thin drizzle of olive oil (take care not to break the cracker). Dollop the fava puree all around and gently smudge it across the carta, covering it with a ¼-inch-thick coating (save any extra for toast). Using a slotted spoon, lift the favas sott'olio from their oil and sprinkle them evenly over the puree. Next, tear over the mint leaves, dotting the puree evenly with them. Finish with a sprinkle of salt, some pepper, and a drizzle of olive oil. Serve immediately.

Carta di Musica

with Crème Fraîche, Chili, and Soft Herbs

1 carta di musica
Salt
Olive oil
⅔ cup crème fraîche
6 Grilled Holland Chilies (page 36), torn into long thin strips
¼ cup chopped soft herb leaves (a mix of marjoram, parsley, and/or fennel fronds)
Freshly ground black pepper

To cook the carta, use tongs to flip-flop it over a medium open flame (on a grill or a gas stovetop) until both sides crisp and singe in spots, less than a minute per side. Once it smokes a bit, turns nutty brown, and smells toasted, lay the crisped carta on a serving board, where it will continue to color.

Season the carta with a pinch of salt and spread out a thin drizzle of olive oil (take care not to break the cracker). Allow the carta to cool slightly, a matter of seconds, so the crème fraîche doesn't melt, then dollop the crème fraîche all over and gently spread it out with the back of a spoon to coat the whole surface in a thin layer.

Drape the grilled chilies here and there, smooth sides face up. Sprinkle the soft herbs all around. Finish with a sprinkling of salt, some pepper, and a drizzle of olive oil. Serve immediately.

Carta di Musica

with Chocolate and Olive Oil

1 carta di musica
2 ounces 70% dark chocolate, roughly chopped
Salt
Olive oil

Preheat the oven to 450 degrees. To cook the carta, use tongs to flip-flop it over a medium open flame (on a grill or a gas stovetop) until both sides crisp and singe in spots, less than a minute per side. Once it is nutty brown and smells toasted, lay the crisped carta on a baking sheet.

Sprinkle the chocolate over the carta and season with salt. Pop the pan into the oven and bake until the chocolate begins to melt, about 2 minutes. Some bits will melt completely while others will stay firm at the center—we like this variety. Pull the pan from the oven and finish the carta with a drizzle of olive oil and another sprinkle of salt. Serve immediately.

CHAPTER 4

Aperitifs & Nibbles

A*PÉRO* IS A KEY MOMENT IN THE DAY FOR THE FRENCH AND ITALIAN ALIKE. THAT IS also true for us at King. In the warmer months, it starts when the sun begins to set and guests arrive onto our terrace for their spritzes and panisse; it's a pause in the day before the main event of dinner.

Apéro in its essence means a light drink and snack to set the tone for the evening ahead. It is often a spritz or a one-two hit like our Suze and Tonic (page 56). These are easy to assemble and only require having the right bottles of bitters on hand. But an apéro can be more of a proper cocktail. It takes a little more work, but when they are as delicious as our beloved Rizzo (page 60) or as beautiful as our Violets for Roses (page 62), they are well worth the effort. In both these cocktails, we like our infused spirits to do the work for us: adding flavor and complexity while working ahead, our favorite combo!

While you do not need a full bar, a few basic tools will come in handy: a cocktail shaker, a strainer, and a jigger. But never fear—if none of these are available to you, all can be substituted with more homely tools: a Mason jar, a piece of cheesecloth, even counting your Mississippis will do the trick.

When it comes to our nibbles, there are myriad options, but the key is to whet the appetite without filling up the belly. These can be as simple as some marinated olives or as elegant as a square of latticed Pissaladière (page 77), served with a cold glass of rosé. We like to serve a simple Artichokes Vinaigrette (page 87) in the summertime, while Roasted Chestnuts (page 67) are coziest in the wintertime.

In the right moment, I will admit to loving apéro more than dinner. It is when your appetite is sharpest and the first sip is always at its coldest and most refreshing. Hosting dinner may take a bit more work, but apéro is always there for you.

—Annie

Suze and Tonic

Suze is a classic French liquor made from gentian root. Pleasantly bitter and surprisingly versatile, it has earthy citrus notes that always refresh. It has no substitute.

You'll notice Suze's neon yellow color straightaway. We drink it (mixed or straight) in tall Collins glasses, stacked with ice. For a wintry rendition, swap in Calvados for the Suze.

Serves 1

1½ to 2 ounces Suze
A good tonic, preferably Fevertree
A broad strip of lemon peel
Ice for glass

Fill a Collins glass with ice—we use large, dense cubes that melt slowly. Pour 1½ ounces Suze into the glass, or increase the pour to 2 ounces for an extra kick. Top with the tonic and stir to combine.

Express the lemon peel over the glass by twisting the peel until its oils burst. Then swipe the strip around the glass's rim and drop it in.

Train to Bayonne

Many autumns ago, Gus, then the head bartender at King, and I came up with this drink and it became an instant hit with our regulars. It asks that you plan ahead and infuse the gin with tarragon; give the bottle at least 2 days to pick up the tarragon's scent, which pairs beautifully with the herbaceous Chartreuse.

We named this after a city in southwestern France, close to the Spanish border, where Chartreuse monks have produced the elixir for ages.

—Annie

Serves 1

1 ounce tarragon gin*
1 ounce Cocchi Americano or similar aromatized wine**
½ ounce green Chartreuse
¾ ounce strained fresh lime juice
½ ounce simple syrup***
A few tarragon leaves to garnish

Place a coupe in the freezer to chill for at least 10 minutes.

Combine the gin, Cocchi, Chartreuse, lime juice, and simple syrup in a cocktail shaker and then pack it with ice, roughly two-thirds full. Cover and shake until the shaker feels quite cold, about 10 seconds.

Strain the cocktail into the chilled coupe. Garnish with the tarragon leaves.

*TO MAKE TARRAGON GIN: Start with a bottle of gin that is at least three-quarters full and stuff it with several branches of tarragon. (For a 750 ml/25.4-ounce bottle, we use about 7 bushy branches.) Cap the gin and let stand until it develops a light green color and smells of a garden, about 2 days on the liquor shelf. Pour the gin through a sieve into an airtight container; discard the spent tarragon. The infused gin keeps for a month in the fridge.

** Cocchi Americano is an aromatized wine, which means it is not sufficiently alcoholic to be shelf-stable. Once it's been opened, store your bottle in the fridge. It will keep for about a month before oxidizing.

***TO MAKE SIMPLE SYRUP: Combine equal parts granulated sugar and water in a pot. Gently heat over low heat until the sugar just dissolves (the timing will depend on the quantity you are making). Let cool to room temperature before using. Covered and in the fridge, simple syrup keeps for at least a month.

The Rizzo

King's kitchen grills Holland chilies almost every day. Typically the chilies are charred, peeled, and seeded. The Rizzo came about as a way to use the discarded skins and seeds—precious as well as flavorful, they infuse tequila with a gentle, smoky heat.

To infuse tequila, combine the skins and seeds of a blistered chili with whatever bottle you have on hand. Set it aside for at least 2 days before tasting and straining. Once strained, taste again and, if necessary, add more tequila until you have attained the desired heat level. As a rule, we don't like the heat to feel punishing, but rather gently warming. Infused bottles keep, capped and in the fridge, for about a month.

Serves 1

FOR THE CHILI-SALT RIM

2 dried red chilies, preferably Calabrian
Salt
A lemon wedge

FOR THE COCKTAIL

1 ounce chili-infused tequila*
1 ounce Campari or similar bitter aperitivo
¼ ounce grapefruit liqueur**
¾ ounce strained fresh lemon juice

To make the chili salt, remove and discard the dried chilies' stem and seeds. Place the chilies in a spice grinder, or use a mortar and pestle. Grind until the chilies crumble. Stir the bashed chilies into ¼ cup salt; there should be an approximate 1:6 ratio of chili to salt. (Leftover chili salt can be used for future rounds of drinks.)

For the chili-salt rim, swipe the lemon wedge over the rim of a double rocks glass. Pour the chili salt onto a plate and slowly roll the rim of the glass over the salt so the salt adheres and forms a crystalline edge. Set the glass aside while you mix the cocktail.

Combine the tequila, Campari, grapefruit liqueur, and lemon juice in a cocktail shaker. Pack it with ice, filling it by roughly two-thirds. Cover and vigorously shake until the shaker feels quite cold, about 10 seconds.

Strain the cocktail into the prepared glass. Top up with fresh ice and serve.

*To make chili-infused tequila, add the skins and seeds of 7 to 10 Grilled Holland Chilies (page 36) to about 17 ounces of tequila (two-thirds of a 750ml/25.4-ounce bottle). Cap the bottle and set it aside until a taste of the tequila pricks your lips, about 48 hours. Strain the infused tequila into a clean bottle by passing it through a fine strainer or a cheesecloth-lined funnel.

**If grapefruit liqueur is hard to find, substitute ¼ ounce grapefruit vodka plus ¼ ounce simple syrup (see page 339).

Violets for Roses

One of our kitchen's most showstopping desserts is the celebratory Pavlova (we have included a similar and just-as-beloved recipe in this book for Eton Mess, page 309). We came up with this recipe because we wanted a cocktail to match its spirit and flair.

Butterfly pea tea, found at specialty shops or online, produces the beautiful deep blue color that defines this drink. Once it is diluted with lemon juice, the color shifts, ranging from a brilliant pink to a stunning violet.

—Laurel Delany, head bartender

Serves 1

¾ ounce rhum agricole or other cane-sugar-based rum
¾ ounce gin
¾ ounce butterfly pea tea syrup*
¾ ounce strained fresh lemon juice
1 egg white
Lavender sprig to garnish

Place a coupe in the freezer to chill for at least 10 minutes.

Combine the rum, gin, tea syrup, lemon juice, and egg white in a cocktail shaker, cover, and shake to blend the liquids, about 10 seconds. (Aerating the liquids before chilling allows the drink to develop a stronger, stiffer foam.)

Uncover the shaker and pack it with ice, filling it roughly two-thirds full. Cover again and vigorously shake until the shaker feels quite cold, about 10 seconds.

Strain the cocktail into the chilled coupe. Garnish with the lavender sprig and serve.

*TO MAKE BUTTERFLY TEA SYRUP: Brew the tea by infusing 1 cup hot water with 2 teaspoons dried butterfly pea flowers until the water turns bright blue, about 5 minutes. (The more dried flowers you use, the more intense the color will be.) Strain the tea by passing it through a fine sieve or a funnel lined with cheesecloth.

Combine the tea with an equal volume of granulated sugar; that is, for 1 cup tea, add 1 cup sugar. Stir the sugar into the hot tea until all dissolved. Once cool, store the syrup in the fridge for up to 3 weeks. Tea syrup made with 1 cup each tea and sugar will be enough for about 10 Violets for Roses.

Braulio Spritz

At King, there is a spritz for every season. Paired with bubbly Prosecco and a splash of club soda, it provides the perfect start to any meal or celebration.

When there is a chill in the air, this is our preferred spritz. It celebrates Braulio, an amaro from the alpine region near Switzerland. The drink's minty flavors always brighten winter's gray.

Serves 1

1 ounce Braulio
or any amaro you have on hand
(other favorites include Cynar and Campari)
1 ounce sweet vermouth, preferably Cocchi*

Splash of Prosecco (freshly popped)
Splash of club soda
A thin orange slice to garnish
Ice

Add a handful of ice to your glass of choice—we serve spritzes in white wine glasses, but any similarly sized glass will do. Add the Braulio and sweet vermouth. Top up with the Prosecco and club soda—we add equal amounts of both, but really it's the bartender's choice. Give a stir and top with the orange slice.

* Vermouth, like Cocchi Americano (see page 59), is an aromatized wine. Keep it in your fridge and finish it before month's end!

Pastis

Winter in New York is hard, dreary, and cold. It's also when everything at King decides to break.

After our first season in Manhattan, we weren't sure if we'd make it. Then, miraculously, there was a day of sunshine and fresh air. We dragged tables and chairs outside and sat in the brightest patch of sunlight available. We were bone-tired but thrilled that spring had finally arrived. To celebrate, we clinked small glasses of cold, milky pastis. I will always associate pastis with the most welcome change of the year.

—*Annie*

Serves 3 partners

4½ ounces pastis,
preferably Henri Bardouin or Ricard

A small carafe of water
Ice

Part of pastis's magic is its pearlescent color, especially when it meets water. We love that the strength of this aperitif depends on how you're feeling between sips. So we always serve a bottle of pastis with small glasses, set out on a tray, along with a carafe of water—dilute or double-down as desired.

Marinated Olives

Unpitted olives are a must for this mix, but other than that, you can use any shape, size, color, and texture you fancy. Allow these to marinate for at least 12 hours in the fridge before giving them an hour or so at room temperature to fully lose their chill before serving.

Makes 4 cups

4 fresh bay leaves
Salt
1 teaspoon fennel seeds
½ teaspoon coriander seeds
Zest of 1 orange, removed in strips with a peeler
Zest of 1 lemon, removed in strips with a peeler
2 dried red chilies, preferably Calabrian
Olive oil (at least 2 cups)
4 cups mixed unpitted olives, such as Castelvetrano, Taggiasca, Picholine, and/or Niçoise
Salt

Combine the bay leaves, a pinch of salt, the fennel seeds, coriander seeds, both zests, and the dried chilies in a small pot. Pour in enough oil so the marinade will ultimately cover the olives, and warm over very low heat until the aromatics bloom and the bay leaves ripple but do not crisp, about 3 minutes. Remove from the heat and let the oil cool to room temperature.

If the olives are in oil or brine, drain them. Transfer to a small bowl, and pour over the infused oil. Mix everything together and then transfer to a sealable container; add more olive oil if needed to submerge the olives. Cover and refrigerate overnight.

These keep for weeks in an airtight container in the fridge. Before serving, bring them to room temperature. Fridge-cold olives do not delight!

Fried Favas

These salty bites need little more to accompany them than a cold beer.

Before frying, the dried favas need to soak for up to 48 hours in the fridge.

Serves 10

4 cups dried favas
3 quarts sunflower oil for deep-frying
Salt
A few pinches of ground dried red chili

SPECIAL EQUIPMENT:
A deep-fry or candy thermometer

Place the favas in a spacious sealable container. Add enough cold water to cover, seal the container, and refrigerate for 2 days.

Drain the favas and pat until bone-dry.

Fill a wide deep pot with the sunflower oil. Secure a deep-fry or candy thermometer to the inside of the pot and heat the oil over medium to medium-high heat. Once it reaches 400 degrees, working in batches to avoid overcrowding, add the favas and fry until they turn chestnut brown, their skins burst, and the beans are crisp, about 4 minutes.

Using a slotted spoon, remove the favas from the oil and drain on a paper-towel-lined plate. While they are still warm, season them evenly with salt and a generous pinch of chili. Serve immediately, while frying up the next rounds. . . .

Roasted Chestnuts

Peeling chestnuts is as enjoyable as eating them. Children are particularly good at the job!

Serves 10

3 pounds chestnuts in the shell
Salt
Olive oil
¼ cup thyme leaves (optional)

Preheat the oven to 425 degrees. To score the chestnuts, place them on a cutting board, flat sides down, and, with a paring knife, carefully cut an X into each round belly, piercing the shells.

Toss the chestnuts with a good pinch of salt, 1 to 2 tablespoons olive oil, and the thyme, if using, in a large bowl. Spread the chestnuts out on a baking sheet in a single layer. Roast in the oven until the skin at the X marks peels back and reveals the chestnuts within, 15 to 20 minutes.

Remove the baking sheet from the oven and tumble the chestnuts onto a couple of tea towels. Bundle the towels around the nuts, forming parcels, and let the chestnuts steam for a couple of minutes, until their shells soften.

Serve warm, straight from their tea towels.

Gruyère and Thyme Gougères

The classic French nibble. Gougères are airy, rich bites of savory pastry that are light and luscious. Don't be afraid of the choux pastry: this dough is simple to make and best when left to rest for a day, so it is party prep friendly.

Serves 10

1½ cups whole milk
102/3 tablespoons (1⅓ sticks) unsalted butter
1½ cups water
Salt
2½ cups all-purpose flour
8 large eggs
2 tablespoons finely chopped thyme leaves
10½ ounces Gruyère cheese, grated
Freshly ground black pepper

Combine the milk, butter, 1½ cups of water, and 1½ teaspoons salt in a medium pot and bring to a boil over medium heat. Once the liquid rumbles, reduce the heat to medium-low and add the flour, stirring vigorously with a wooden spoon until a shiny, uniform paste forms. Beating the dough will require some muscle, but stick with it until the flour no longer tastes raw, about 5 minutes.

Remove from the heat and transfer the hot dough to the bowl of a stand mixer fitted with the paddle attachment. Beat on medium to medium-low speed until the dough cools to room temperature (the sides of the bowl side will no longer feel warm), about 15 minutes.

Once it is tempered, keep paddling the dough while you crack in the eggs one at a time. Add the next egg only once the previous one has been incorporated. When all the eggs have been added and the batter looks smooth and glossy, beat in the thyme, Gruyère, and 1 teaspoon pepper until evenly distributed.

Transfer the batter to a container, cover, and refrigerate. You can use it after an hour, but a longer rest (10 to 12 hours) ensures that the gougères rise higher and bake up lighter.

Preheat the oven to 400 degrees. Line two large baking sheets with parchment paper. When ready to bake, spoon or pipe small blobs, about half the size of a Ping-Pong ball, onto the pans, spacing them about 2 inches apart. (If you don't want to bake all the gougères now, leftover dough holds, covered in the fridge, for up to 2 days.)

Bake the gougères in the oven until they puff, crisp, and turn golden, about 18 minutes. If needed, bake in batches but always serve straight from the oven.

Mushroom Toasts

These toasts, cut up and shared, are a wonderful nibble for a group. To turn it into lunch for a few, keep whole and serve with a green salad.

Serves 10

3 cups Confit Chanterelles (page 192), held in their oil
10 thick slices crusty bread, such as filone or sourdough
1 garlic clove, halved lengthwise
A handful of parsley leaves, roughly chopped

Drain the mushrooms, reserving their oil, and add them to a small pot. Add enough of the reserved oil to cover them by ½ inch and heat over medium-low heat until the mushrooms are warmed through, about 5 minutes; keep the heat low and steady so the oil never comes up to a simmer.

Meanwhile, for the toast, heat the oven's broiler. Dip a pastry brush into the some of the mushroom oil and paint it onto the slices of bread, coating both sides evenly. Lay the slices on a baking sheet and broil, turning once, until toasted and golden, 1 to 2 minutes per side. (This can also be done in a large heavy skillet on the stovetop over medium-high heat.) Transfer the toasts to a cutting board and rub each with a cut side of the garlic clove.

Using a slotted spoon, lift the mushrooms out of their oil, allowing the excess to drain off back into the pot, and spoon the mushrooms onto the toasts. Finish with a generous sprinkling of parsley and slice each toast into bite-sized pieces. Share while warm.

Save the leftover confit oil for another batch.

Panisse

These fried ribbons of cooked chickpea batter have been on our menu since our Friends and Family service. While the menu changes every day, these return night after night.

Panisse are a traditional street food from Nice (the Italian version from Liguria is called *panelle*). Creamy and salty, they are impossible to tire of. But making them is not easy: the batter is temperamental, requiring both time (they need to be made a day ahead) and attention. The results more than reward the committed and brave.

Serving these hot and crisp, just as they come out of the oil, is essential.

Serves 10

FOR THE BATTER

Kosher salt
Olive oil
3½ cups chickpea flour

FOR FRYING

2 to 3 quarts sunflower oil for deep-frying
Leaves from a handful of sage sprigs (at least 10 sprigs)
Salt

Fill a large heavy pot with 1 quart salted water and ¼ cup olive oil and bring to a boil over high heat. Reduce the heat to a simmer and carefully stream in the chickpea flour while whisking constantly to prevent lumps. Once all the flour has been added, reduce the heat to low, switch to a wooden spoon, and give the pot a good stir. Gently cook, stirring often so the batter doesn't stick to the bottom of the pot (treat this like polenta). After an hour, the batter should have a deep nutty flavor. No better way to check than taste . . .

Despite your best intentions, the batter will look like a lumpy porridge at this stage. Most mornings, it draws a crowd of cooks—a couple of dollops make a hearty breakfast. Remove from the heat and use an immersion blender (or smooth it in a food processor) to blitz the batter (in batches, if necessary) until completely smooth, a few minutes. Taste and add salt as needed.

Lightly oil a 9-by-13-inch baking pan. Pour in the batter, spreading it evenly. Allow it to cool and set at room temperature, then transfer to the fridge for an overnight rest. The batter needs at least 8 hours of down time, and it will hold for about 24 hours.

To fry the panisse, pour 3 inches of sunflower oil into a wide deep pot over medium heat. While the oil warms, slice the firm chickpea batter into long ribbons approximately ½ inch wide. Once the oil is at 340 degrees, start frying the ribbons, working in batches so as not to overcrowd the pot. Upon contact, the panisse should sizzle; fry until they puff and crisp all over, about 5 minutes. With a slotted spoon or tongs, transfer the panisse to a tray lined with paper towels.

Once this first batch is fried and the pot is clear, drop a few sage leaves into the oil and fry them until crisp and sharp green, a few seconds. Remove from the oil and scatter them over the panisse. Season with salt and immediately serve hot while you fry up the next round, scattering more of the sage leaves over each batch.

Socca

Socca is a chickpea flour pancake from the South of France. A good one is crisp on the exterior, custardy within, and rich with the flavor of olive oil. You may be alarmed by the quantity of oil used in this recipe, but you cannot scrimp—it is key to transforming the loose batter into something with crunch.

Use this recipe as the base for seasonal toppings, adding them right before the socca broils. Socca is especially useful for putting all sorts of loose ends from the fridge to good use. A whole one, served with a salad, could be a meal for one; sliced into bite-sized pieces, it will serve a few people as a nibble.

The batter can rest, covered in the fridge, for up to 4 days. It only improves with age.

Makes 6 soccas

5 cups chickpea flour
Olive oil (at least 6 cups)
Salt

Put the chickpea flour in a large bowl and gradually drizzle 6 cups of water down one side, pouring it into a single spot; as you pour, whisk the puddle until smooth and widen it by pulling in flour from the puddle's edges. Continue whisking until the batter is smooth and has the consistency of paint. Let the batter rest at room temperature for at least 2 to 3 hours, or let rest overnight, covered and in the fridge.

Position an oven rack 12 inches away from the broiler element and turn on the broiler to preheat. Set an 8-inch broilerproof frying pan over high heat and add about ¾ cup olive oil. As the oil warms, stir the batter to incorporate any sediment that has settled. The batter should pour easily, but if it's become too thick, stir in enough splashes of water to loosen it (again, it should have the consistency of paint).

Add about 1 cup of batter to the hot pan, just enough so the oil casts a thin film over the pancake's top. Quickly swirl the pan around to spread out the batter: A Socca should be thinner than an American pancake but thicker than a French crepe. Immediately lower the heat to medium and, when the socca sputters and bubbles, a matter of seconds, sprinkle it with salt (and, if using, the toppings of your choice; see the variations that follow).

Once the socca's edges set and crisp, after 2 to 4 minutes, lift up one edge with a thin spatula and peek: If it is golden, loosen the bottom with the spatula, place the pan in the broiler, and cook the socca until its top crisps but the inside remains a bit fudgy, 3 to 5 minutes. Carefully remove the pan from the oven and pour off any excess oil into a heatproof container. Slide the socca onto a plate lined with paper towels to absorb the oil.

Slice and eat. Socca is best hot, but it is also good at room temperature. You can make more soccas immediately, or hold the batter, covered in the fridge, for the next day.

Socca
with Pine Nuts, Onions, and Sultanas

Makes 6 soccas

Olive oil
4 medium red onions, thinly sliced
¼ cup sultanas or golden raisins
1 batch Socca batter (page 73)
½ cup pine nuts, toasted
Salt

Set a large frying pan over medium-low heat and swirl in 2 to 3 tablespoons olive oil. Add the onions and cook gently, stirring often, until they collapse and lightly caramelize, 15 to 20 minutes. If they start to brown too quickly, lower the heat.

Meanwhile, put the sultanas in a small bowl and add just enough hot water to cover. Set aside to plump, about 5 minutes, then drain and pat dry.

Cook the soccas as instructed on page 73, but before broiling each one, scatter one-sixth of the caramelized onions, pine nuts, and sultanas evenly over it. Season with salt, place the pan under the broiler, and finish cooking as directed.

Socca
with Ceci, Rosemary, and Anchovy

Makes 6 soccas

1 batch Socca batter (page 73)
3 cups cooked chickpeas (see page 15), drained
12 anchovy fillets, torn lengthwise in half
Salt
2 tablespoons rosemary needles

Cook the soccas as instructed on page 73, but before broiling each one, scatter one-sixth of the chickpeas over it. Lightly press the chickpeas into the batter and then drape one-sixth of the anchovies over the socca along with the rosemary needles. Season lightly with salt, place the pan under the broiler, and finish cooking as directed.

Socca
with Fennel Seeds, Sliced Fennel, and Fennel Fronds

Makes 6 soccas

3 fennel bulbs, bushy stalks still intact
Salt
2 tablespoons fennel seeds
1 batch Socca batter (page 73)

Separate the fennel stalks from the bulbs and reserve. Halve the bulbs, tip to root, and discard the tough outer layer of each one (or reserve for another use, like stock). Thinly slice the fennel crosswise into paper-thin slivers.

Bring a large pot of salted water to a boil over a high heat. Add the sliced fennel and blanch until its color lightens, about 30 seconds. Drain, let cool, and pat dry.

While the fennel cools, remove a handful of fronds from the stalks and roughly chop enough of them to get 3 tablespoons. Discard the stalks (or reserve for a stockpot down the road).

Cook the socca as instructed on page 73, but before broiling each one, scatter one-sixth of the blanched fennel slices, fennel fronds, and fennel seeds over it. Season lightly with salt, place the pan under the broiler, and finish cooking as directed.

Socca
with Zucchini Blossoms and Anchovy

Makes 6 soccas

1 batch Socca batter (page 73)
18 zucchini blossoms, stamens removed
12 anchovy fillets, rinsed and halved lengthwise
Salt

Cook the soccas as directed on page 73, but before broiling each one, scatter one-sixth of the toppings evenly over it by first gently tearing the zucchini blossoms into halves or quarters, depending on size, and lightly pressing them into the batter, and then draping the anchovy fillets all over the socca. Season lightly with salt, place the pan under the broiler, and finish cooking as directed.

Pissaladière

This onion and anchovy tart, which comes from Nice, is served all across southern France. Traditionally it is made with a yeast dough, but we prefer the rather more indulgent use of puff pastry. Store-bought puff is fine here, but our own rough puff is very forgiving and delicious so we suggest giving it a go. . . .

Serves 10

FOR THE TOPPING

1 cup olive oil
4 large red onions, thinly sliced
Salt
2 garlic cloves, thinly sliced
20 anchovy fillets,
rinsed and halved lengthwise
⅓ cup Niçoise olives, pitted and torn in half
3 to 4 tablespoons roughly chopped thyme leaves
Freshly ground black pepper

FOR THE PASTRY

1 batch Rough Puff Pastry (page 39)
or 1 pound frozen puff pastry (in one block)
All-purpose flour for dusting

Choose a large wide pot to cook the onions; they should fill it by no more than half. Add the olive oil, onions, and a pinch of salt (season lightly here, as the anchovies are coming) and cook over medium-low heat, stirring frequently to prevent sticking, until the onions soften and start to collapse, about 20 minutes. Add the garlic and continue cooking until the onions completely soften and turn very sweet, at least 1½ hours longer. When you think they are done, continue for another 30 minutes! The onions should darken and reduce by about three-quarters of their original volume. Remove from the heat and let cool completely.

Preheat the oven to 350 degrees. Line a baking sheet with parchment paper. Remove the pastry from the fridge and lightly flour a work surface. Roll the dough out into an 11-by-16-inch rectangle about ¼ inch thick. If the dough is too firm to roll easily, let it stand briefly at room temperature, but it's important that the dough remain cool to the touch. If it warms, refrigerate it until chilled again.

Lay the dough on the lined baking sheet pan. Prick it all over with a fork (this helps ensure an even rise) and place another sheet of parchment on top of it. Place a lightweight baking sheet on top to gently weigh the dough down and keep it from puffing up too much.

Bake the puff until golden brown (lift up the top baking sheet to check), 20 to 25 minutes. Remove from the oven and let the dough cool for at least 10 minutes.

(Continued)

Spread the onions evenly over the dough, leaving a ½-inch border all around the edges. Starting at one corner, about 1½ inches from the end of the dough rectangle, arrange a line of anchovies in a 45-degree diagonal line across the dough. Arrange another diagonal line parallel to the first one and about 1½ inches from it. Continue with the remaining anchovies until the entire surface of the dough is covered with parallel lines. Then repeat the process with the remaining anchovies, arranging them in diagonal lines that run in the opposite direction, forming a tight diamond grid (see page 76) all over the surface of the tart.

Place a torn olive in the center of each diamond. Sprinkle the thyme over the top and finish with a drizzle of olive oil and a few grinds of pepper.

Bake the pissaladière on the oven's top rack until the anchovies melt a bit and the edges of the dough color, 15 to 20 minutes. Let cool for 10 minutes, then slice into squares and serve warm, with a glass of rosé.

Leek and Chèvre Tart

This puff pastry tart with goat cheese and young leeks is an early celebration of spring. You can serve it as a nibble or as a main course with a green salad.

Serves 10

2 medium leeks
½ cup dry white wine
2 fresh bay leaves
1 garlic clove, thinly sliced
1 tablespoon roughly chopped thyme leaves
Olive oil
Salt

1 batch Rough Puff Pastry (page 39)
or 1 pound frozen puff pastry (in one block)
1 large egg yolk
½ cup crème fraîche
8 ounces fresh chèvre
Freshly ground black pepper

To clean the leeks, split them lengthwise in half and rinse them thoroughly under cool running water to remove all the grit between the layers. Trim away and discard the root ends. Chop off the dark tops (save these for a stockpot down the road). Slice the white and pale green portions into ¼-inch-wide half-moons. You should have 2 to 3 cups sliced leeks. Check to make sure the slices are clean; if necessary, give them another rinse under cool water.

Transfer the leeks to a large heavy pot and add the white wine, bay leaves, garlic, ½ tablespoon of the thyme, and ¾ cup olive oil. Season generously with salt and bring to a simmer, then reduce the heat to medium-low and braise the leeks, stirring occasionally to prevent sticking, until they turn meltingly soft and most of the wine has evaporated, 20 to 30 minutes. Remove from the heat and let the leeks cool to room temperature.

To bake the tart, preheat the oven to 400 degrees. Line a baking sheet with parchment paper. On a floured work surface, roll out the pastry to a ¼-inch thickness. Transfer the pastry to the lined sheet pan and prick it all over with a fork (this helps encourage an even rise).

Remove and discard the bay leaves from the pot of leeks and, with a slotted spoon, evenly scatter the leeks over the pastry, leaving a 1-inch border all around. Bake in the oven until the pastry rises and turns lightly golden, about 20 minutes.

Meanwhile, whisk the yolk with the crème fraîche in a small bowl.

Remove the tart from the oven shelf and, working quickly, crumble the chèvre into walnut-sized pieces over it (leaving the border untouched) and then scatter over the remaining ½ tablespoon thyme. Brush (or drizzle) the crème fraîche mixture over the tart, spreading it evenly.

Slide the tart back into the oven and bake until the edges of the dough turn a rich golden brown and the cheese melts and darkens in spots, 10 to 20 minutes. Remove from the oven and let cool for at least 10 minutes.

Grind pepper over the top of the tart and drizzle it with olive oil. Slice and serve.

Tourte de Blettes

Angeles Chavarria, affectionately known as Tina, is King's executive chef. This recipe for a classic Provençal tart filled with cooked greens is hers. It requires a day of rolling and cooking, so she saves it for Sunday lunch, when there's plenty of time to make the pastry and squeeze the Swiss chard bone-dry. We suggest you do the same, or make the filling and pastry dough in stages and keep both in the fridge until you're ready to bake.

Serves 10

FOR THE DOUGH

2 cups all-purpose flour,
plus more for dusting
Kosher salt
10⅔ tablespoons (1⅓ sticks) unsalted butter,
diced and chilled
¼ cup ice water

FOR THE FILLING

Salt
3 bunches Swiss chard (about 2½ pounds),
washed and stems trimmed
2 medium yellow onions
1 garlic clove
Olive oil
½ teaspoon fennel seeds, ground in a spice
grinder, or ½ teaspoon ground fennel
½ teaspoon ground dried red chili,
preferably Calabrian
1 cup plus 2 tablespoons pine nuts
¼ cup grated Parmesan cheese
¼ cup crème fraîche
¼ cup roughly chopped marjoram leaves
Freshly ground black pepper
1 large egg
1 tablespoon heavy cream
2 tablespoons granulated sugar

SPECIAL EQUIPMENT:

A 10-inch fluted tart pan
with a removable bottom

To make the dough, combine the flour and 1 teaspoon salt in a large bowl and add the butter. Using your fingertips, pinch the butter into the flour, creating thin flat flakes. Once the two are combined, gradually add the ice water, mixing with your fingers until a shaggy dough forms.

Turn the dough out, divide it in half, and pat each half into a 2-inch-thick disk. Wrap the disks in a cloth or plastic wrap and chill until firm, at least 30 minutes.

Remove one disk of dough from the fridge. Roll it out between two sheets of lightly floured parchment into a ¼-inch-thick round that is 12 inches across. If it feels sticky, dust with a little extra flour as necessary. Gently lay the round of dough into a 10-inch fluted tart pan and carefully fit it into place, pressing it evenly over the bottom of the pan and up the sides.

Roll out the second disk of dough to 10 inches across and lay it on a lightly floured baking sheet. Refrigerate the dough round and tart shell for at least 30 minutes. (The dough can be held, covered and in the fridge, for a day.)

(Continued)

To prepare the filling, bring a large pot of salted water to a boil over high heat. (If necessary, blanch the chard in batches to avoid overcrowding.) Once the water is at a rumble, add the chard and blanch until the stems are completely tender and taste sweet, about 5 to 7 minutes. Using tongs, transfer the chard to a colander set in the sink to steam-dry. Pour out the pot's water and wipe it clean.

Slice the onions and garlic wafer-thin. Pour about 2 tablespoons olive oil into the cleaned pot and set it over medium heat. Stir in the ground fennel, ground chili, garlic, onions, and pine nuts and cook, stirring, until the onions have softened and the pine nuts are toasted, 6 to 8 minutes. Remove from the heat.

Using your hands, wring the blanched chard dry and then, with a kitchen towel, squeeze it bone-dry. Finely slice the greens and add them to a large bowl. Stir in the onion mixture, Parmesan, and crème fraîche, then stir in about 2 tablespoons olive oil and the marjoram. Add enough salt and pepper so the filling tastes well seasoned and delicious. Let cool to room temperature.

Remove the chilled tart shell from the fridge and preheat the oven to 400 degrees. Spread the cooled filling evenly in the tart shell.

Whisk the egg with the heavy cream in a small bowl and season with salt. With a pastry brush, paint the pastry's rim with this egg wash. Remove the pastry round from the fridge and lay it over the filling, centering it. Using a fork, seal the edges of the dough by pressing them together all around. Paint the top crust with the egg wash and sprinkle with the sugar.

Place the tart on a baking sheet and bake in the oven for 20 minutes. Lower the temperature to 350 degrees and continue baking until the pastry browns and pulls away from the edges of the pan, about 20 minutes longer. Remove the tart from the oven and let rest for 20 minutes before removing the sides from the pan.

Slice the tart and serve warm with a green salad.

Petit Aioli

Petit aioli is the bite-sized version of a celebratory French meal, the grand aioli, where a myriad of boiled vegetables and seafood are served with a giant bowl of garlicky aioli. This starter shares the same spirit but will leave you room for a main course. Having multiple pots of boiling water on the go at once will make this recipe's assembly far quicker and easier. Once the pots are rumbling, it's simply a matter of conducting the orchestra so each element cooks to its ideal point.

Everything can be done in advance, which is as appealing as the garlicky aioli at the center of this feast.

Serves 10

1 pound small potatoes, preferably new potatoes or fingerlings
2 fresh bay leaves
Salt
Olive oil
A small handful of parsley stems (optional)
1 garlic clove, smashed
1 cup Cassis Blanc or similar dry white wine
10 to 12 large shrimp or langoustines (about 1 pound), preferably with heads and tails still attached
16 large mussels (about 1 pound), scrubbed and debearded
10 quail eggs
2½ pounds green beans, preferably haricots verts or runner beans, topped and tailed
15 to 20 small carrots, bushy tops removed
15 to 20 radishes, preferably French breakfast
2 medium zucchini, sliced into ½-inch-thick coins
2 to 3 lemons, cut into wedges
3 cups (1½ batches) Rouille (recipe follows)

Put the potatoes and one bay leaf in a medium pot, add enough cold water to cover the potatoes by 1 inch, and season with salt. Bring the water to a boil over medium heat and cook until the largest potato is tender at its center, about 15 minutes. Drain the potatoes, transfer to a bowl, and season with salt and olive oil; let cool to room temperature.

Meanwhile, fill a large wide pot about one-third full with cold water and add the parsley stems, if using; a good pinch of salt; the garlic clove; the second bay leaf; and the wine. Bring the water to a boil over high heat. Once it is rumbling, add the shrimp (if necessary, top up the pot with enough water to keep them *just* covered), then add the mussels; these should mostly sit on top of the shrimp so they steam. Cover the pot and steam-poach until the mussels open and the shrimp turn pink, 4 to 6 minutes. Use tongs to transfer the opened mussels and the shrimp to a large bowl; if some mussels require a bit more time, cover the pot again and continue cooking until the stubborn mussels yield, a few minutes more.

Discard the cooking water or reserve it to use as a fumet or as a fish stock for the rouille (recipe follows). Arrange the cooked shellfish on a tray in a single layer. Let cool to room temperature and then refrigerate for at least an hour to chill. (The shellfish will hold, covered in the refrigerator, for up to 24 hours.)

Bring a small pot of salted water to a boil over high heat; prepare an ice water bath. Carefully lower the quail eggs into the boiling water and cook for 3½ minutes for a softly set center. Drain and plunge the boiled eggs into the ice water bath to stop the cooking, then remove from the water once cooled and set aside.

Bring a medium pot of salted water to a boil over high heat. Add the beans and cook until al dente, about 3 minutes. Transfer the cooked beans to a colander set in the sink, and add the zucchini to the boiling water. Boil until just tender, 1 to 3 minutes. With a slotted spoon, transfer the zucchini to the colander with the green beans. Add the carrots to the boiling water (if necessary, top up with more water so they are just submerged) and blanch until their centers are just tender, about 4 minutes. Drain and add the carrots to the colander with the other vegetables. Allow everything to steam-dry, then transfer to a bowl and toss with salt to taste.

To serve, break out your finest (and largest) platter. Arrange the vegetables, chilled shellfish, and lemon wedges around a bowl or two of the delicious rouille in the center of the platter. Finish everything with a squeeze of lemon juice, a sprinkle of salt, and a drizzle of olive oil.

Rouille

This garlicky sauce, originating in Marseille, is typically a garnish for fish and seafood soups—most notably that city's bouillabaisse. Making it with homemade fish stock is best, but the broth from simply steaming shellfish works well too.

Makes 2 cups

1 cup roughly torn stale bread (crust removed)
4 garlic cloves
½ cup fish stock or reserved shellfish broth (from recipe above), or cold water
2 generous pinches saffron threads
1 large egg yolk
Salt
½ teaspoon cayenne pepper or ground dried red chili
Juice of ½ lemon
Olive oil (at least 2 cups)

Place the bread and garlic cloves in a small bowl and add the fish stock and saffron. Let soak until the bread absorbs the stock and is stained by the saffron threads, about 10 minutes.

Squeeze the soaked bread over the bowl to remove excess liquid and transfer it to a cutting board; leave the liquid and garlic in the bowl. Run a knife through the bread a couple of times to make a paste; then transfer it to a medium bowl and, using a Microplane, grate in the soaked garlic cloves. Add the egg yolk, a pinch of salt, the cayenne, and the lemon juice and whisk everything together. Whisking constantly, gradually add about 2 cups olive oil, a little at a time (much as you would with an aioli; see page 22), until a thick sauce forms.

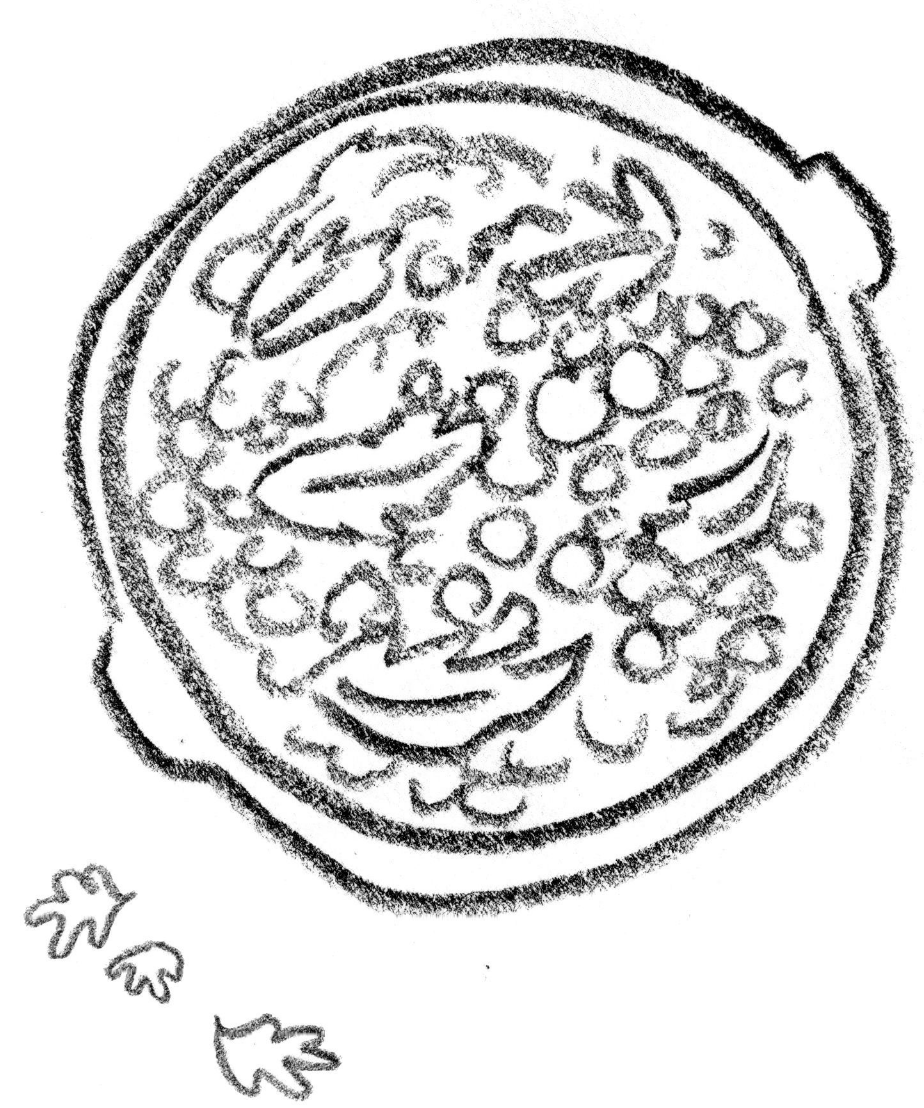

Artichokes Vinaigrette

Whole globe artichokes, simply boiled, are the perfect vehicle for this vinaigrette. But they're also very good with small bowls of melted butter or just lemon and olive oil.

Toothed leaves scattered around the table are the ultimate sign of leisurely feasting, signaling the start of a great party. . . .

Serves 6

FOR THE ARTICHOKES

6 large globe artichokes
3 fresh bay leaves (optional)
6 whole black peppercorns
3 garlic cloves
2 sprigs of thyme
Salt

FOR THE VINAIGRETTE

2 tablespoons roughly chopped thyme leaves
2 cups Mustard Vinaigrette (page 29)

Rinse the artichokes and snap off the small woody leaves around the base of each one. Trim off about ½ inch from the bottoms of the stems. Place the artichokes in a tall wide pot along with the bay leaves, peppercorns, garlic, and thyme sprigs. Add cold water to cover and season generously with salt.

Place a small plate on the artichokes to prevent them from bobbing up, bring the water to a boil over medium heat, and cook until the bases of the artichokes are soft, about 1 hour. To check that they're ready, tug on a central leaf of one artichoke; it should come away with ease. Or check by poking a stem with a sharp knife; there shouldn't be any resistance.

While the artichokes cook, stir the chopped thyme into the vinaigrette; set aside.

When the artichokes are ready, drain them and pat dry. Cut the stems off at the base—these are a chef's treat at King, but if you're feeling generous, you can serve them along with the artichokes. Stand the artichokes up on a platter, fanning out a few layers of their leaves to make room for some of the vinaigrette. Ladle over some of the vinaigrette, making sure it runs into the artichokes' many pockets. Serve the remaining vinaigrette in small bowls for dipping.

CHAPTER 5

Salads

WE LIKE OUR SALADS BIG AND BOLD. MOUNDS OF PERKY LEAVES WILL ALWAYS SIT AT the center of the table and are rarely demoted to the side of our plate. With little to hide behind, they are the purest reflection of each season with every component—the handfuls of leaves, the soft herbs, or slivers of raw or marinated veg—carefully selected for its contribution to the bowl.

In the spring and summer, we use delicate lettuces—tender and often a little sweet. These include everything from frilly fava leaves and pea shoots to citrusy sorrel, Bibb lettuces, and pale green baby gems (sometimes they're ruby red). Tina loves her sunny, morning market trips to the Greenmarket at Union Square, where she handpicks the leaves for the menu that day. She returns back to King with her shopping basket filled with purslane or wild rocket from H.O.G. Farm or Lani's Farm. The leaves get laid out on Table 25, where she then wraps them in a damp paper towel to keep them fresh for dinner service. The leaves are so tender and delicious that they only require a gentle touch and just a few seasonal peaks—shavings of zucchini, perhaps some young favas, a big pinch of torn mint or basil, and maybe some lemon zest.

By deep winter, when we are scratching our heads as we write the menu each gray morning, we cheer on the arrival of the chicories! Belgian endive and Treviso! Puntarelle! Grumolo! Pink endive! They bring a brightness both in flavor and color to the fridge, and with so many varieties to enjoy, they keep us going until spring. Waxy chicory leaves are often sharp, robust, and slightly bitter—they pair especially well with punchier dressings: Puntarelle likes generous amounts of vinegar-soaked anchovies (see page 96) tossed through, and Treviso takes kindly to Lucy's blood orange vinaigrette (page 98).

We keep our dressings simple—at most they require only four or so ingredients. King's go-to vinaigrette is made with three parts extra virgin olive oil (see page 29) to one part acid. Often the acid is freshly squeezed lemon juice (we juice the lemons as we go), but vinegar is substituted for heartier needs such as the winter leaves (or when we're dressing tomatoes). Every salad that leaves our pass, from a composed plate to the pinch of watercress accompanying a chop, gets seasoned, even if we're simply tossing some greens in the resting juices of Braised Rabbit (page 260). Crucially, nothing is dressed until just before it hits the plate.

And when it comes to dressing leaves we use our hands as tongs, delicately tossing the leaves to make sure the leaves are lightly coated—glossy, never soggy. And taste, taste, taste as you toss so that you may tweak as you go—a little more salt? A drop more acid? A pinch of pepper. Then taste again. . . .

Much of the time, before the leaves hit the table, we may finish them with a final lift. For salty contrast, often a chalky cheese, sharp pecorino, or a gooey Gorgonzola, or a grating of a toasted walnut or hazelnut for something earthier, and if we are in need of a briny hit or extra brightness, a flurry of bottarga di muggine is followed by some lemon zest.

At the table, we tend to forgo forks and enjoy the leaves from our hands. For some reason, we think they taste better that way.

Salade Verte
with Anchoïade

The addition of Little Gems and watercress steers this salad away from a classic crudité plate. Don't feel bound by the vegetables listed below. Rather, let the season guide you, remembering that crunch is king. We also like making this salad with fennel, cucumber, celery hearts, cauliflower florets, asparagus, snap peas, and so on. . . .

We favor a soft-boiled egg here, but to each their own.

Serves 4 to 6

Salt
2 or 3 large eggs
6 small radishes, preferably French Breakfast
6 small white turnips, greens trimmed
6 small or baby rainbow carrots, peeled if the skins look dry or dirty
½ lemon
Freshly ground black pepper
Olive oil
2 heads Little Gem lettuce
1 bunch watercress, tough stems discarded (about 2 cups)
6 tablespoons Anchoïade (page 23), plus more as needed
2 or 3 anchovy fillets, held under olive oil

Bring a small pot of salted water to a boil over high heat. Carefully lower the eggs into the pot, reduce the heat, and simmer for about 7 minutes. Drain the eggs and run under cold water to cool, then peel and halve them. The yolks should be just set but remain fudgy at the center.

Cut the radishes and turnips into quarters. Slice the carrots lengthwise into ½-inch spears. Add everything to a medium bowl and season with a squeeze of lemon juice, salt and pepper, and 1 to 2 tablespoons olive oil. Toss well and let the vegetables marinate while you prepare the leaves.

Remove any wilted or bruised outer leaves from the Little Gems. Snap off all the crisp pretty leaves and add them to a large salad bowl. When you reach the hearts, quarter them lengthwise and add to the bowl.

Toss the watercress into the salad bowl and pour the anchoïade around the inside of the bowl. Gently toss the leaves around until they pick up a light coating. Taste and adjust the seasoning with salt, lemon, and/or more dressing as needed, until the leaves taste punchy. Add the marinating vegetables, tossing until they are evenly dispersed.

Pile the salad high on a large platter and arrange the eggs on top. Drape half an anchovy fillet over each egg yolk and then season the eggs with pepper. Or, if assembling individual plates, top each with a halved egg dressed with half an anchovy fillet and some pepper.

Baby Gems

with Green Almonds, Mint, and Pecorino

Make this salad when firm and fuzzy produce peaks. The snap peas should be sweet, the favas tender, and the green almonds plump.

Green almonds can be tricky to find, but while they are not essential, they are worth the hunt. Use them whole, nipping off their small stalks and then slicing off thin rounds just before serving (otherwise, they will discolor!).

Double-podding favas is a faff, but if they are not in peak form, their skins are too tough to eat. Any favas you don't use for this salad can be used to make smashed favas with pecorino (see pages 18 and 51).

Serves 4 to 6

1 cup sugar snap peas
½ cup green almonds (see headnote)
Grated zest of 1 lemon; lemon reserved and halved
A small handful of mint leaves, torn into pieces
½ cup double-podded fava beans or Favas Sott'olio (page 176)
2 heads Little Gem lettuce, leaves separated
Salt
Olive oil
2 cups pea shoots
A piece of pecorino cheese for grating

Slice the sugar snaps on the bias into oblong shards, as thin as possible. Slice the green almonds into equally thin rounds, and add them both to a large bowl. Toss with a squeeze of lemon juice so they don't oxidize. Add the mint, favas, and Little Gem leaves. Season with salt, another squeeze of lemon juice, and a dribble of olive oil, about 2 tablespoons. Toss with your hands, checking that every leaf is slicked, and then taste and adjust with more salt, lemon juice, and/or oil as needed. The salad should taste bright and delicious. Mix in the pea shoots, tossing them in delicately, as they're prone to wilting.

Mound the salad on a large serving plate and shave over some pecorino, using a sharp knife or a vegetable peeler. We use a chef's knife to shave broad, thin pieces off the cheese block. Finish with lemon zest and a drizzle of olive oil.

Agretti, Sorrel, Purslane, and Asparagus Salad
with Bottarga

This salad celebrates spring's first delights. Some of these ingredients may be new to you and could take some time to find, but if you're curious, they're worth seeking out to make a salad that defines our kitchen in the months of March and April.

Serves 4 to 6

Salt
1½ cups agretti or samphire, rinsed
6 to 8 large asparagus spears
½ lemon
Olive oil
2 cups baby spinach
1½ cups sorrel
½ cup purslane, mâche, or pea shoots
One 4-ounce stick bottarga di muggine, peeled

Fill a small pot with lightly salted water and bring to a boil over high heat. Add the agretti and boil until tender, about 5 minutes. Drain in a colander and let cool.

Snap the woody bottoms off the asparagus and discard (or save for stock). Slice the tender stalks and tips on the bias into thin slivers.

When the agretti is cool, add it to a large bowl, along with the asparagus, and dress with a squeeze of lemon juice, salt, and olive oil to taste. Add the baby spinach, sorrel, and purslane and, using your hands, gently toss everything together. The seasoning on the agretti and asparagus will carry over enough to lightly coat the salad leaves. Taste and see if more seasoning is needed and add more salt and/or olive oil as necessary, but note that the lemony-ness of the sorrel means you won't need additional lemon juice.

Spread the salad out on a large plate, so you can see all the components. Finish by grating over some bottarga di muggine, passing it over a Microplane until the salad is covered in a coating of golden flurries. Serve immediately.

Puntarelle and Endive Alla Romana

This is King's take on Italy's puntarelle alla Romana. Puntarelle's season is short, and as we never seem to buy enough to sate ourselves, we stretch whatever we have with endive. It mimics puntarelle's crunch nicely and stands up to the bracing anchovy dressing as well.

Preparing the puntarelle does takes a little effort, but it is a do-ahead kitchen job; at the very last minute, all that's really required is drying and dressing. You will want to give the puntarelle a few hours to rest in the ice bath so the pieces crisp and curl properly. Toss the greens intentionally for a glossy, emulsified finish.

Serves 4 to 6

FOR THE SALAD

1 large head puntarelle (1¼ pounds)
2 Belgian endives (about ½ pound each)

FOR THE ANCHOVY DRESSING

18 to 20 anchovy fillets, finely chopped
Scant 5 tablespoons red wine vinegar
¼ teaspoon crushed dried red chili, plus more as needed
Freshly ground black pepper
Olive oil

Set up an ice bath and set a large sieve in it. To prepare the puntarelle, remove its soft, dark leaves; discard or reserve for another use (at King, we treat these like spinach and braise them slowly). Once you hit the wispy pale inner leaves that are attached to long white stalks that resemble fingers, snap these off the stalks and add them to the sieve in the ice bath. Now cut off the stalks: One by one, bend each stalk back near its base until it snaps—this is your separation point. Discard the woody lower parts of the stalks and sliver the tender upper portions lengthwise, on the bias, into thin strips, ⅛ inch wide or less. Yes, we know the stalks are hollow, but you can slice them all up regardless. Add the sliced puntarelle to the sieve.

Let the puntarelle stand in the ice bath until very crisp, at least 2 to 3 hours; add more ice as needed to keep it cold. (Prepared puntarelle holds for about a day in an ice bath in the fridge.)

To prepare the endives (this can be done up to an hour or so before serving), chop 1 inch off the top of each head, separating these leafy bits, and add to the sieve with the puntarelle. Slice the endive's midsections crosswise into ½-inch-wide crescents. Stop slicing once you hit the cores, about 2 inches up from the base, and snap off the leaves surrounding the cores. Add them, along with the rest of the sliced endive, to the sieve. Halve the cores lengthwise and trim away the browned bits at the base. Slice the cores on the bias into long, thin shards, ⅛ inch wide or less. Add to the sieve.

To make the dressing, combine the anchovies, vinegar, red chili, and some pepper in a small bowl and let the anchovies macerate until they disintegrate at the edges, at least 10 minutes.

When you're about ready to serve (no sooner!), lift the sieve out of the ice bath and drain the puntarelle and endive very, very well: Dry them in batches in a salad spinner until bone-dry.

Place the puntarelle and endive in a large bowl. Spoon the anchovies out of the vinegar bath, tilting out most of the macerating liquid, and spoon the anchovies, with a little of their vinegar, over the salad, tossing to lightly coat. Taste and season with salt and more runoff vinegar if necessary. The salad should taste bright and well seasoned.

Pour about 2½ tablespoons olive oil over the salad and toss until the leaves are glossy and uniformly coated. Toss again with intent! This is a sturdy salad, and it must be vigorously mixed so that the dressing works itself into the leaves. Taste again and adjust the seasoning as necessary with more olive oil, chili, pepper, and/or runoff vinegar.

Winter Leaves in Lucy's Dressing
with Blood Orange, Olives, and Almonds

Lucy Gibson, a beloved King chef who is now the head chef at our sister restaurant in Rockefeller Center, Jupiter, came up with this dressing. It is made with blood orange juice, citrus zest, and smashed fennel seeds. Bright, bitter-sweet, and punchy, it gives many of our winter salads flair. Since freshly squeezed orange juice doesn't keep, the dressing *must* be made on the day it is used. Also, do keep the dressing's acid separate from the oil until the salad is assembled.

Any bitter radicchio will do here, but our favorites are Treviso Tardivo (for its lovely plumed leaves) and Rosa del Veneto (for its broad, waxy pink ones). Both are heirloom varieties with wonderful snap. That said, regular radicchio, including the tightly balled heads found at most grocery stores, will work here.

This salad can stand alone, but it pairs nicely with grilled fish (see page 231), duck confit, or most roasted birds.

Serves 4 to 6

FOR THE DRESSING

Finely grated zest of 2 blood oranges; oranges reserved
¼ teaspoon freshly ground fennel seeds
Pinch of crushed dried red chili, preferably Calabrian
1¼ tablespoons red wine vinegar
1 tablespoon lemon juice

FOR THE SALAD

¼ cup whole unblanched almonds
2 heads radicchio, preferably a mix of Treviso, Rosa del Veneto, and/or other varieties
2 small fennel bulbs, stalks and fronds still attached
Salt
4 blood oranges, peeled and supremed
3 tablespoons roughly torn, pitted Taggiasca olives
Olive oil

Preheat the oven to 375 degrees. To make the dressing, combine the zest, ground fennel seeds, chili, red wine vinegar, and lemon juice together in a small bowl. Juice the oranges and add 2½ tablespoons of their juice to the bowl; reserve the remaining orange juice.

Spread the almonds in a single layer on a small baking sheet and toast in the oven until golden brown, 10 to 15 minutes. Remove from the oven.

Using a very sharp knife, slice all but 8 of the roasted almonds lengthwise into fine shards (it's best to slice or chop toasted nuts while still warm, as they harden as they cool). Set the remaining almonds aside.

To prepare the radicchio, remove and discard any tatty outer leaves. Chop off about 3 inches from the top of each head. Place the tops in a large salad bowl. Slice the midsections crosswise, moving from the top down to the root ends; stop slicing once the white core becomes pronounced. Add the slices to the salad bowl. Trim away the brown bits at the base of each core, keeping as much of it intact as possible. Snap off any leaves surrounding the stems and add them to the salad bowl. Slice the stems lengthwise into thin slivers, ⅛ inch thick or less, and add them to the bowl.

Remove the fronds from the fennel stalks and set them aside. Cut off the stalks (these are very good for stocks!) and halve the bulbs lengthwise, top to root. Using a mandoline or a very sharp knife, shave the bulbs, starting from a cut side, into paper-thin slivers. Add these to the salad bowl.

Sprinkle the salad with salt. Whisk the orange dressing until it looks more or less uniform, quickly spoon 3 to 4 tablespoons of it around the salad bowl's inside walls, and toss the leaves until they pick up a light coating. Mix in the orange segments, sliced almonds, olives, and the reserved fennel fronds. Have a taste and adjust the seasoning as necessary. Drizzle over about 3 tablespoons olive oil and toss until the leaves glisten. Taste and season with more orange juice, olive oil, and/or salt as necessary.

When plating, show off the radicchio's curls by standing the tops upright. Tuck the orange segments, sliced almonds, and olives all around, so they peek out here and there. Finely grate over the reserved whole almonds (much like you would a hunk of cheese).

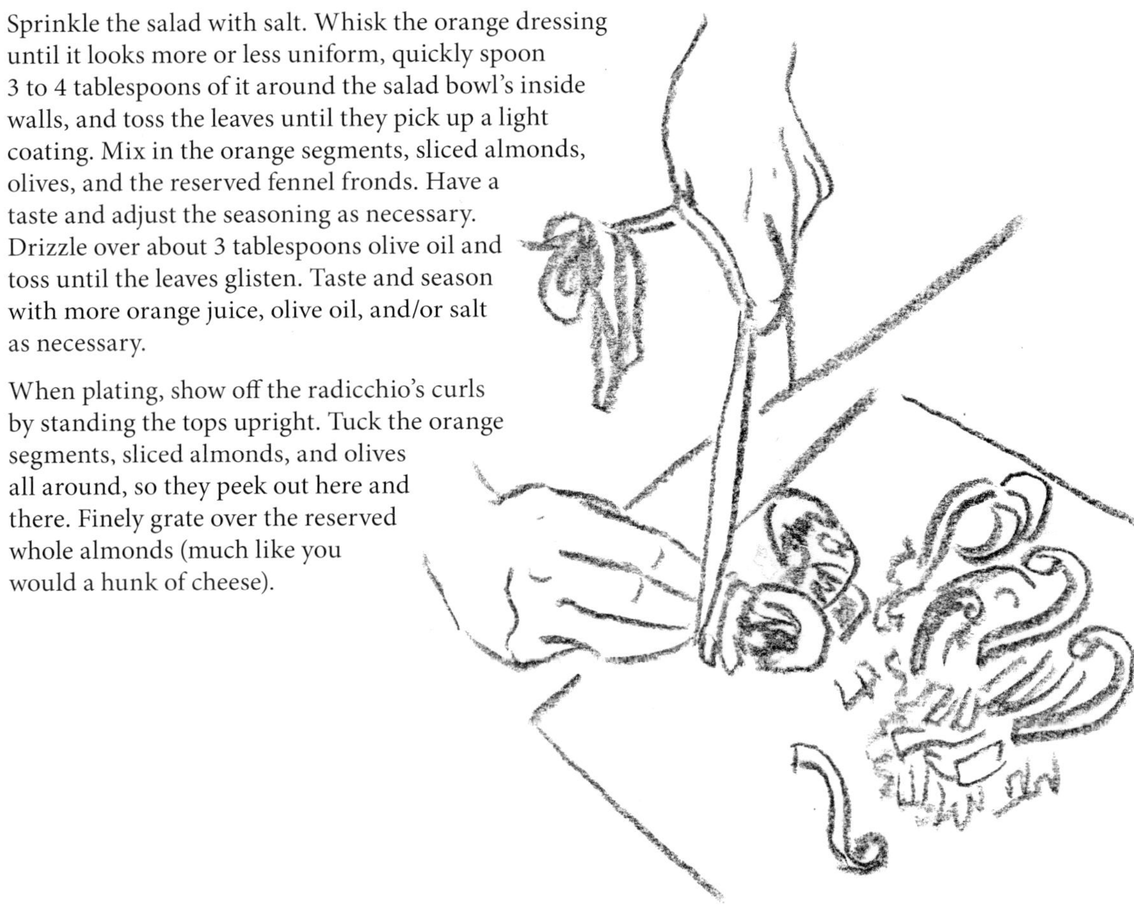

Madame Moriaz's Chèvre and Tomato Salad

In the forty years that I have known Madame Moriaz, she has not aged. Perhaps it's her appetite for good cheese or the odd Ricard? But I think it's due to the sun-drenched life she leads running her family's hotel on the Côte d'Azur, an hour east of Marseille.

The cheese trolley at the hotel's restaurant boasts all the regional gems, but my favorite, starting when I was young, has always been the marinated chèvre, drenched in olive oil and packed with herbs.

Individual fresh chèvre are tricky to find, so you can slice thick rounds from a log. It's best to let the cheese marinate for at least a few hours, or overnight in the fridge, before serving. I always marinate a little more than needed, so there's extra for spreading on bread. Adding a bowl of French Tapenade (page 26) would also be welcome.

—Jess

Serves 4

FOR THE MARINATED CHÈVRE

2 goat cheese crottins (4 to 6 ounces each) or a log of fresh goat cheese (8 to 12 ounces)
Olive oil (at least 4 cups)
2 tablespoons thyme leaves
12 to 16 rosemary needles
2 dried red chilies
A good pinch of fennel seeds
2 bay leaves
6 whole black peppercorns

FOR THE CROUTONS

¼ loaf day-old rustic bread, crust removed
Olive oil
Salt

FOR THE SALAD

1½ cups cherry tomatoes, preferably Datterini or Sungolds, or a combination
Salt
Olive oil
Freshly ground black pepper
2 large heirloom tomatoes (about 2 pounds)
Leaves from 2 to 4 sprigs of mint
½ lemon

To make the marinated chèvre, if using crottins, slice them in half across their equators. If using a log, slice it into 2-inch-thick rounds. To marinate the cheese, choose either a large Mason jar or a shallow dish large enough to hold the cheese rounds plus a little wiggle room for the herbs and oil.

If using a jar, pour in a little olive oil and add a chèvre round. Add a generous pinch or two each of the thyme, rosemary, the dried chilies, and fennel seeds, a bay leaf, and a few

(Continued)

peppercorns. Then add a bit more oil, another chèvre round, and more seasonings. Continue layering until all the chèvre is stacked and dressed. Pour in enough olive oil to fully submerge the cheese and seal the container. Or, if you are using a dish, cover the bottom with a thin pool of olive oil and add half the seasonings. Add the goat cheese rounds, sprinkle over the remaining seasonings, and pour in enough olive oil to submerge the cheese. Cover the cheese with a sheet of parchment paper.

Let the crottins sit for at least a few hours at room temperature, or cover and refrigerate overnight.

To make the croutons, preheat the oven to 450 degrees. Slice the bread into wafer-thin slices.

Choose a baking sheet large enough to hold the croutons in a single layer (or use a few sheets). Grease the pan with a tablespoon of oil and sprinkle with a pinch of salt. Lay the bread on the pan and season the slices with a little olive oil and salt. Bake on the oven's top rack until the slices are crisp and golden brown, 5 to 7 minutes. Flip the slices and toast for about another minute. Transfer the croutons to a rack to cool. (They will keep in an airtight container for up to a day.)

To make the salad, halve the cherry tomatoes across their equators. Set a sieve over a large bowl and pinch each halved tomato over the sieve, squeezing its belly and seeds into it (reserve the pinched tomatoes). Press on the captured seeds with the back of a spoon to extract all their juice; discard the seeds. Add the pinched tomatoes to the bowl with the tomato juice and season with salt, about 2 tablespoons olive oil, some pepper, and a little squeeze of lemon juice.

Core the heirlooms and slice them into chunky wedges. Add to the bowl with the cherry tomatoes, tear in the mint leaves, and gently toss. Taste and season with more salt or oil as needed.

Place a marinated crottin or slice of cheese on one side of each plate. Top it with about 1 tablespoon of the marinade and a few of its herbs. Arrange a tumble of tomato salad alongside the cheese. At the restaurant, we stand a crouton up between the two, like a sail. If you'd rather serve this family-style, arrange the tomato salad, the croutons, and the marinated chèvre on serving plates, stacking the croutons up high.

Radicchio
with Persimmon, Hazelnuts, and Gorgonzola

Bright winter fruit, bitter leaves, toasted nuts, and blue cheese make this salad full-spectrum. Swap out the Gorgonzola or hazelnuts for another cheese or nut as inclined. But be sure to use Fuyu persimmons. No other winter fruits have their color, texture, and taste.

Serves 4 to 6

4 ripe Fuyu persimmons
½ teaspoon thyme leaves, chopped
Salt and freshly ground black pepper
Olive oil
¼ cup hazelnuts
2 heads Treviso and/or other radicchio, preferably a combination
½ lemon
¼ cup crumbled Gorgonzola cheese

Preheat the oven to 450 degrees. Tear each persimmon into 8 chunky wedges—we like the ragged edges of torn fruit, but slicing is also an option. Put the persimmons in a bowl and toss with the thyme, a pinch of salt, some pepper, and 1 to 2 tablespoons olive oil.

Spread the persimmon wedges out on a baking sheet and roast until they soften and lightly caramelize, 15 to 20 minutes. Remove from the oven and let cool.

Meanwhile, spread the hazelnuts out on a small baking sheet and roast until aromatic and a rich golden brown, about 10 minutes. Remove from the oven, and once the nuts are cool enough to handle, crush using a mortar and pestle or a rolling pin until they shatter into chunky, uneven pieces. Let cool completely.

Remove and discard the outer tatty leaves from the radicchio. Snap the good leaves into a large salad bowl. If some are too big for large bites, tear them into more manageable pieces. For a Treviso head, slice off the top half and thinly slice the rest into ½-inch-wide rounds, working from the cut side down; transfer to a large salad bowl.

Season the radicchio with a pinch of salt, a squeeze of lemon juice, and 1 to 2 tablespoons olive oil. Toss, taste, and add more salt, lemon juice, and/or olive oil until the salad is a little glossy and tastes sharp. Mix in the nuts, roasted persimmons, and Gorgonzola and season once again with salt if needed.

Mound the salad on a serving plate or platter, the taller the better, and serve.

CHAPTER 6

Soups

SEASONAL, FLEXIBLE, FRUGAL, AND CAREFULLY MADE, SOUPS ARE AN INTEGRAL PART OF the home kitchens of France and Italy. It follows, then, that they are integral to our kitchen as well.

The Italians' mastery of bread-, bean-, and water-based soups—*cucina povera* at its most comforting—is a source of constant inspiration. And the full-bodied French pureed soups are among the best we've ever had. From both camps come scores of baked soups, quick soups, and involved slow-cooked soups, all represented in this chapter.

Ever-present is our fridge-sweep soup, less of a recipe and more of a formula applied to whatever vegetables are on hand (or about to turn). To begin, make a sofrito (Italian) or mirepoix (French) by slowly braising a combination of chopped onion, celery, carrot, fennel, and/or leeks in olive oil—cook this for much, much longer than you might think is necessary. Then add some cooked beans or blanched greens, or both, and cover everything with liquid, submerging the pot's contents by about an inch. Bean water (see page 15) is our preferred cooking liquor, but water or broth are reached for too. Simmer everything until the vegetables go completely soft and their flavors deepen and resonate. To give the soup body without heft, puree half the contents of the pot (no cream is necessary) and then combine with the rest of the soup. Or, alternatively, give your fridge-sweep a Tuscan finish and lay slices of day-old bread over its top, drizzle on lots of olive oil, and bake until a golden lid forms.

Anything (truly) can become a soup. Like the French and Italian cooks we celebrate, the only rule we religiously follow is that we always use what's in season and on hand. With that in mind, we ask that the recipes within this chapter be thought of as suggestions rather than prescriptions. The precise amount of each ingredient matters less than what you actually have to work with. If there are more herbs on hand, use them. Less zucchini, that's fine. If you're trying to get rid of six ribs of celery, not three, use them all. Often a spare tomato torn into a sofrito is a good idea. . . .

We hope these humble dishes, our most beloved soups, teach you how to think resourcefully about ingredients, to cook with intuition, and, as ever, to taste at every stage.

Soupe au Pesto

It's hard to go wrong when some of spring's most delicious produce comes together in a pot. But this French vegetable soup is particularly delicious thanks to attentive dicing, quick cooking, and partial blitzing.

After shelling the peas and favas, use the pods to make a fresh vegetable stock—simmering them, along with whatever else makes sense (carrots, onions, any soft herbs in the fridge . . .) in lightly salted water until a spring-green taste emerges.

Do spend time cutting all the vegetables into very little pieces so they will fit, along with the artichokes and favas, in the belly of a large spoon.

Pureeing half the soup at the end gives it the texture of something laden with cream, although it is not. As is classic with this vegetable soup, we finish off each helping with a drizzle of pesto.

Serves 6

FOR THE SOUP

3 small yellow onions, thinly sliced
Salt
Olive oil
1 cup shelled fava beans (about 1½ pounds favas in the pod)
10 baby artichokes, prepped (see page 110) and quartered
2 small zucchini, diced into ½-inch pieces
6 cups warm vegetable broth, plus more as needed
2 cups English peas
1 cup thinly sliced asparagus (cut on the bias)
⅓ cup roughly chopped mixed soft herbs (mint, parsley, and/or basil leaves)

TO FINISH

½ cup Pesto (recipe follows)

Place a heavy pot over medium to medium-low heat, add the onions, along with a pinch of salt, and 3 tablespoons olive oil, and cook gently until very soft and translucent, about 5 minutes. Increase the heat slightly, stir in the favas and artichokes, and cook, stirring often, until the artichokes are al dente, about 10 minutes. To check, poke a large artichoke quarter at its thickest point with the tip of a knife: You want a little resistance at the very center, but that's it.

Stir in the zucchini and cook until soft at the edges, about 5 minutes. Pour in 6 cups of vegetable broth, increase the heat to medium-high, and bring to an active simmer. Once the soup has rumbled for a moment, reduce the heat to a gentle simmer and cook until the favas and zucchini have completely softened and the broth is flavorful, about 15 minutes. The favas will wrinkle and brown as they soften.

Add the peas and asparagus and simmer until both are just cooked and bright green, 3 to 5 minutes. (If your asparagus isn't very fresh, or it's very fibrous, add to the pot a minute or so

(Continued)

before adding the peas.) Once all the vegetables are tender, stir in the herbs. As soon as their color sets, 30 seconds or less, turn off the heat and let the soup cool until hot but no longer scalding.

Transfer half the soup to a blender or food processor and puree until smooth. Stir the puree back into the pot and stir in enough olive oil so the soup takes on a glossy sheen, about ½ cup. Season with salt and more olive oil to taste, stopping only once sips are rich and creamy.

Let the soup settle further off the heat; its flavor will only improve. Once lukewarm, after 30 minutes or more, taste and season again as necessary with salt and olive oil. Serve in bowls, with generous helpings of pesto drizzled on top.

ARTICHOKE PREP

Hold a whole artichoke in one hand and snap away the small dark leaves near the base.

Then continue snapping off leaves until you reach the tender light-colored ones. Stop once all the leaves are tender, from the base up to the pointy top. Discard the snapped-off leaves or save for another use (like a vegetable stock).

Holding the artichoke, take a sturdy vegetable peeler and trim the base, working from the lower leaves down to the stem, until smooth and tender.

Set the artichoke on a work surface and trim away the thin, fibrous bottom of the stem end. Now, cut away the pointy leaves at the point where they start to darken, so the artichoke's top is flat.

With a small spoon, scoop out the fibrous heart from the center. Once the choke has been removed, run your finger along the resulting cavity and scoop further if any prickly hairs remain.

As you prep each artichoke, place them in a bowl of water with a lemon or two squeezed in to prevent them from discoloring.

Pesto

A good pesto is about two things: the quality of the ingredients and the intensity of the color. To make it bright green, stream in hot water as you puree it to set the basil's electric green.

Makes 2 cups

4 packed cups basil leaves
1 cup pine nuts
1 garlic clove, crushed
1 cup grated Parmesan cheese
Salt
Olive oil (at least 1 cup)

Combine the basil, pine nuts, garlic, Parmesan, and a teaspoon of salt in a blender or small food processor and blitz until you have a coarse mixture. Scrape down the sides of the jar or bowl as needed between pulses. With the blade running, stream in about 1 cup olive oil. Once a sauce has formed, loosen it by whizzing in a thin stream of very hot water, ½ cup or less, depending on the desired consistency. Season with salt to taste.

Use immediately or store in a container in the fridge with some olive oil poured over top to prevent oxidation.

Potato Watercress Soup

This soup is sexier than its name suggests. The potatoes and crème fraîche give it a silky body without adding bulk. And the peppery cress adds more interest than most green soups offer.

Its three essentials are squeaky clean leeks (remove all the grit between the layers), a flavorful stock (homemade, of course), and a mindful cooking time (boil the cress until emerald green and no longer).

Serves 6 to 8

1 leek, split lengthwise and washed well
3 tablespoons unsalted butter
Salt
4 cups diced (1-inch cubes) peeled Yukon Gold potatoes
4 cups chicken stock, homemade (see page 35)
3 bunches watercress, woody stems discarded and roughly chopped (about 6 cups)
2 tablespoons crème fraîche, plus more to finish
Freshly ground black pepper

Remove and discard the dark green tops of the leek and slice the white and light green portions into ½-inch-wide rounds. Wash the slices again, as there is likely to still be some sand there despite all your efforts. Dry thoroughly.

Melt the butter in a medium pot over medium heat. Add the leek, season with a pinch of salt, and cook gently until the slices soften but do not pick up any color, about 5 minutes.

Stir in the potatoes, coating them in buttery leeks. Pour in the chicken stock, increase the heat to medium-high, bring the soup to an active simmer (a few large bubbles should break the surface at a time), and cook until a large piece of potato is soft enough to be crushed with the back of a spoon, about 15 minutes. Stir in the watercress and simmer just until it is wilted and a sharp emerald color, 1 to 2 minutes. (If the cress cooks too long, its color will dull. . . .)

Remove from the heat and puree the soup with an immersion blender until smooth. Or, if you don't have an immersion blender, puree in batches in a food processor or blender, and return all the soup to the pot. Whatever the device, run the blade for longer than you might be inclined—at least a minute or more—so the greens fully break down and the soup is velvety soft.

Stir the crème fraîche into the soup and season it with more salt and with pepper to taste. Serve hot in bowls, topped with dollops of crème fraîche.

Pappa Pomodoro

Tuscans know a thing or two about bread soups. And this, their most cherished, requires only a handful of ingredients. It does, however, demand patience: the tomatoes must be blanched, peeled, crushed, seasoned, and slow-simmered even before meeting with the bread that turns their stewed juices into this hearty classic, a thick soup that feels part porridge.

Please save this recipe for late summer when—and only when—tomatoes are ripe and juicy. Do not attempt to make this with canned tomatoes, no matter their quality. The results will be disappointing rather than astonishing. Stale bread is a must—anything fresh just leaves a starchy slop.

Serves 4 to 6

Salt
8 pounds ripe tomatoes
Olive oil
2 garlic cloves, thinly slivered
A handful of basil leaves, plus more to garnish
Freshly ground black pepper
1 large loaf country bread, white or sourdough, 1 to 2 days old
Extra virgin olive oil for serving

Bring a large pot of salted water to a boil over high heat. As it comes up, lightly score the top and bottom of each tomato with a cross mark. Set up a large ice bath.

Working in batches, plop the tomatoes into the boiling water and place a plate on top of them to stop them from bobbing up. Blanch until the skins begin to peel away at the score marks, 1 to 2 minutes. With tongs, remove the plate (careful, it's hot!), and transfer the tomatoes to the ice bath using a slotted spoon. Turn off the heat but keep the blanching water on the stove, as you may need it to loosen the soup later.

Once the tomatoes are cool enough to handle, remove them from the ice bath and peel away their skins. Place the peeled tomatoes on a cutting board and halve them crosswise. With a small spoon, scoop out their seeds and pulp and discard them. Cut out all their eyes. Place the cleaned, hollowed-out tomatoes in a large bowl. Season with salt and a generous pour of olive oil, 2 to 3 tablespoons. Mash the tomatoes up with your hands until they have broken down into large chunks.

Place a wide heavy pot over medium heat. Pour in 3 tablespoons olive oil and stir in the slivered garlic, basil leaves, and a pinch each of salt and pepper. Gently fry the aromatics until the garlic's scent blooms, 1 to 2 minutes (don't let it brown!).

Stir in the crushed tomatoes, plus all their juices, and gently simmer over low heat until the sauce thickens slightly, 30 to 45 minutes. Be careful not to overreduce it; the sauce should remain loose—you do not want this jammy. If you accidentally reduce the tomatoes too much, add a small ladleful or two of the reserved blanching water. Toward the end of the cooking time, season the soup with salt to taste.

Meanwhile, cut away and discard the bread's crust. Tear its interior into long straggly scraps, approximately 2 inches across and as long as the loaf will allow. If the loaf is not dry enough (which means that it will absorb too much liquid and bloat more than desired), toast the scraps on a baking sheet in a 300-degree oven until its excess moisture evaporates, about 20 minutes; do not allow the bread to pick up any color.

Lay the dry scraps over the top of the soup, completely covering it with a solid "lid." Gently cook over low heat until the bread absorbs some of the soup, about 5 minutes. Turn off the heat and let the soup stand, undisturbed, until it is at room temperature and the bread has fully absorbed it, at least 30 minutes.

With a large spoon, fold the bread into the soup while breaking it up. Taste and season with salt as you go. Stop mixing before the texture becomes uniform. If the pappa starts to look dense or claggy, loosen it with splashes of the reserved blanching water to reach a textured, porridge-like consistency that's still fresh and light.

Serve in bowls, with a few torn basil leaves over the top and lots of extra virgin olive oil.

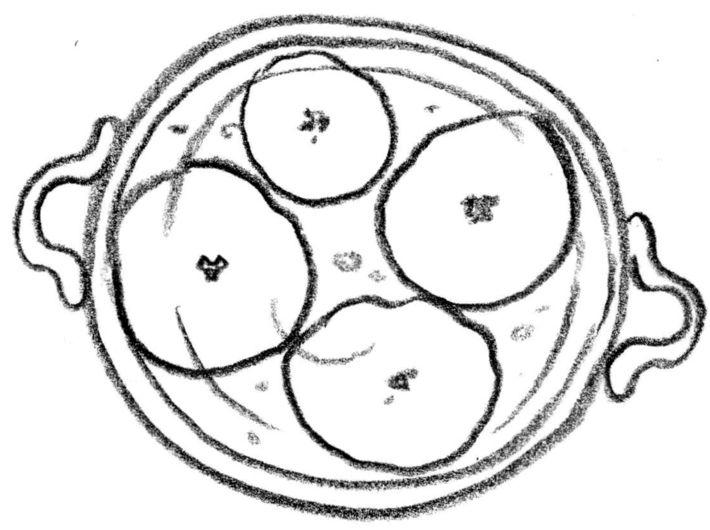

Raclette Soup

The best thing that came from our pandemic experience was this soup.

After New York City shut down, we tried everything to breathe life into our restaurant. And the most treasured result was a pop-up raclette window. On weekends, during the first long winter, we'd slide open the bar's accordion doors so neighbors and friends could gather out on the terrace. Blankets and mulled wine kept everyone warm as we scraped raclette over boiled new potatoes, cornichons, and pickled onions. At the end of each weekend, we were left with heaps of trimmings from the half wheels of raclette. And from those scraps, we made this soup. Served on Monday evenings, it gave the comfort we all needed.

Serves 6

1¾ pounds waxy potatoes, peeled
1 large head savoy cabbage (about 1½ pounds)
1 day-old large loaf country or sourdough bread
Salt
4 large garlic cloves
About 4 cups hot chicken stock, homemade (see page 35) or store-bought, if not using the reserved cabbage blanching water (see method)
16 to 20 anchovy fillets, rinsed
Olive oil
⅓ cup of thyme leaves
Freshly ground black pepper
1¾ pounds raclette or Gruyère cheese, cut into ¼-inch-thick slices
A 3-ounce wedge of Parmesan for grating

Roughly chop the potatoes into cubes the size of cherries. Remove the tatty outer leaves from the cabbage and discard. Snap off 8 to 10 of the outer leaves and reserve them. Once you come to the tighter leaves and core, roughly chop the cabbage into cubes the same size as the potatoes.

Cut away and discard the bread's crust. Slice the bread into ½-inch-thick slices.

Fill a large pot with salted water, add one garlic clove and the potatoes, and bring to a boil over medium-high heat. Reduce the heat slightly and boil until the potatoes are just tender, 10 to 15 minutes. Using a slotted spoon, transfer the potatoes to a colander to drain.

Add the diced cabbage to the pot and boil until tender, about 5 minutes. Remove it with a slotted spoon and add it to the colander with the potatoes.

With the pot at a rumble, taste for salt; the water can become too salty as it reduces. If necessary, top up with fresh water to dilute it; the water should be flavorful, not Dead Sea–salty). Add the whole cabbage leaves and blanch until they soften at their thickest point, about 5 minutes. Move them to the colander and reduce the heat to a very gentle simmer.

(Continued)

If you are not using chicken stock, this blanching water can serve as your vegetarian alternative; keep it at a very gentle simmer. If you are using chicken stock, discard the blanching water or save it for another use (it will be full of flavor) and bring the broth to a gentle simmer when ready to proceed.

Preheat the oven to 450 degrees.

Slice 2 of the remaining garlic cloves into thin slivers. Roughly chop about 8 of the anchovy fillets. Set a wide heavy pot (approximately 13 inches wide and 5 inches high) over medium heat and gently warm 3 tablespoons olive oil, along with the slivered garlic, thyme, and plenty of pepper, until the garlic sizzles. Stir in the chopped anchovies and let them melt into the oil, about 2 minutes. Stir in the blanched potatoes and the chopped cabbage and cook until everything is coated in the anchovy oil, a few minutes. Season boldly with salt and pepper (raclette is not a hugely salty cheese). Turn off the heat and transfer all but 1 cup of the potato-cabbage mixture to a medium bowl. Spread what's left over in the bottom of the pot in a thin layer.

Grill or toast the sliced bread until it is golden brown on both sides, about 1 to 2 minutes. Split the remaining garlic clove in half and rub the warm toasts on both sides with the cut sides of the garlic clove, then season each slice with salt and olive oil (again on both sides), adding enough so the bread glistens.

Arrange a layer of toast over the potato-cabbage mixture in the pot. Follow with a layer of sliced raclette and then 1 or 2 of the blanched whole cabbage leaves. Spread another layer of the potato-cabbage mixture on top, followed by another layer of bread, cheese, and cabbage leaves. Continue until the pot is about four-fifths full, ending with a layer of the potato-cabbage mixture.

Pour the warm chicken stock or blanching water into the pot until everything is just submerged. Add more stock or water if necessary. Cover the top with a lid of the remaining toasted bread, pressing down lightly so everything is snugly packed. Finish by covering the bread with the remaining bits of cheese, lots of grated Parmesan, a lattice of the remaining anchovies (see page 116), and a generous drizzle of olive oil.

Cover the pot with a lid or with a sheet of aluminum foil, crimping the edges to seal. Bake in the oven until the bread softens and the raclette cheese melts, about 20 minutes. Uncover and continue baking until the Parmesan melts, the top looks golden, and the raclette is bubbling around the pot's edges, 20 to 30 minutes. Remove the soup from the oven and let it settle for about 10 minutes.

Scoop out helpings of the piping-hot soup and finish each bowl with an olive oil drizzle and lots of pepper. Make sure every bowl has a ladle or two of the steaming broth.

Ribollita

Ribollita is a Tuscan magic trick performed with stale bread, beans, kale, and water—with the help of fresh-pressed olive oil. It's *cucina povera* at its most delicious. Versions of this hearty soup are seen all over Tuscany, especially after the harvested olives are pressed in the fall and the first frost deepens cavolo's flavor in November.

At the River Café, we celebrated these moments as Tuscans do: making pots of ribollita and dousing the bowls with fresh green oil. King's version is a cherry-picking of what Jess and I learned in London and what we've come to favor in our own kitchen.

It's essential to cook the sofrito here for far longer than you might imagine. Just keep going as the vegetables break down, adding more oil and stirring. Do not undercook the cavolo either: It must be soft, soft, soft! As with most bread soups, make sure your loaf is stale. It has to want the delicious kale water and olive oil poured over it. Use plenty of both, the first ribollita of the season is always a celebration.

—Clare

Serves 6

2 medium carrots
2 medium red onions
1 head celery, outer ribs removed and reserved for another use
Olive oil
Salt
2 garlic cloves, finely chopped
3 whole canned tomatoes, drained
2 bunches cavolo nero (about 1 pound), stems removed
4 cups cooked borlotti beans (see page 15), held in their cooking liquor
½ loaf stale white bread, crust removed and sliced 1 inch thick

Cut the carrots, onions, and celery into ¼-inch dice or smaller.

Pour ½ cup of the olive oil into a large heavy ovenproof pot, add a large pinch of salt (always season sofrito well from the beginning) and the diced vegetables, and gently stew over medium-low heat until the vegetables break down and caramelize, at least 30 minutes. This step *must* take a while—it is essential for building flavor. As the sofrito cooks, keep it moving so it doesn't burn and add splashes of oil as necessary to keep things juicy.

Once the diced vegetables are meltingly soft and very sweet, add the garlic and sauté until its scent blooms, about 5 minutes. Stir in the tomatoes, breaking them up as you stir. Once they've reduced, about 5 minutes, taste. If the sofrito is delicious, move on. If not, keep gently stewing until it is irresistible.

Preheat the oven to 400 degrees.

(Continued)

Meanwhile, fill a medium pot with at least 8 cups lightly salted water and bring to a rolling boil over high heat. Add the cavolo nero and boil until completely tender, about 10 minutes. Remove the leaves from the pot and transfer to a colander; keep the blanching water at a gentle simmer. Dry the greens thoroughly and slice them into thin strips (if you stack and roll the leaves, this goes quickly).

Remove 2 cups of the borlotti beans from their cooking liquor and puree in a food processor until completely smooth. If necessary, thin the puree with splashes of olive oil or the bean cooking liquid.

Once the sofrito is good and soft, stir in the remaining whole borlotti beans, the bean puree, and the sliced cavolo until thoroughly combined. Pour in just enough of the cavolo's blanching water to cover everything in the pot by ½ inch (about 6 cups should do). Increase the heat to medium and simmer until the flavors meld and your ribollita looks nice and thick, about 5 minutes. Taste and season lightly with salt. Turn off the heat (but don't discard the cavolo's blanching water yet!).

Lay the sliced bread over the soup, fully covering it. Drizzle this lid with lots of olive oil, enough to dampen and color the bread. Transfer the ribollita to the oven and bake until the top browns and the soup thickens, about 30 minutes. Remove from the oven and let rest for 10 minutes.

LIFT UP A CORNER OF THE SOUP'S BREAD LID AND CHECK: If things look claggy or dry (you want this dense but still soupy), stir in a few splashes of the warm cavolo blanching water and re-cover the soup with the bread lid. Let it cool for about 20 minutes more, until it is just warm.

Use a large spoon to stir the soup, breaking up the bread strips, and then season the ribollita with salt and pepper. Take care not to overwork the soup—it should end up moist and textured, with crusty bits of seasoned bread dotting the pot. If necessary, add more splashes of the cavolo water so the ribollita is silky and a little spongy.

Serve in bowls at just above room temperature, doused with lots of freshly pressed olive oil.

Pasta e Fagioli

Sade was the first person we hired. She'd never gone to culinary school, nor had she worked in a restaurant kitchen. But three years later, she was King's head chef. When she made this soup for lunch one day, it stopped us in our tracks. It was gentle and nourishing, just like Sade.

—Jess and Clare

Sade says, for this endlessly variable classic, "I use Italian white beans and roll out malloreddus to mimic the bean's shapes. Do the same, or feel free to use a small dried pasta, like ditalini, instead. Depending on what is on hand, swap a pancetta rind in for the Parmesan. The key is creating a super-creamy base by cooking the sofrito for a very, very long time.

"If you want to use your own pasta, make it a day in advance. If not, this comes together in one slow afternoon. Either way, don't add the pasta to the pot until just before serving. I don't measure out precise amounts; rather I throw in about six handfuls—and bear in mind that the pasta will continue to expand as the bowls settle at the table."

Serves 6

Olive oil
½ cup finely chopped celery heart
½ cup finely chopped carrot
½ cup finely chopped red onion
2 whole dried red chilies, preferably Calabrian, crushed
Salt
3 garlic cloves, thinly sliced
Needles from 4 sprigs of rosemary, finely chopped
4 whole canned tomatoes, drained
About 3 cups cooked cannellini or coco beans (see page 15), held in their cooking liquor
6 ounces Malloreddus (page 138) or dried ditalini
Grated Parmesan cheese for finishing
Freshly ground black pepper

Warm about 3 tablespoons olive oil in a large pot over medium-low heat. Add the diced celery, carrot, and onion, the dried chilies, and a pinch of salt and cook until the sofrito is extremely soft and sweet, 30 minutes at the minimum. Stir it throughout, and add more oil if it ever looks dry.

Add the garlic and rosemary to the sofrito—ideally a well of oil has pooled in the center; if it hasn't, just add enough oil to create one. Fry the aromatics in the oil until the garlic tans but does not brown, 1 to 2 minutes. Add the tomatoes, smashing them up while stirring, and cook until they tint the sofrito, about 10 minutes.

(Continued)

Drain the cooked beans, reserving their liquor, and add to the pot, stirring to coat them in the sofrito. Increase the heat to medium-high and add enough of the reserved bean cooking liquor to cover the pot's contents by about an inch; if you don't have enough bean liquor, add water or stock as needed. Bring to a simmer and cook until the pot's flavors marry, about 5 minutes.

Turn off the heat and, using a slotted spoon, transfer about one-quarter of the beans from the pot to a food processor (don't worry if some of the sofrito clings to them). Puree until completely smooth, then stir the puree back into the pot. Return the soup to a simmer and gently cook until the flavors meld, about 5 minutes. Check for salt, adjust it as needed, and keep the soup at a bare simmer over low heat.

Just before serving, bring a medium pot of salted water to a rolling boil. Add the malloreddus and cook until it bobs to the surface, about 1 minute. Or, if you are using dried pasta, cook it only halfway (check the package's instructions for timing). With a slotted spoon, remove the pasta from the pot and add it to the just-simmering soup; keep the pot of pasta water to the side. Increase the heat and bring the soup to a quick, active boil. Let the pasta finish cooking in the soup until it is al dente, 3 to 5 minutes. If the soup looks too dense, add a couple ladlefuls of the pasta water to loosen it.

We like this soup creamy and stretchy, never thick or gloopy! Turn off the heat and season the soup with a generous dusting of grated Parmesan, some black pepper, and a good drizzle of olive oil. Serve immediately.

CHAPTER 7

GIVEN HOW INFLUENCED WE ARE BY ITALIAN KITCHENS, YOU MIGHT BE SURPRISED that we offer just one pasta a night. Initially this was out of necessity. In our opening months, when it was just the two of us plus Sade in the kitchen, we simply couldn't make more than one fresh pasta a day. Each morning, one of us would head down into the basement and hand-crank out as many portions as possible. Most days, we ran out.

But once we could produce more, we kept just the one dish because we'd come to regard it as our ode to the "primi." We still make pasta from scratch every day, with extreme care, and dress it with loving consideration.

Pasta falls into two broad categories: pasta fresca and pasta secca.

Associated with southern Italy, where eggs and dairy were traditionally not readily available, pastas seccas are made with water and semolina flour (coarsely milled hard-durum wheat with a high gluten content). These are often extruded from machines, but since we do not have one at King, we make this type of pasta less often, reserving the process for slower days when there's time to hand-roll and then dry the dough. On such occasions, we sit around a table and roll shapes like Malloreddus (see page 138), dimpling each one with our thumbs or a pasta paddle, just like the nonnas do. For serving any of the sauces we pair with our dry pastas, you can substitute a good-quality store-bought version of the same shape.

But most of our pastas are fresh, and they take their cues from Italy's central Emilia-Romagna region. Enriched with eggs, our pasta dough strays a bit from tradition as it's made with a blend of semolina and Italian "00" flour, a very fine farina. We like the toothy bite that the semolina brings. Thanks to the dough's structure, our fresh pastas—pappardelle, farfalle, tagliarini, and tagliatelle—stand up well to rich sauces made with butter and cheese or to dense, meaty braises.

Just as the Italians do, we like to mark special occasions with stuffed pastas. The dough we use for these is a little more pliable, made with just 00 flour and egg yolks. It is rich and has a velvety finish. Once the sheets are rolled out, we stuff them with various purees that mark the season. Or we fill the parcels (be they ravioli or cappellacci) with ricotta enlivened with braised greens or, perhaps, a sweeter accent (see page 163). To finish, a light buttery sauce or some excellent olive oil is all that's required.

Fresh Pappardelle, Tagliarini, and Farfalle

This recipe yields enough dough to easily serve six, with a little extra to account for lost scraps as well as a practice portion. Any extra portions will hold, uncovered, on a semolina-dusted tray in the fridge for a couple of days. Extra dough will also keep for a couple of days, tightly covered in the refrigerator.

Here we call for mixing the dough in a bowl (easier for the home cook and, maybe, the pasta novice). But at King, we make ours on a wooden bench—mounding the flour up high and then cracking the eggs into a well in the center. Once you get the hang of working in the eggs and kneading the dough in a bowl, you'll likely move to the bench—or a wooden cutting board—as well.

Makes about 21 ounces, enough for 6 servings

1½ cups (260 grams) semolina flour,
plus more for dusting
⅔ cup (100 grams) 00 flour
14 large egg yolks (250 grams)

Pile the semolina and 00 flours into a large bowl and stir to combine. Make a well in the center and add the yolks to the well. Using a fork, slowly whisk the yolks in a circular motion to combine them. Then gradually pull in enough flour from the well's sides to form a slurry, and continue mixing until the two are mostly combined.

Gather everything together in the bowl and knead the scraggy bits and loose flour into a more-or-less uniform mass. If the dough needs some encouragement, knead in a flick or two of cold water to bring it together.

If you are making the dough entirely by hand, move it to a work surface and knead it until smooth. After each stretch-and-pull motion, rotate the ball 45 degrees. Kneading may feel like a challenge, but after 10 or so minutes, it should come together. Stick with it!

Alternatively, if you have a stand mixer, fit it with the dough hook, transfer the dough to the bowl, and knead on medium-low speed for 7 to 10 minutes.

Whether making it by hand or with a mixer, the dough is ready when a poke receives a very slow bounceback.

Cover the ball with a tea towel to prevent drying out and let it rest for at least 30 minutes. Covered and at room temperature, it will hold for about 1 hour.

To roll out the pasta, cut the ball into quarters. Work with one piece at a time, keeping the remaining quarters covered.

Dust a work surface lightly with semolina flour. Using a rolling pin, flatten the dough just enough so it will pass through the pasta roller's widest setting. Run the dough through the rollers, catching it as it emerges.

Reduce the width between the rollers and run the dough through the rollers again. Continue reducing the width between the rollers, one click at a time, as you roll the dough through the machine and the sheet thins and elongates, about 12 inches long. An extra dusting of semolina may be needed, either on the bench or the rollers, if things start to feel sticky.

For the final pass through the rollers, they should be on their finest setting and the pasta sheet should emerge paper-thin, 1⁄16 inch thick or less.

Lay the sheet out horizontally on a work surface lightly dusted with semolina. Starting at the far left end, fold about 5 inches of the pasta sheet over itself. Continue flip-flopping 5-inch folds down the sheet until you reach the right end of the sheet.

Once the pasta sheet is all folded up, run the "booklet" through the pasta rollers to start the rolling process all over again. The first pass should be through a setting that is wide enough that the booklet is just lightly compressed. Make sure to run the dough through the rollers so a side showing the folds leads the way; changing the feed's direction after each roll will build up the gluten and give the dough a sturdy texture. Continue reducing the width between the rollers and running the dough through them. Once the sheet is rolled and elongated, lay it out and fold it as before.

Repeat the roll and fold *two* more times, but for the final pass, stop when the sheet of dough is approximately ⅛ inch thick. Transfer the first sheet to a dusted baking sheet and repeat with the remaining dough.

For Tagliarini or Pappardelle

Lay one pasta sheet, about 5 inches by 12 inches, horizontally on a work surface lightly dusted with semolina. Moving across the sheet, cut it, from top to bottom, at 5-inch intervals. Stack the resulting rectangles on top of one another, lightly dusting each one with semolina to prevent sticking.

Attach the pasta cutting device to your machine if it's not affixed. Handle one rectangle at a time, passing it through the cutter:

For tagliarini,
cut the sheet into ⅛-inch-wide strands

For pappardelle,
cut it into 1-inch-wide ribbons

In either case, catch the pasta as it emerges from the cutter and lay each bundle on a tray lightly dusted with semolina. Repeat with the remaining rectangles.

Or, if your pasta machine doesn't have a cutting attachment, roll up each sheet into a cigar shape and slice through the roll at intervals to achieve the desired width. When you roll the sheet, make sure to capture the sheet's length so the strands are as long as possible! Unfurl the the strands and arrange in bundles on a semolina-dusted tray to prevent sticking.

Held, covered, at room temperature, the pasta will keep for a couple of hours. Covered and in the fridge, it holds for a day.

For Farfalle

We like our farfalle large so that each bow tie is easier to make and provides a lot of surface area for the sauce. These ones are larger than what you would buy in a shop.

Unlike most fresh pastas, these do best when left to dry for at least 6 hours, or overnight, before cooking.

Lay one pasta sheet out on a work surface lightly dusted with semolina flour.

With a frilled pasta wheel or a sharp knife, cut the strip into 2½-inch squares. Separate them slightly, to afford some room for maneuvering. Fill a spray bottle with cool water (or use a damp pastry brush) and lightly mist (or dampen) the face of each square.

To form the bow ties, with your thumb and forefinger, accordion-fold the square and pinch the center together. Firmly pinch this point shut to set the shape. If the pasta has dried out and does not stick properly, lightly remist it and try again. Place the bow tie on a semolina-dusted tray and repeat, forming more bow ties with the remaining squares. Then repeat the process with the remaining pasta sheets.

Refrigerate, uncovered, for at least 6 hours. These will keep for a couple of days in the fridge.

Ravioli Dough

This is a rich, super-silky, all-yolk dough. The recipe makes enough for any of the stuffed pasta recipes that follow, with some extra in case of any failed attempts! Any scraps can be added to soups (in particular, Pasta e Fagioli on page 121) or even just hot chicken stock (see page 35) topped with plenty of grated Parmesan.

Makes 1 pound, enough for 6 servings

2 cups (250 grams) 00 flour,
plus more for dusting
14 large egg yolks (250 grams)
Semolina flour for storing

Pile the flour into a large bowl. Make a well in the center and add the yolks. Using a fork, slowly whisk the yolks in a circular motion while gradually pulling in enough of the flour from the well's sides to form a slurry, then continue mixing until the two are mostly combined.

Gather everything together in the bowl and knead the scraggy bits and loose flour into a more-or-less uniform mass. If the dough needs encouragement to come together, knead in a flick or two of cold water.

If you are making the dough entirely by hand, move it to a work surface and knead it until smooth. After each stretch-and-pull motion, rotate the ball 45 degrees. Kneading may feel like a challenge, but after 10 or so minutes, it should come together.

Alternatively, if you have a stand mixer, fit it with the dough hook, transfer the dough to the bowl, and knead on medium-low speed for 7 to 10 minutes.

Whether making it by hand or with a mixer, the dough is ready when a poke receives a very slow bounceback.

Cover the ball with a tea towel to prevent drying out and let it rest for at least 30 minutes. Covered and at room temperature, it will hold for about 1 hour. Covered and kept in the fridge, it will keep for up to 24 hours.

To roll out the pasta, cut the ball into quarters. Work with one piece at a time, keeping the remaining quarters covered.

Lightly dust a work surface with flour. Using a rolling pin, flatten the dough just enough so it will pass through the pasta roller's widest setting. Run the dough through the rollers, catching it as it emerges.

Reduce the width between the rollers and run the dough through them again. Continue reducing the width between the rollers, one click at a time, as you roll the dough through the machine and the sheet thins and elongates. An extra dusting of semolina may be needed, either on the bench or the rollers, if things start to feel sticky.

For the final pass through the rollers, they should be on their narrowest setting and the pasta sheet should emerge paper-thin, 1⁄16 inch thick or less.

Lightly dust a work surface with semolina and lay the sheet of pasta out horizontally on it. Starting at the far left end, fold about 5 inches of the pasta sheet over itself. Continue flip-flopping 5-inch fold down the sheet until you reach the other end.

Once the pasta sheet is all folded up, run the "booklet" through the machine's rollers to start the rolling process all over again. The first pass should be through a setting that is wide enough that the booklet is just lightly compressed. Make sure to run the dough through the roller so a side showing the folds leads the way; changing the feed's direction after each roll will build up gluten and give the dough a sturdy texture. Continue reducing the width between the rollers and running the dough through them again. Once the sheet is rolled and elongated, lay it out and fold it up as before.

Repeat the roll and fold two times in total. After the final roll, lay the sheet out on a work surface that has been lightly dusted with flour, with a long side toward you, and fill the ravioli as directed below. Repeat with the remaining pasta sheets and filling.

TO FILL AND SHAPE THE RAVIOLI

Remove the filling from the fridge. Sprinkle two baking sheets with a ¼-inch-thick layer of semolina. (For a pound of dough, which makes about 70 pieces, you will need at least two pans.)

Lightly mist the pasta sheet with cold water (a spray bottle is best, but a pastry brush works too). Starting 2 inches in from the left end of the sheet and one-third of the way down from the top, pipe out or spoon a small dollop of filling onto the dough; the exact amount will depend on your recipe. Continue dotting the filling at 3-inch intervals all down the sheet (the exact spacing may depend on your recipe as well), placing the last dollop of filling no less than 2 inches from the sheet's right end.

Lightly mist the pasta sheet with water once more. Fold the sheet's lower edge up over the dollops of filling so it meets the top edge. Moving from left to right, gently dab the top of each dollop to round it out. Run your finger over the seam where the two edges meet, sealing it shut. Moving from left to right, press down and trace around the "belly" of each ravioli to seal it while pushing out any trapped air.

Using a knife or pasta cutter, trim off ½ inch from the two ends of the filled sheet. Now trim the top edge, creating a straight edge. Finally, separate the ravioli by slicing through the halfway point between the rounded bellies. Arrange the ravioli on a semolina-dusted pan and set aside until ready to cook. Repeat with the remaining dough and filling.

The ravioli will hold at room temperature for 1 to 2 hours. Left uncovered on the semolina-dusted trays, they will keep for a couple of days in the fridge.

KCB 7/27
RICOTTA

Malloreddus
(Gnocchetti Sardi)

Sardinia's "little gnocchi" found their way onto the menu when our pasta machine broke one morning. We needed something for our sauce that could be rolled easily by hand. We quickly made a dough and started thumbing it into little ridged shells. We haven't stopped since. Since this is a lot to ask of one thumb alone, we usually form malloreddus in communion, just as we do when podding piles of favas.

These do require time to dry out. Overnight, uncovered, in the fridge is best, but a few hours on the kitchen table while you make your soup or sauce will do.

Without the saffron, these can be added to vegetable soups (see pages 109 and 112) or to rich sausage ragùs, as is done in Sardinia. With or without the saffron, these nuggets have a good bite and ridges that absorb sauces and soups perfectly.

This recipe can serve anywhere from 4 to 8 people. Used more sparingly in a light brothy dish like our Malloreddus with Mussels, Ceci, and Bottarga (page 168) or Pasta e Fagioli (page 121) it will feed up to 8 diners. If sauced with a ragù, it will serve 4 people.

Makes 1 pound, enough for 4 to 8 servings

2 pinches saffron threads (optional)
¾ cup plus 2 tablespoons (200 ml) boiling water if using saffron, warm water if not using saffron
4¼ cups (400 grams) semolina flour, plus more for dusting

If using the saffron, finely crumble the threads between your thumb and forefinger into a small bowl. Pour over 2 tablespoons of the boiling water and steep the saffron until its color blooms and the water cools to room temperature, about 10 minutes. Then add the remaining ¼ cup water; this second addition need only be warm, not boiling.

Add the semolina to a large bowl. Slowly pour the warm saffron water into the flour, tilting it into a single spot at first and then stirring with your hand until evenly distributed. Capture any stray saffron threads and work them into the dough. Or, if you're not using saffron, simply add all the warm water to the semolina and stir to combine.

Once the dough is damp and workable (not wet and gloppy), turn it out onto a work surface lightly dusted with semolina. Ideally, you won't need any extra flour for kneading the dough, but, if it's sticking to the work surface, dust it with more semolina so the dough moves easily without sticking. Knead until a smooth ball that is slightly springy to the poke forms, about 6 to 8 minutes. If using the saffron, it will tint your dough a lovely amber color, and once you've finished kneading, it should be uniformly colored.

Wrap the dough in a tea towel and let it rest until it relaxes, at least 30 minutes. Covered, the dough holds at room temperature for 6 to 8 hours; well-covered in the fridge, it will keep for about 2 days.

To shape the pasta, cut the ball into 6 equal portions. Work with one piece at a time, keeping the remaining pieces covered with a towel to prevent drying out. Using the palms of your hands, working on a flour-dusted surface, roll one piece of dough out into an elongated sausage about ⅓ inch in diameter.

Next, moving from left to right, cut through the "sausage" at ¼-inch intervals, making loose dumplings.

If you have a wooden gnocchi board, take one nugget and gently press down on it with your thumb, dragging it down the board while lightly pressing it into its ridges; allow the pasta to curl against your thumb before releasing it. The nugget should be curled and shell-shaped. If you don't have a board, use the back of a fork, rolling the dumplings down its arch so the tines form ridges. Repeat with the remaining nuggets. Arrange the shaped malloreddus on a tray that's been generously dusted with semolina, spreading the pieces out to prevent sticking.

Repeat with the remaining dough. These will keep in the fridge, uncovered, for about 2 days.

Crespelle

Crespelle, Italian crepes, can go sweet or savory. They are eaten plain, stuffed, or sauced. We serve savory crespelle at King, adding Parmesan and nutmeg to the batter for flavor.

Make the batter in advance of cooking; it requires at least a few hours of rest, and, if you like, it holds very well for a day. As ever with this type of pancake, your first will be a casualty. Take it as an opportunity to determine how much batter to pour into the pan (nonstick is best) and how to control the heat's intensity.

Makes 12 to 14 crespelle

1 cup (130 grams) all-purpose flour, sifted
Salt
¼ cup finely grated Parmesan cheese
A small nub of nutmeg
2 cups whole milk
4 large eggs
Unsalted butter for cooking the crespelle (about 3 tablespoons)

Combine the flour, a teaspoon of salt, and the Parm in a medium bowl. Using a Microplane or a similar tool, grate in the nutmeg.

Make a well in the center of your dry ingredients. Whisk together the milk and eggs in another bowl. Slowly pour the wet ingredients into the dry, dribbling the liquid into a single spot and whisking out from the well's center to prevent lumps. Allow the batter to rest for at least an hour so it thickens slightly. At room temperature, it happily sits for about 2 hours; covered and in the fridge, it holds overnight.

To cook the crespelle, heat an 8-inch nonstick crepe or frying pan over low to medium-low heat. Add about ½ teaspoon butter, swirling to coat the pan's bottom evenly with a thin film; using a pastry brush for this helps. When the pan is hot, ladle in a conservative amount of batter—about ¼ cup to start—and immediately swirl it over the pan's bottom to fully cover it with a thin sheet. When the crespelle's edges start to show browning, 1 to 2 minutes, loosen it with a thin spatula and flip it like a pancake. Cook on the second side until browned in spots, about 1 minute more. Move the cooked crespelle to a cooling rack and make another one, adjusting the heat and amount of batter as necessary to ensure that each one comes out thin and pretty. Repeat until all the batter is used; cooked crespelle keep for a day.

Dress these up as suggested in the following two recipes, or fill them as desired.

Crespelle 'Mbusse
with Bone Marrow

'Mbusse means "wet crepes" in the local dialect of Abruzzo. To turn our crespelle green, we add blanched parsley puree to the basic batter. To account for the extra moisture it introduces, we reduce the amount of milk slightly.

These green ribbons float in bowls of chicken stock along with a roasted marrow bone for a light but indulgent meal that comes together somewhat quickly, as all the components, save for the marrow bones, must be prepared in advance.

Serves 4

FOR THE CRESPELLE

Salt
2 cups parsley leaves
2 large eggs
2 tablespoons finely grated Parmesan
½ cup all-purpose flour
¾ cups whole milk
A small nub of nutmeg

FOR ASSEMBLY

Four 2-inch-tall marrow bones
Salt and freshly ground black pepper
4 cups chicken stock, preferably homemade (see page 35)
½ teaspoon butter
A small nub of nutmeg

To make the parsley puree for the batter, bring a small pot of salted water to a boil over high heat. Add the parsley and blanch until the leaves soften and turn sharp green, about 5 minutes. Drain in a colander and quickly run the parsley under cold water to fully cool it. When the parsley is cool enough to handle, squeeze it to remove excess water. Then squeeze again to wring out any remaining water.

Put the parsley in a food processor, add the eggs, and whiz to make a completely smooth puree, 2 to 4 minutes. Add the Parmesan, flour, milk, and a few gratings of nutmeg and whiz again until the batter is completely smooth; stop to scrape down the sides now and again as necessary. Season with salt to taste.

Let the batter rest so it thickens slightly, at least 1 hour. At room temperature, it will happily sit for about 2 hours. Covered and in the fridge, it holds overnight.

Preheat the oven to 400 degrees. Generously season the marrow bones on all sides with salt and pepper. Stand the bones up in a small roasting pan and roast in the oven until they caramelize and smell deliciously meaty, about 1 hour.

While the bones cook, make the crespelle and heat the chicken stock in a medium pot over low heat. To cook the crespelle, heat an 8-inch nonstick crepe or frying pan over low to

(Continued)

medium-low heat. Add about ½ teaspoon butter, swirling to coat the pan's bottom evenly with a thin film; using a pastry brush for this helps. When the pan is hot, ladle in a conservative amount of batter—about ¼ cup to start—and immediately swirl it over the pan's bottom to fully cover it with a thin sheet. When the crespelle's edges start to show browning, 1 to 2 minutes, loosen it with a thin spatula and flip it like a pancake. Cook on the second side until browned in spots, about 1 minute more. Move the cooked crespelle to a cooling rack and make another one, adjusting the heat and amount of batter as necessary to ensure that each one comes out thin and pretty. Repeat until all the batter is used; cooked crespelle keep for a day.

Stack all the crespelle and roll them up to form a large cigar. With a chef's knife, slice through the roll to form ¼-inch-wide ribbons.

When the marrow bones are cooked, bring the broth to an active simmer over medium-high heat and taste for seasoning.

Ladle the steaming broth into shallow bowls and then unfurl the crespelle, adding a handful of ribbons to each bowl. Stand a marrow bone in each bowl and finish off with a fine grating of nutmeg. Spear a small spoon or fork into each marrow bone so that guests can tease out the cupped marrow and eat it straight or mix it into their bowls.

Spinach and Ricotta Crespelle
with Fonduta

Bubbling and rich, these crespelle are stuffed with a spinach filling, rolled up, and baked. The result resembles a casserole of stuffed cannelloni, but crespelle are a little spongy and nuttier in flavor.

This dish, excellent in the colder months, also does well at parties, since everything can (mostly) be prepared in advance. Only the fonduta is poured over at the last minute before the dish browns and finishes in the oven.

Serves 6

3⅓ pounds spinach, washed and tough stems removed
Salt
Olive oil
Butter for greasing the baking dish
12 to 14 Crespelle (page 140)
1½ cups full-fat ricotta cheese, at room temperature
⅔ cup finely grated Parmesan cheese (about 3 ounces), plus extra for finishing
1 cup warm Fonduta (page 28)
A small nub of nutmeg

Begin by preparing the spinach puree: Boil the greens in a medium pot of heavily salted water until their stems soften, about 3 minutes. Drain in a colander and let the excess water steam off.

Once the spinach is cool enough to handle, wring out the leaves to remove excess water, then wring out again, removing every drop of water. Once it is bone-dry, add half the spinach to a food processor, along with 2 to 3 tablespoons olive oil, and whiz to form a velvety-smooth puree, 1 to 2 minutes. Taste and blitz in salt as needed, then set the puree aside. Finely chop the remaining spinach and set it back in the colander.

Preheat the oven to 500 degrees. Rub a knob of butter, about 1 tablespoon, over the inside of a 12-by-16-inch baking dish that is approximately 2 inches high.

To fill the crespelle, lay one down on a work surface and dot the top half with dobbles of ricotta, about 1½ tablespoons. Next, dobble a similar amount of chopped spinach over the crespelle's top half and follow with the same amount of spinach puree, so the ricotta, puree, and chopped spinach cover the top half of the crespelle with alternating proportional dots. Sprinkle some of the Parmesan all over the crespelle and then roll it up, starting at the top and moving down to the bottom. As you roll it up, carefully tuck the filling back into the pancake as necessary without pressing down forcefully, so the filling stays fluffy.

Lay the crespelle seam side down in the prepared dish. Repeat with the remaining crespelle and filling, packing them into the dish into a snug single layer.

Ladle over the warm fonduta so it pools between the rolled crespelle and covers the top in a generous blanket. Finish with a hearty grating of Parmesan, dusting the entire top.

Bake on the oven's top rack until the filling is warmed through, about 10 minutes. Check on doneness by poking a fork into the middle of a crespelle in the dish's center. Hold it in place for 5 seconds, then touch the tines to your lip: If they feel hot, remove the dish from the oven and turn on the broiler. If they don't, bake for a few more minutes.

Slide the dish under the broiler and watch it like a hawk: Once brown bubbles form around the top of the crespelle, 2 to 4 minutes, remove the baking dish. Sprinkle over a little more Parmesan (a thin dusting) and finely grate over a bit of nutmeg with a Microplane (or similar tool), remembering that a little goes a long way. Serve immediately.

Tagliarini
with Boiled Lemons, Almonds, and Bottarga

The sauce for this pasta is a variation on pesto that swaps parsley in for basil and almonds for pine nuts and adds finely chopped boiled lemons. It is always served at King with a final flurry of grated bottarga di muggine, which makes it especially dazzling, but if you don't have any at hand at home, it is just as tasty without.

Serves 6

½ cup roughly chopped parsley, plus more if needed
Salt
1 garlic clove, thinly sliced
1 cup blanched whole almonds
Olive oil
2 tablespoons finely chopped boiled lemons (see page 25)
21 ounces (1 batch) fresh tagliarini, homemade (see page 128) or store-bought
About 1½ ounces bottarga di muggine, peeled, for finishing (optional)

To make the sauce, put ¼ cup of the parsley in a mortar, along with a good pinch of salt, and bash it into the garlic with the pestle until a bright green paste forms. (A small food processor is a fine substitute for the mortar and pestle; just blitz until smooth.)

Place the almonds in a blender or a small food processor and pulse until they break into pebbly, irregular bits. Add the parsley paste and the remaining roughly chopped parsley and pulse to combine, stopping once the almonds take on a light green hue; if they do not color, add a little more chopped parsley (a few tablespoons should do) and pulse again. Blitz in ¼ cup water and then, as the blade runs, stream in about ½ cup olive oil, enough to make a loose pesto-adjacent sauce. Taste and add salt as necessary.

Scrape the sauce into a medium bowl and stir in the chopped boiled lemons. Cover with a dribble of olive oil to prevent oxidation. This holds for about 4 hours at room temperature or overnight in the fridge.

When ready to make the pasta, bring a large pot of salted water to a rolling boil over high heat; the water should taste highly seasoned (not seawater salty, but flavorful). Add the pasta, stirring to make sure it doesn't stick together. Cook for about 2 minutes, or until 30 seconds shy of al dente.

Meanwhile, as soon as the pasta goes into the water, add the almond-parsley sauce to a large frying pan set over medium-low heat. Add ¾ cup of the hot pasta water (scoop it from the pot) and gently warm the sauce, stirring out any lumps.

Once the pasta is ready, remove it with tongs or a slotted spoon and add it to the warm sauce; keep the pot of pasta water hot. Add another ¼ cup of the pasta water to the sauce and increase the heat to high. Toss the pasta, coating it in sauce, splashing in extra hits of the pasta water as necessary. Cook the pasta in the sauce for about 1 minute; the sauce should be glossy and loose and cloak all the strands. Taste and season with salt as needed.

Grate a generous flurry of the bottarga di muggine over the pasta and finish with a drizzle of olive oil.

Tagliatelle
with Zucchini and Clams

This is basically spaghetti alla vongole, with a hefty dose of grated zucchini.

Always wash clams properly (leave them in a bowl set under running water until the bottom of the bowl is utterly grit-free). Use the large holes on a box grater to shave the zucchini here; the slivers should approximate the width of the tagliatelle. Last but not least, wait until the whole dish comes together before adding salt—you never know how salty clams are until they've opened.

Serves 6

Salt
2 medium zucchini (about 1½ pounds)
3 garlic cloves, finely sliced
A fat pinch of crushed dried red chili
Olive oil
2 pounds of small clams, preferably Manila, scrubbed and soaked
1½ cups dry white wine
21 ounces (1 batch homemade) fresh tagliatelle (see page 128), or similar dried pasta
A large handful of finely chopped parsley

Bring a large pot of salted water to a boil over high heat. The water should taste highly seasoned (not seawater salty, but flavorful).

Meanwhile, grate enough of the zucchini on the widest holes of a box grater to yield 2 cups; set aside.

ONCE THE WATER IS AT A RUMBLE, START ON THE CLAMS: Warm the garlic and dried chili with ⅓ cup olive oil in a large wide pan over medium heat. Allow the garlic to sizzle in oil, 1 to 2 minutes, but before it begins to color, then stir in the clams and wine. Increase the heat to high, stir to distribute the seasonings evenly, and cover with a lid. After a few minutes, the clams should hiss. Leave them undisturbed for about 3 minutes longer and then peek to see if they have opened; most likely, some will remain shut. With tongs, move the opened clams to a clean bowl, then cover the pan again and continue steaming the closed shells. After a minute or two, check again and add the newly opened clams to the bowl; if some just won't open after a few tries, discard them. (The goal is to cook the clams until they just open and no longer.) Drain the precious pan juices in a sieve set over a bowl; discard the trapped grit. Set the clams aside.

Wipe out the pan if necessary and set it back on the stove. Pour enough of the reserved clam juices into the pan to cover the bottom with about ¼ inch of liquid (keep any remaining liquid by the stove). Turn the heat under the pan to low and swirl about 2 tablespoons olive oil into the clam liquid, adding enough so it tastes briny and buttery.

Drop the tagliatelle into the boiling water, stirring to ensure it doesn't stick together. When the pasta is almost tender but retains some bite, after 2 to 3 minutes, using tongs, transfer the tagliatelle to the pan with the clam drippings; keep the pot of pasta water hot.

Immediately turn the heat under the pan to high and add the grated zucchini along with the opened clams, tossing well. Cook, stirring constantly until the briny drippings cloak the pasta and the zucchini no longer tastes raw, 1 to 2 minutes. If the sauce looks dry or needs loosening, add a splash of the hot pasta water and toss until it emulsifies. If a little brininess is required, add a splash of the reserved clam drippings (any leftovers will work as fish stock). When the pasta is al dente and well seasoned, turn off the heat and stir in the parsley and a good glug of olive oil, about 2 tablespoons. Taste again and adjust, adding more salt and/or oil until bites are briny, sweet, salty, and irresistible.

Farfalle
with Fonduta, Walnuts, and Black Pepper

Supersize your farfalle! We like them large to mop up this rich, cheesy sauce. This recipe for "Action-Women Bow Ties" is for Angeles, Sade, Maya, and Alissa—the line cooks who first made them.

You can make the farfalle with our classic Fonduta (page 28), but we like the addition of tangy Gorgonzola for this pasta. When it's time to add the Parmesan, whisk in 1½ cups crumbled Gorgonzola as well.

Serves 6

1½ cups roughly chopped walnuts
Salt
Olive oil
21 ounces (1 batch) fresh farfalle (see page 128), dried overnight, or 16 ounces dried farfalle

3 cups Fonduta (page 28), made with the addition of 1½ cups crumbled Gorgonzola cheese (see headnote)
Freshly ground black pepper
A small piece of Parmesan cheese for grating

Preheat the oven to 350 degrees. Place the walnuts in a small bowl and season them with a pinch of salt and a drizzle of olive oil, about ½ tablespoon. Toss and spread the nuts out on a small baking sheet.

Toast the nuts in the oven for 3 to 4 minutes, then give the sheet a shake. Continue toasting the walnuts until they are golden brown and aromatic, 5 to 7 minutes more. Remove from the oven and let cool.

Bring a large pot of salted water to a rolling boil over high heat. The water should taste highly seasoned (not seawater salty, but flavorful). Add the pasta, stirring to ensure it doesn't stick together.

As soon as you've dropped the pasta into the pot, set a wide pan over low heat. Add the Gorgonzola fonduta, along with a generous grinding of pepper, and warm the sauce over low heat. Once the pasta is just shy of al dente, after about 3 minutes, use a slotted spoon to transfer the bow ties to the pan with the fonduta, add a cup of the hot pasta water (just scoop it from the pot), and swirl until the sauce is silky and loose. Keep the pot of pasta water hot.

Increase the heat to medium-high and toss everything together, adding a smidge more of the reserved pasta water to loosen as necessary. After a minute or less, the pasta should be cooked al dente and well coated and the sauce should look glossy. Turn off the heat and crumble over the walnuts, rubbing them between your fingers as you do so. Finish the pasta with a pinch of pepper, a grating of Parmesan, and a drizzle of olive oil.

Pappardelle
with Saffron and Speck

Toothsome pappardelle is the ideal vehicle for this rich, fragrant, marigold sauce—it is not meant to be subtle!

If you like, use pancetta or bacon instead of speck or prosciutto; the lardons may take a little longer to crisp. If using one of these, add a tablespoon of cold water to the pan and gently cook the lardons in the water. The pork's fat will render as the water evaporates and eventually provide enough fat for crisping it without the need for extra oil.

Serves 6

10 slices (about 140 grams) speck or prosciutto
3 cups heavy cream
3 garlic cloves, peeled
5 very generous pinches saffron threads
Salt
21 ounces (1 batch) fresh pappardelle, homemade (see page 128) or store-bought
Olive oil
Freshly ground black pepper

Cut half the slices of speck crosswise into ½-inch-wide matchsticks. Place a large nonstick skillet over low heat and add the matchsticks, taking care not to overcrowd the pan (if necessary, cook the speck in batches or use two pans). Gently fry until the speck crisps up, 5 to 7 minutes. Transfer to a plate lined with paper towels and blot off the excess fat.

Combine the cream, garlic, the remaining slices of speck, the saffron, and a good pinch of salt in a medium pot and bring the cream to a gentle simmer over low heat. Slowly cook until the cream reduces by one-third, about 35 minutes; stir frequently to prevent the cream from boiling over. Season with salt and allow the cream to stand, with the aromatics and speck so the flavors intensify, for at least 30 minutes.

Choose a wide pan that is large enough to hold the pasta and the sauce. Hold a strainer over the pan and pour the cream through it, pressing on the captured aromatics to extract all their flavor; discard the spent aromatics and set the pan aside.

Bring a large pot of salted water to a boil over high heat. The water should taste highly seasoned (not seawater salty, but flavorful). Drop in the pappardelle, stirring to make sure it doesn't stick together, and boil until just shy of al dente, about 3 minutes.

Meanwhile, as soon as you've added the pasta to the pot, set the pan of cream sauce over medium-low heat, add ½ cup of the pasta water (scoop it out of the pot), and gently warm the sauce. Finish with a drizzle of olive oil.

When the pasta is ready, use a slotted spoon to move it to the simmering cream sauce. Turn the heat up to medium-high and add an extra splash of reserved pasta water if necessary; the sauce should be silky. Cook, tossing the pasta, until it is al dente and lightly coated with sauce, about 1 minute.

Turn off the heat and scatter over the fried speck and a generous amount of pepper. No Parmesan—nothing to distract from the golden strands.

Pappardelle
with Wild Boar Ragù

Civet de sanglier is a wild boar ragù from France's Haute Savoie region. This recipe celebrates autumn's hunt. It's typically eaten in November, when boar are especially plump after gorging on the fallen acorns and chestnuts.

It's worth seeking out wild boar for this recipe. If that's not possible, swap in a cut of beef that's good for stewing, like shank or brisket.

This ragù is also delicious with polenta or boiled potatoes. Whatever the accompaniment, make it at least one day ahead of time, as it requires at least a night's rest after braising.

Serves 6

FOR THE RAGÙ

1¾ pounds boneless wild boar (cut from the leg) or beef shank, cut into 2-inch cubes
Salt and freshly ground black pepper
1 tablespoon all-purpose flour, plus more if needed
2 tablespoons unsalted butter
Olive oil
4 medium shallots, minced
1 cup ½-inch diced bacon or pancetta
6 juniper berries, roughly crushed using the side of a heavy knife
Zest of half an orange removed in strips with a vegetable peeler
¼ cup finely chopped thyme leaves
3 fresh bay leaves
4 garlic cloves, thinly sliced
3 cups Mondeuse or other fruity red wine
½ cup Cognac

FOR THE PAPPARDELLE

21 ounces (1 batch) fresh pappardelle, homemade (see page 128) or store-bought
1 to 2 tablespoons unsalted butter

Preheat the oven to 375 degrees. Heavily season the boar cubes all over with salt and pepper. Set aside to allow the meat to come up to room temperature, at least 30 minutes if it's straight from the refrigerator.

When ready to cook the ragù, lightly dust the cubes of meat with the flour. Heat a tablespoon of the butter and 2 tablespoons olive oil in a wide, heavy ovenproof pot over high heat. Once the fat bubbles, add the seasoned meat, spreading it out in a single uncrowded layer; if necessary, brown in batches. Once a golden crust has developed on one side of the cubes of meat, reduce the heat to medium and brown the remaining sides. When a crust has developed all around, about 8 minutes total, transfer the boar to a tray, and turn off the heat. Pour off all but a thin film of fat

(Continued)

from the pot and wipe up any burnt patches with a paper towel, leaving all the tasty golden bits in place, and return the pot to medium heat.

Add the remaining tablespoon of butter to the pot and let it melt, then stir in the shallots and diced bacon, reduce the heat to medium-low heat, and cook until the shallots soften but do not color and the bacon renders some of its fat but does not crisp, about 5 minutes.

Push the shallots and bacon to one side and add a tablespoon of olive oil to the pot's empty side, along with the juniper berries, strips of orange peel, thyme, bay leaves, and garlic, and wait for the garlic to sizzle and the aromatics to bloom, 1 to 2 minutes. Stir everything together, return the browned meat and all its accumulated juices to the pot, and increase the heat to medium-high. Deglaze the pot with the red wine and Cognac, stirring to release the browned bits on the bottom of the pot.

Bring the liquid to a simmer and cover the braise with a cartouche (see page 15) and then a lid. Transfer the pot to the oven and braise until the meat is completely spoon-tender and the sauce has the viscosity of a light gravy, about 2½ hours. After an hour, check that the meat is just popping up above its braising liquid; if necessary, add a splash or two of water.

Remove the braise from the oven, taste for seasoning, and adjust with salt if necessary. Pull out and discard the spent bay and orange peel. With a spoon, break up the meat into threads. Let the ragù cool to room temperature and then give the braise a long rest in the fridge, at least 12 hours, or, better, for up to 2 days.

When ready to serve, remove the pot from the fridge and let stand for at least 30 minutes.

Bring a large pot of salted water to a rumbling boil over high heat. The water should taste highly seasoned (not seawater salty, but flavorful). Drop in the pappardelle, stirring to make sure it doesn't stick together, and boil until just shy of al dente, about 3 minutes.

Meanwhile, as the water heats, scoop the sauce into a pan large enough to hold the pasta and sauce and set it over medium-high heat. Scoop out a generous splash, about ¾ cup, of the simmering pasta water and add it to the pan to loosen the ragù. Keep the ragù at a gentle simmer over low heat as the pasta cooks; if the sauce looks at all dry, add more splashes of pasta water.

Use tongs or a slotted spoon to move the almost-cooked pasta to the simmering sauce. Add a few more splashes of hot pasta water to the pan, starting with ¼ cup and adding more as necessary; the ragù should appear loose but not watery. Increase the heat to high and toss the pappardelle in the sauce until it absorbs some of the ragù but retains some bite, about 1 to 2 minutes. Add the butter, turn off the heat, and toss until the the pasta looks glossy. Taste for salt and adjust as necessary.

Transfer to a serving platter and serve immediately. No need for cheese.

Pumpkin Cappellacci

Joseph Trivelli, a head chef at the River Café, has magic hands, especially when it comes to making pasta. Most mornings, I would watch him thread ream after ream of pasta through the machine, like an eager octopus, while writing up the day's lunch menu and also making a soup. One day, he found the time to teach me how to make fresh pasta as well. These cappellacci ("little hats" in Italian) were my first efforts.

Mine weren't as uniform as the ones Joseph put up on his tray, but they were served anyway. "They look homemade," he said. Yours will too.

Traditionally, cappellacci are filled with just pumpkin. But tradition need only take you so far. We add some ricotta into the pureed squash for extra richness. If you'd rather not use ricotta, swap in another cup of pumpkin.

—Jess

Serves 6

FOR THE FILLING

3 cups Smashed Pumpkin (page 191), at room temperature
1 cup fresh ricotta cheese
Salt
Olive oil

FOR THE CAPPELLACCI

1 pound Ravioli Dough (page 134), rolled out as directed
Semolina flour for dusting
Salt
8 tablespoons (1 stick) unsalted butter
1 cup sage leaves
An 8-ounce hunk of Parmesan cheese for grating
Olive oil

To make the filling, combine the pumpkin and ricotta in a bowl; the filling will be relatively dense. Season with salt to taste. Cover and refrigerate until cold (it is easier to work with the filling when it is chilled).

To assemble the cappellaci, generously dust two baking sheets with semolina. Transfer the filling to a piping bag fitted with a ½ inch tip and pipe it out, or use a spoon to dollop blobs of filling onto the pasta sheets.

Dust your work surface with semolina to prevent the pasta from sticking and then place one sheet of pasta on it. Cut the sheet into 4-inch squares. Fill a clean spray bottle with water and lightly mist the pasta sheet; or use a wet pastry brush to lightly dampen the pasta. Pipe or spoon a walnut-sized dollop of filling into the center of each square.

(Continued)

Lift up the bottom right corner of one square and fold it over the filling to meet the top left corner, forming a triangle. Then lift up the corners with your forefingers and thumbs and pull them together so one corner overlaps the other by a little more than a ½ inch and pinch them together to seal the seam, then lift the top of the triangle straight up so the cappellacci stands up and resembles a pope's pointy cap. Place the cappellacci on a semolina-dusted baking sheet and repeat with the remaining filled squares. (If the dough dries out, simply mist it again.) Then repeat with the remaining pasta sheets and filling.

Once all the cappellacci are formed, refrigerate the pans for 1 hour. (If necessary, these can rest overnight, but any longer and the bottoms will become soggy.)

When ready to serve, bring a large pot of salted water to a rumbling boil over high heat. The water should taste highly seasoned (not seawater salty, but flavorful). Remove the cappellacci from the fridge and add half to the boiling water, gingerly stirring to prevent sticking, and boil until the hats bob to the water's surface, about 5 minutes.

Meanwhile, as soon as the pasta goes into the pot, add the butter to a large pan, one that is wide enough to hold the pasta comfortably, turn the heat to medium, and toss in the sage leaves, swirling to combine. Once the butter foams and the sage leaves crisp, add a couple of splashes of the pasta water to the pan to create an emulsion. Keep the sauce over low heat while the pasta finishes cooking.

Using a slotted spoon, transfer the cooked cappellacci to the warm butter sauce. Add the remaining uncooked cappellacci to the boiling water and cook as before until they bob to the surface. Once cooked, with a slotted spoon, add to the first batch in the butter sauce and warm over low heat.

Immediately serve the cappellacci on hot plates—don't forget the sage leaves! Finish with freshly grated Parmesan and a drizzle of olive oil.

Potato, Ricotta, and Chicoria Ravioli
with Ricotta Salata

Potato, pasta, and a bitter green is a quintessential Italian combination. We mash boiled potatoes and seasoned softened greens together and then stuff the filling into delicate pasta parcels, which we finish off simply with lots of olive oil and thin shavings of ricotta salata.

If you can't find chicory, use dandelion greens, broccoli rabe, or if you have them, the outer leaves of puntarelle (see page 96). Any of these will lend this filling the bitterness it requires.

Serves 6

FOR THE FILLING

1 Yukon Gold potato (4 to 6 ounces)
Salt
2 bunches (about 1 pound) chicory or other bitter greens
Olive oil
2 pinches fennel seeds, crushed
A pinch of crushed dried red chili

FOR THE RAVIOLI

1 cup fresh ricotta cheese
1 pound Ravioli Dough (page 134), rolled out as directed
Salt
Very good olive oil for finishing
Semolina flour for dusting
A chunk of ricotta salata for grating
Zest of a lemon

To make the filling, put the potato in a small pot and add just enough water to cover. Season the water heavily with salt, bring to a boil over medium heat, and cook until the potato is tender at its center, about 15 minutes. Drain, wipe the pan dry, and return the potato to the hot pot so its excess water steams off.

Meanwhile, fill a medium pot with salted water and bring it to a rumble over high heat. Add the greens and simmer, pushing the leaves down with a wide spoon to submerge them every now and again, until the stems are completely soft when squeezed between your thumb and forefinger, about 15 minutes.

Drain the leaves and when they are cool enough to handle, wring them out to release excess water. Then wring them out again and blot dry with a kitchen towel; the greens must be bone-dry, or the filling will be soggy. Finely chop the greens on a cutting board and then run your knife through the mound until everything is properly minced.

Warm ½ cup olive oil, the fennel seeds, and dried chili in a small pot over low heat. Stir in the greens and braise until the leaves absorb the oil's seasoning, 2 to 3 minutes. Meanwhile, peel the potato and chop it into cubes.

(Continued)

Transfer the cooked greens and all their oil to a large bowl. Add the potato and mash everything together with the back of a spoon until the potato crumbles into pea-sized bits. Let cool completely.

Fold the ricotta into the cooled filling to loosely combine; you're not after uniformity, but rather a chunky mash. Taste and add enough salt so it tastes full-bodied and delicious. If necessary, add more olive oil. The filling holds for up to 2 days, covered in the fridge.

To form the ravioli, dust two baking sheets with semolina, then dust a clean work surface with semolina. Lay a sheet of dough horizontally on the work surface. Spoon a dimple of filling (about the size of half a large cherry) 2 inches in from the left edge, placing it one-third of the way down from the top of the sheet. Continue dotting dimples of filling at 5-inch intervals down the sheet, stopping about 2 inches from the right end.

Fill a clean spray bottle with water and lightly mist the pasta sheet, or use a damp pastry brush to moisten the pasta. Fold the top of the sheet down over the filling, aligning the edges. Using your fingers, press down on either side of each mound of filling, pushing out any trapped air and partially sealing the ravioli, then pinch the ends of the sheet closed. Next, press down along the upper seam to seal the sheet (see page 135).

Use a frilly ravioli cutter or a knife to trim the top edge of the sheet, making a straight edge. Then cut between each mound of filling to separate the ravioli, and arrange them on a semolina-dusted baking sheet. Repeat with the remaining pasta sheets and filling.

The ravioli can rest for about an hour at room temperature, or hold them, covered in the fridge, for up to 24 hours.

To cook, bring one large pot of salted water to a boil and cook the ravioli in two batches. The water should taste highly seasoned (not seawater salty, but flavorful). When the water's rumbling, add half the ravioli to each pot. Once the ravioli bob to the water's surface, about 4 minutes, use a slotted spoon to lift them from the water, allowing them a moment to drain before transfering the ravioli to a warm serving platter.

Drizzle with olive oil. Then, using a knife, shave off shards of ricotta salata over the ravioli, or alternatively use the largest holes of a box grater. Finish with a flurry of lemon zest and serve immediately.

Celeriac and Chestnut Ravioli
with Sage, Butter, and Prosciutto

Celeriac and chestnut filling is a winter treat—sweet, smooth, and luxurious. In addition to using it to stuff ravioli, we serve it as an accompaniment to pork chops and scallops.

The filling can be made up to 2 days in advance. If you can't find chestnuts, peeled hazelnuts are a good alternative.

Serves 6

FOR THE FILLING

1 quart whole milk
1 medium head celeriac (about 1 pound), peeled and cut into 1-inch dice
5 sage leaves
1 garlic clove
Salt
2 cups chestnuts in the shell, shells scored (see page 67)

FOR THE RAVIOLI

Semolina flour for dusting
1 pound Ravioli Dough (page 134), rolled out as directed
Salt
8 tablespoons (1 stick) unsalted butter
A generous handful of sage leaves
6 to 12 slices prosciutto
Olive oil

To make the filling, pour the milk into a medium pot and add the celeriac, sage, and garlic. Season with a generous pinch of salt and bring everything to a simmer over medium-high heat. Reduce the heat to medium and cook, stirring occasionally to prevent the milk from boiling over, until the celeriac is soft enough to be crushed with the back of a spoon, about 15 minutes.

Remove the pot from the heat and discard the garlic and sage. Using a slotted spoon, transfer the celeriac to a food processor, leaving the celeriac-infused milk in the pot.

Add the scored chestnuts to the pot of milk, cover, and simmer until the chestnuts are soft to the poke of a sharp knife, about 20 minutes. Remove one chestnut, carefully peel it, and check that it's potato-soft. If not, continue cooking the chestnuts, adding a bit more milk or some water if necessary so they remain submerged, until soft. Using a slotted spoon, remove the cooked chestnuts from the milk (reserving the cooking liquid) and transfer to a colander.

While they're still warm but not piping hot, peel the chestnuts and discard the shells. Peel off their papery skins and remove any clingy fibers—a good paring knife and patience are necessary.

Transfer the chestnuts to a food processor, add the celeriac, and puree until the filling is silky-smooth and glossy, about 5 minutes. If necessary, blend in a few tablespoons of the reserved milk. Season with salt—the puree should taste equal parts sweet and savory.

(Continued)

Allow the filling to cool completely and then spoon it into a piping bag or hold it in a container and use a spoon for doling it out. The filling holds, covered in the fridge, for up to 2 days. Just before piping out the filling, snip off about ½ inch of the piping bag's tip, if using one.

When ready to assemble the ravioli, dust two baking sheets with semolina flour. Dust a clean work surface with more semolina flour and lay a sheet of pasta horizontally on it. Pipe or spoon a dimple of filling, about the size of half a large cherry 2 inches in from the left end of the pasta sheet, placing it one-third of the way down from the top of the sheet. Continue dotting dimples of filling at 5-inch intervals down the sheet, stopping about 2 inches from the right end.

Fill a clean spray bottle with water and lightly mist the pasta sheet; or use a wet pastry brush to lightly dampen the pasta. Fold the bottom of the sheet up over the filling, aligning the edges.

Using your fingers, press down on either side of each mound of filling, pushing out any trapped air and partially sealing the the ravioli, then pinch the ends of the sheet closed. Next, press down along the top seam to seal the sheet (see page 135).

Use a frilly ravioli cutter or a knife to trim the top of the sheet, making a straight edge. Next, cut between each mound of filling to separate the ravioli and arrange them on a semolina-dusted baking sheet. Repeat with the remaining pasta sheets and filling.

These hold in the fridge for up to 24 hours.

When ready to cook, bring a large pot of salted water to a boil over high heat. The water should taste highly seasoned (not seawater salty, but flavorful). When the water is rumbling, lower the heat to medium-high and drop in half the ravioli.

As soon as you've added the ravioli to the pot, place a large pan over medium heat and add half the butter and half the sage. Once the butter bubbles and the sage crisps, 1 to 2 minutes, ladle ¼ cup of pasta water (just scoop it out of the pot) and swirl the sauce until an emulsion forms, about 1 minute. Season with salt and keep the sauce warm over low heat.

Once the ravioli bob to the water's surface, 3 to 4 minutes, check that the edges have softened but retain some bite. With a slotted spoon, transfer the ravioli to the sage-butter sauce. Swirl the pan to prevent the pasta from sticking while you cook the remaining ravioli. Once cooked, add to the pan with the other ravioli and a splash or two of pasta water if needed.

Serve immediately, draping the prosciutto over the top of the ravioli. Finish with a drizzle of olive oil.

Quince and Ricotta Ravioli
with Thyme and Hazelnuts

The slightly sweet filling for these ravioli is balanced by the addition of thyme and roasted hazelnuts. Store-bought membrillo is a good substitute for homemade, but our recipe is on page 38 if you find time on a weekend morning.

Serves 6

FOR THE FILLING

One 16-ounce container full-fat ricotta cheese
1 cup Quince Preserves (page 38) or store-bought membrillo
Salt

FOR THE RAVIOLI

Semolina flour, for dusting
1 pound Ravioli Dough (page 134), rolled out as directed on page 134
Salt
8 tablespoons (1 stick) unsalted butter
2 teaspoons thyme leaves
Olive oil
16 to 20 hazelnuts, toasted

To make the filling, place the ricotta in a sieve set over a large bowl. Set a weight on the ricotta (a small plate and a jam jar should do it) and set aside to drain for at least 1 hour. (The ricotta can be drained overnight in the fridge; it won't give off much water, but draining it ensures that the filling won't make the ravioli soggy.)

Meanwhile, if using homemade quince preserves, place them in a medium bowl and give them a stir to ensure they have the consistency of a loose, spreadable jam (they should dribble off a spoon). If they are too tight, add a splash of warm water and stir to combine; set aside to cool.

Or, if using store-bought membrillo, place it in a small pot, add ¼ cup or so of water, and warm over medium-low heat, stirring, for a few minutes, until the membrillo melts. It should be loose enough to drizzle but still thick. If necessary, add another splash of warm water. Transfer to a large bowl and let cool completely before using.

Add 1½ cups of the drained ricotta to the quince preserves, swirling the cheese through them until well combined. Taste and add more ricotta if necessary, until the tastes aren't cloying; the preserves should not overwhelm the ricotta's delicacy. Check for seasoning and add salt if necessary, then scoop the filling into a piping bag, or transfer it to a bowl and use a spoon for doling it out. The filling can be held in the fridge, covered, for up to 2 days.

When ready to assemble the ravioli, dust two baking sheets with semolina flour. Dust a clean work surface with more semolina flour and lay a sheet of pasta horizontally across the surface.

(Continued)

Pipe or spoon a dimple of the filling, about the size of a small walnut, 2 inches in from the left end of the pasta sheet, placing it one-third of the way down from the top of the sheet. Continue dotting dimples of filling at 5-inch intervals down the sheet, stopping about 2 inches from the right end.

Fill a clean spray bottle with water and finely mist the pasta sheet; or lightly dampen the sheet with a wet pastry brush. Fold the bottom of the sheet up over the filling, aligning the edges.

Using your fingers, press down on either side of each mound of filling, pushing out any trapped air and partially sealing the ravioli, then pinch the ends of the sheet closed. Next, press down along the top seam to seal the sheet (see page 135).

Use a frilly ravioli cutter or a knife to trim the top of the sheet, making a straight edge. Then cut between each mound of filling to separate the ravioli, and arrange them on a semolina-dusted baking sheet. Repeat with the remaining pasta sheets and filling.

These hold in the fridge for up to 24 hours.

When ready to cook the ravioli, bring a large pot of salted water to a boil over high heat. The water should taste highly seasoned (not seawater salty, but flavorful). When the water is rumbling, lower the heat to medium-high and drop in half the ravioli.

As soon as you have added the pasta to the boiling water, place a large pan over medium heat and add half the butter and half the thyme. Once the butter bubbles and the thyme's scent blooms, after 1 to 2 minutes, add a ladleful of pasta water, about ¼ cup (scoop it directly from the pot), and swirl or whisk the sauce until an emulsion forms, about 1 minute. Season with salt and keep the sauce warm over low heat.

Once the ravioli bob to the water's surface, after 3 to 4 minutes, check that their edges have softened but retain some bite. With a slotted spoon, transfer the ravioli to the pan of simmering thyme-butter, increase the heat to medium to medium-high, and cook, swirling the pan to prevent sticking and spooning the sauce over the ravioli to cloak each parcel, for 1 to 2 minutes. If the sauce is too tight, loosen it with another splash of pasta water. Taste for salt and adjust as necessary, then spoon the pasta and sauce onto individual plates or a large platter. Cook the remaining ravioli and finish them in butter sauce as described above.

Drizzle the ravioli with olive oil and finely grate over the hazelnuts, passing each nut over a Microplane.

Gnudi Verde

Gnudi, featherlight balls of a "nude" ricotta filling, are essentially poached dumplings. Their name translates as "naked," and as such, they come scantily dressed at King, with just a drizzle of new-season olive oil. For a little more finery, though, we've turned these gnudi green, folding a sweet pea puree into the ricotta base.

No flour is added to the mix, making these tricky to assemble but ethereal in the end. Draining and pressing the fresh ricotta to remove excess moisture is critical; otherwise, the gnudi would break apart when boiled. These merit all the effort they require and then some.

Plan to start preparing the gnudi at least 2 days in advance. Once formed, they must rest on a bed of semolina to firm before cooking. To finish, we like to garnish the plates with pea shoots and thin slices of prosciutto, but if you can't get the shoots, or you're avoiding meat, simply omit one or both.

Serves 4 to 6

1½ pounds (24 ounces) fresh ricotta cheese
Salt
½ garlic clove
1 cup English peas
¼ cup mint leaves, plus more to garnish
Olive oil
1 large egg
1 large egg yolk
4 ounces Parmesan cheese, finely grated, plus more to finish
3 cups semolina flour, plus more for dusting
8 tablespoons (1 stick) unsalted butter
3 ounces thinly sliced prosciutto
A handful of pea shoots to finish (optional)
Freshly ground black pepper

Place the ricotta in a sieve set over a large bowl. Set a small plate and a weight (such as a jam jar) on top of the ricotta. Let drain in the fridge for 12 to 24 hours.

Fill a medium pot with salted water, add the garlic, and bring to a boil over high heat. Add the peas and blanch until soft and bright green, about 3 minutes; moments before draining the peas, add the mint leaves to blanch for a couple of seconds. Drain.

Add the peas, garlic, and mint to a blender or food processor. Add 1 tablespoon olive oil and 1½ teaspoons salt and whiz until a very smooth puree forms, 1 to 2 minutes. Taste and season with more salt if needed (but tread lightly, as more seasoning will be coming later). Spread the puree out on a sheet pan or dish and let cool completely.

Transfer the drained ricotta to a large bowl, add the egg, egg yolk, Parmesan, and pea puree, and fold everything together until well combined, then taste and season with salt; this should be flavorful but delicate. Spoon the mixture into a piping bag or a large ziplock bag and

(Continued)

refrigerate the filling until slightly firmed, at least 2 to 3 hours; it will hold for 1 to 2 days in the fridge.

To form the gnudi, sprinkle a baking sheet with enough semolina flour to make a ¾-inch-thick bed. Snip off ½ inch from the tip of the piping bag. Pipe the dough into parallel logs that run length of the pan, spacing them at least ½ inch apart. With scissors or a sharp knife, cut through the logs at 2-inch intervals to make little nuggets. Dust more trays with semolina as needed and repeat the piping and snipping with the remaining dough. Between piping out batches, refrigerate the bag to prevent softening.

Dust your hands with semolina, roll one nugget into a uniformly round ball, and place it back on the pan. Repeat with the remaining nuggets, spacing the formed gnudi ½ inch apart to prevent sticking. Cover the pan with plastic wrap and refrigerate for 3 hours.

Remove the gnudi from the fridge, dust your hands with semolina, reroll each one, taking care to form a light, even semolina dusting around it, and return to the pan. Cover the gnudi and refrigerate until firm, or up to 2 days.

When ready to cook, fill a wide pot with salted water (the wider the better, so the gnudi don't bump together and break apart) and bring to a boil. Remove the pan from the fridge and comb through each to gently loosen the gnudi.

Reduce the heat under the pot to a gentle simmer; only a few bubbles should burst at a time. Be gentle when cooking the gnudi, or they will break! Working in batches to avoid crowding (and prevent breakage), carefully shake off the semolina dusting from about half of the gnudi to the quietly simmering water. Cook until the gnudi float to the surface, about 2 minutes, then allow them to bob at the surface to finish cooking, about 1 minute more.

Meanwhile, as soon as you've added the gnudi to the pot, add half the butter to a large wide pan set over medium heat (it should be large enough to comfortably hold the poached gnudi in a single layer). When the butter foams, add about ¼ cup of the pasta water to the pan (scoop it directly from the pot), swirl to form an emulsified sauce, and then lower the heat to a quiet simmer to keep the sauce warm.

Using a slotted spoon, carefully transfer the cooked gnudi to the warm butter sauce. Increase the heat to medium so the sauce just simmers. (Keep the gnudi water at a simmer.) Delicately swirl the gnudi in the butter sauce, turning to coat them evenly. Add more splashes of pasta water if needed so the sauce stays silky and loose. Once the gnudi are glossy, turn off the heat and tear in a small handful of mint leaves to garnish. Spoon onto individual plates (or onto a large platter) and pour whatever remains of the butter sauce on top. Cook the remaining gnudi and then finish them in butter sauce as described above.

Once all the gnudi are plated, drape the prosciutto over them, tearing the slices into polite bites. Finish with pepper, grated Parmesan, a thin scattering of pea shoots, if you have them, and a drizzle of olive oil.

Malloreddus
with Mussels, Ceci, and Bottarga

This recipe lives somewhere between a pasta and a soup. Its sweet, briny notes capture the Sardinian sunshine. The saffron helps with that as well.

If you decide to make homemade malloreddus, prepare it and the chickpeas well in advance (the malloreddus require 6 to 8 hours of rest once rolled). Alternatively, good-quality store-bought dried cavatelli works well.

Serves 6 to 8

Olive oil
2 garlic cloves, thinly sliced
2 pinches saffron threads
¼ teaspoon fennel seeds, smashed
¼ teaspoon crushed dried red chili, preferably Calabrian
Salt
4 pounds mussels, cleaned and debearded
1 large heirloom tomato (about 1 pound)
2 cups Vermentino or similar dry white wine
3 cups halved Sungold tomatoes
2 cups cooked chickpeas (see page 15), drained
10 ounces (about 2 cups) Malloreddus (page 138), made with saffron, or dried cavatelli
1 tablespoon unsalted butter
1 lemon, cut into 6 to 8 wedges
A small handful of mint leaves to garnish
A 1- to 2-inch nub of bottarga di muggine, peeled (optional)

Select a large wide pot that's big enough to hold the mussels in a single evenish layer. Set the pot over medium-low heat and add ⅓ cup olive oil, half the garlic, half the saffron, the fennel seeds, chili, and a pinch of salt. Heat the aromatics over medium-low heat until the garlic sizzles but does not color, 1 to 2 minutes. Add the mussels and then quickly tear in the heirloom tomato, ripping it in half or into quarters. Pour in the wine and give the pot a jiggle before covering it. Steam the mussels until they just open, about 6 minutes.

Meanwhile, set a strainer over a large bowl. As the mussels pop open, move them to the strainer using tongs or a slotted spoon. If any stubborn mussels remain unopened after 6 or so minutes, cover the pot and steam for a few minutes more, then add them to the strainer once the shells finally open. If after a few extra minutes, any mussels remain unopened, discard them.

Pour the pot's contents into the strainer, capturing all the briny drippings in the bowl below. Lift up the strainer of mussels, wait for the excess liquid to drain off, and then set on a rimmed plate; remove and discard the tomato. Set the bowl of cooking liquid aside.

Once they are cool enough to handle, pluck all the mussels from their shells, placing them in a clean bowl, and discard their shells.

(Continued)

Set a small sieve over a medium bowl and pinch the halved tomatoes so their bellies and seeds fall into the sieve. Set the squeezed tomatoes aside on a plate, and press on the captured seeds and pulp to extract as much juice as possible. Remove the sieve and discard the seeds; add the captured tomato juice to the mussels' cooking liquor.

Set a large heavy pot over low heat. Add a tablespoon of olive oil and the remaining garlic and saffron. Once the scents bloom but before the garlic colors, 1 to 2 minutes, add the squeezed tomatoes to the pot. Heat until the tomatoes warm through, about 2 minutes, then add the cooked chickpeas and about half of the mussels' cooking liquor. There should be enough to cover the chickpeas by at least 1 inch; if not, top up the pot with water. Simmer until the chickpeas have absorbed the delicious broth's flavor, 3 to 5 minutes. Remove from the heat and set aside.

Fill a tall medium pot with salted water and bring to a boil over high heat. Add the malloreddus or cavatelli and boil until just shy of al dente. If using malloreddu, this will take 35 minutes; if using store-bought, refer to the box's directions and cook for 1 to 2 minutes less than the recommended time.

Meanwhile, as soon as you've added the pasta to the pot, stir the mussels into the pot of chickpeas. When the pasta is done, reserve 2 cups or so of its cooking water (you may not need the pasta water, but you'll have it just in case . . .) and drain the pasta.

Gently warm the chickpeas and mussels over medium heat, and once the liquid is simmering, toss in the pasta. Increase the heat to medium-high and simmer until the pasta is cooked to al dente and the flavors have melded, a minute or so. The final dish should be silky and a bit soupy, so add more of the mussels' cooking liquor if necessary (the liquid will tighten as it sits, so make this a bit looser than you want); if you run out of the mussels' liquor, use some of the reserved pasta water. Toss in the butter (to keep things juicy) and season with salt to taste.

Quickly ladle helpings into warm bowls and garnish each with a lemon wedge, some torn mint leaves, and a fine grating of bottarga di muggine, if using. Drizzle with olive oil and serve immediately.

CHAPTER 8

Vegetables

WHEN IT COMES TO VEGETABLES, WE LEAN WHOLESALE INTO SEASONALITY. WEEKLY trips to the Greenmarket, led by Tina, are year-round sources of inspiration. The vegetables that change subtly throughout their season are a particular delight.

We cook such sensitive vegetables accordingly. At the start of their life, when the vegetables are young and tender, we serve them raw, in salads, or maybe simply boiled and dressed with a little lemon and olive oil. Any number of sauces are delicious here, but our Bagna Cauda (page 24) and Anchoïade (page 23) always work because their intensity brings life to all kinds of vegetables. A little later, once the vegetables mature, growing larger and bolder, we cook them twice, first boiling and then, perhaps, slowly braising. The first pass tenderizes them and the second layers in flavor. In Italy, they call this practice *ripassata,* meaning "re-cooking."

We cook greens—spinach, dandelions, cavolo nero, and chard—throughout the year and we always double-cook them. First boiled until truly soft, they are then drained (very thoroughly) and primed for a second cook. We finish them off, most often, in a garlic-and-chili-infused olive oil, cooking the greens until they are saturated and very delicious.

Near the end of a vegetable's life, we like to stew and crush it, so any wooliness or excess water evaporates and the flavors intensify. Honeynut squash, large zucchini, and late-season favas all turn creamy and rich when cooked to the point of collapse.

Peas Sott'olio

Serves 8

1 garlic clove, halved lengthwise
4 cups English peas
Leaves from 6 or so large mint branches
Olive oil (at least 2 or 3 cups)
Salt

Bring a medium pot of (unsalted) water, with the garlic clove, to a boil over high heat. Add the peas and boil until they are just plump and turn sharp green in color, about 2 to 3 minutes. Add the mint leaves and let them cook for a minute or so, until their color sets. Drain the peas in a colander and let steam-dry for a moment.

Transfer the peas (and garlic and mint) to a medium bowl. While everything is still quite hot, pour over enough olive oil to fully submerge the peas, 2 to 3 cups. Season with salt and let cool for at least 10 minutes.

Remove peas from the oil with a slotted spoon and serve warm or at room temperature.

Artichokes Sott'olio

These artichokes can confidently stand alone or go with grilled fish and meat. They can also be torn into pieces and tossed with pasta, or placed whole on the grill briefly for an outdoor antipasto.

Serves 6

3 pounds baby artichokes (about 24), prepped (see page 87)
8 sprigs of thyme
8 parsley stems
8 sage leaves
Olive oil (at least 1½ cups)
Salt

Combine the artichokes, thyme, parsley, sage, 1½ cups olive oil, and a palmful of salt in a large pot that's wide enough to hold the artichokes in a single layer. Add enough cool water to just cover, then place a cartouche (see page 15) over the artichokes and set a heat-resistant plate on top to keep them submerged (to prevent bobbing is to prevent discoloration). Bring to a simmer over medium heat and simmer until the artichokes' bases are tender to the poke of a knife, about 20 minutes; when checking, test a larger artichoke for doneness, as these will take longer.

Remove from the heat and let the artichokes cool completely in their oily cooking liquor.

The artichokes hold, submerged in the cooking liquor and covered, in the fridge for up to 4 days.

Favas Sott'olio

To double-pod or not will depend on the size of your favas and your own inclination. We prefer smaller tender favas (almost pea-sized) left in their skins. With larger ones (thumbnail size up), we remove the inner skin. Double-podding is always necessary late in the season once the shells have toughened.

Serves 8

1 garlic clove, peeled
5 pounds fava beans, double-podded (see below)
A handful of mint leaves
Olive oil (at least 2 cups)
Salt

Bring a medium pot of (unsalted) water, with the garlic, to a boil over high heat. Add the favas and boil until they are completely soft, 2 to 4 minutes. If your favas are whoppers, they will take longer; taste and see. Add the mint leaves and let them cook until their color sets, a minute or less. Drain the favas in a colander.

Quickly blot the favas dry and then transfer them, with the garlic and mint, to a medium bowl. While everything is still hot, pour over enough olive oil to fully submerge the favas, 2 to 3 cups. Season with salt and let the favas cool in the oil for at least 10 minutes. Serve warm or at room temperature.

Favas sott'olio will hold at room temperature for a few hours. Covered and in the fridge, they hold for up to 2 days. Longer, and they may sour.

HOW TO DOUBLE-POD FAVAS

Pop open the long pods and pull out the fava beans. Discard the pods (or use them in a stock).

Bring a large pot of water to a boil over high heat. Set up an ice bath. Add the beans to the boiling water and cook until they turn bright green, about 2 minutes.

Drain the favas from the pot and plunge them into the ice bath to cool completely.

One at a time, lift a fava out of the ice bath and, with your thumbnail, pierce the skin near its sprout. Now peel back the skin a bit and pop out the tender bean. Discard the skins.

Asparagus
with Anchovy Butter

Spring asparagus needs nothing more than a bit of butter and an anchovy or two.

Serves 8 to 10

Salt
5 bunches asparagus (3 to 4 pounds)
Olive oil
1 cup Anchovy Butter (recipe follows), tempered

Bring a large pot of salted water to a boil over high heat. Meanwhile, rinse the asparagus and snap off and discard their woody ends (where the whitish part turns green). When the water is rumbling, add the asparagus and foil until just tender, about 3 minutes. Taste a fat spear: it should be slightly toothsome but mostly tender.

Drain the asparagus in a colander and allow to quickly steam-dry, then toss them in a large bowl with enough olive oil, about 2 tablespoons, to glisten. While they are still quite warm, transfer the asparagus to a warm platter and dollop generous spoonfuls of the anchovy butter all around. If the asparagus stack up in a pile, drop a few tablespoons of butter between the layers to distribute it.

Serve these warm and buttery.

Anchovy Butter

As with all our sauces, we like this one bold. Add dollops to hot carte di musica, grilled steaks or lamb chops, a piece of white fish, a handful of asparagus spears. . . . Always make more than you think you need. What isn't used will be polished off at breakfast, on toast.

Makes 2 cups

½ pound (2 sticks) unsalted butter, at room temperature
½ cup anchovy fillets (about 30), rinsed and roughly chopped
Juice of ½ lemon, strained
Salt and freshly ground black pepper

Combine the butter, half the anchovies, and the lemon juice in a blender or food processor and blend until the butter forms soft peaks and the anchovies are evenly dispersed (or use a bowl, a wooden spoon, and a strong wrist).

Transfer the anchovy butter to a bowl and fold in the remaining anchovies. Add salt and pepper to taste.

Braised Artichokes

These herby artichoke bonbons are cooked until soft and caramelized. Do not worry if they fall apart slightly. Just make sure to fry them for long enough and in enough oil that they crisp and turn completely fudgy within.

Serves 6 to 8

Olive oil
5 bay leaves
1 head garlic, halved across its equator
3 pounds baby artichokes (about 24), prepped (see page 87) and held in lemon water
Salt
2 cups dry white wine
Leaves from 4 sprigs of rosemary, finely chopped
Leaves from 4 sprigs of thyme, finely chopped
A small handful of sage leaves

Choose a pot that's wide enough to hold the artichokes in a single layer, essential for browning! (If necessary, use two pots.) Add ¾ cup olive oil, the bay leaves, and the garlic head, placing it cut side down, and gently warm the oil over medium heat. (Split everything between the two pots if using two.)

Meanwhile, drain the artichokes and dry thoroughly. Add them to the hot fragrant oil and season with salt. Stir to fully coat the artichokes in oil, then turn the heat up to full blast. Pour in the wine and cover with a cartouche (see page 15). Once the wine bubbles, reduce the heat to medium-low and simmer until the artichokes are tender at their thickest point, about 15 minutes.

Remove the cartouche and turn the heat up to high once more, driving off any water so the artichokes caramelize. Once the pot is dry, after 5 or so minutes, reduce the heat to medium or medium-high and stir in the rosemary, thyme, and sage leaves; they should gently fry.

Continue cooking and browning the artichokes, frequently shaking the pot, letting the artichokes settle, and then shaking again, until the artichokes are sweet and golden all around, about 25 minutes. As they cook, add more olive oil as necessary to crisp the leaves that fall off and to prevent scorching.

Turn off the heat, check the seasoning, and adjust with salt as needed. Serve warm or at room temperature.

Favas Braised in Milk

This recipe will look strange, but if you end up with shriveled, slightly gray favas coated in milk curds, that is actually correct. Trust the recipe, and make sure to cook everything long enough. It won't look like much, but the taste will surprise!

Serves 8

Olive oil
2 garlic cloves, thinly sliced
A small handful of sage leaves
½ teaspoon fennel seeds, lightly crushed
4 cups shucked fava beans
(about 8 pounds of fava pods)
Peel of 4 lemons
3 cups whole milk
Salt

Combine ¼ cup olive oil, the garlic, sage, and fennel seeds in a wide deep pan and gently warm over medium-low heat. Once the oil is fragrant but before the garlic colors, a minute or so, add the favas and lemon peel and stir, coating the favas in the scented oil, then pour in the milk. Season with 2 teaspoons salt and cover the braise with a cartouche (see page 15).

Gently simmer until the favas soften and crumple, about 30 minutes. This will depend on the favas' size, so it's best to start checking and tasting at the 15- or 20-minute mark. The beans are ready once all the milk has cooked off and the curds are starting to caramelize. Remove from the heat.

The favas are as good at room temperature as they are warm.

Braised Lettuce and Peas

. . . or petits pois à la Française, as they say in France!

Serves 8 to 10

6 heads Baby Gem lettuce or
3 small heads romaine (about 1½ pounds)
5 tablespoons unsalted butter
Olive oil
5 shallots, thinly sliced
Salt
3 tablespoons all-purpose flour
⅔ cup dry white wine
3 cups chicken stock, preferably homemade (see page 35)
4 cups English peas
½ cup mint leaves

Remove all the tatty outer leaves from the Baby Gems and then cut away any brown bits from their root ends while keeping the heads intact. Quarter the heads lengthwise and set aside.

Heat the broth in a medium pot over medium-low heat. Meanwhile, place a wide heavy pan over medium heat and add the butter, 1 tablespoon olive oil, the shallots, and a pinch of salt and cook until the shallots have softened but not picked up any color, 5 to 8 minutes.

Increase the heat to medium-high, and when the butter foams, stir in the flour to form the base of the roux. Lower the heat to medium and cook, stirring constantly to prevent scorching, until the roux is blond in color, about 4 minutes. Pour in the wine, stirring to deglaze, and then slowly add the warm broth about one ladleful at a time, stirring without pause. Whisk to break up any lumps and then let everything bubble so the roux thickens slightly, a couple of minutes. Season with salt.

Stir in the peas, season with a little more salt, and simmer until the peas turn bright green and plump, 1 to 2 minutes. Stir in the lettuce quarters and cook until their outer leaves wilt slightly and their centers soften but still retain some bite, about 2 minutes.

Remove from the heat and season with salt as needed. Tear over the mint and finish with a drizzle of olive oil. Serve warm.

Boiled Baby Zucchini

Young squash have a delicate flavor and a firm texture, which makes them perfect for boiling.

If female zucchini with their blossoms still attached are available, quickly add them to your basket. Use the cheerful yellow flowers as a garnish or in the seasoning.

Serves 4

1 garlic clove, peeled
12 to 14 baby zucchini, preferably with flowers attached
Salt and freshly ground black pepper
Olive oil
Finely grated zest of 1 lemon; lemon halved and reserved
2 to 3 tablespoons minced parsley

Bring a large pot of salted water to a boil over high heat; as it comes up, add the garlic clove. Snap off the squash blossoms, if you have them, and set aside.

Add the squash to the pot and boil until they are soft and yield to a knife's poke, 8 to 10 minutes. (Baby zucchini are about 6 inches long; anything larger will have to cook for longer, until tender.) Drain the zucchini in a colander and steam-dry.

Add the zucchini to a large bowl and season with a generous pinch of salt, some pepper, and 2 to 3 tablespoons olive oil. Add a squeeze of lemon and jiggle the bowl to coat all the zucchini with the seasoning. Taste and add more lemon juice, olive oil, and/or salt as needed.

Arrange the zucchini on a serving dish. If you have them, tear the reserved flowers in half and remove their stamens, then tear the yellow flowers over the platter, dressing it up. Finish with a sprinkle of the minced parsley and lemon zest.

Confit Tomatoes

This is probably summer's most versatile, lowest-effort dish. It scales up or down effortlessly and never fails to impress.

Use whatever variety of tomato is at peak ripeness, and confit many more than you think you need. The recipe below calls for larger tomatoes—dramatic showstoppers. But we also apply this formula to small or baby tomatoes, covering them with oil and gently cooking them until they puff and soften. With smaller varieties, like cherry or Sungold tomatoes, reduce the cooking time by about 20 or 30 minutes. We spoon these (with their oil) over meat or fish, sometimes adding chopped olives and soft herbs to this drizzle as well. The variations are infinite. . . .

Stored under oil, either version will keep for days. And they both provide lots of leftover oil, stunning all on its own. Use it for everything: dressings, for dipping bread, pastas, etc.

Serves 8 to 12

7 pounds large ripe heirloom tomatoes
A head of garlic, cloves separated but skins left intact
2 large handfuls basil leaves
Salt
Olive oil (at least 6 cups)

Preheat the oven to 450 degrees. Place the tomatoes in a deep roasting pan large enough to hold them in a snug single layer, and add the garlic cloves, basil, and a few generous pinches of salt. Pour enough olive oil into the dish so only the tomatoes' very tops are exposed (the upper ½ inch or so). Roast the tomatoes in the oven until the oil simmers, about 15 minutes. Turn the heat down to 350 degrees and confit the tomatoes until they fully soften but still hold their shape, about 45 to 55 minutes more (really, though, this depends on size!). To test, pierce a tomato with the point of a knife at its thickest point: it should meet no resistance.

Remove the pan from the oven and let the tomatoes cool in their oil for at least 15 minutes. Serve warm or at room temperature. Once the tomatoes disappear, strain the tomato oil and keep it in an airtight container in the fridge.

Tian

A classic Provençal tian tastes as dazzling as it looks. Mixed summer vegetables, tomatoes, zucchini, and eggplant, all thinly sliced, get packed into a buttered dish and roasted until softened and juicy.

The key is to season everything from the beginning and cook the tian for long enough that the top browns and the vegetables yield. If your eggplant is massive, halve it before slicing it to approximate the size of the sliced tomatoes and zucchini.

Serves 6

2 to 3 garlic cloves, 1 split, the other(s) thinly sliced
2 to 3 tablespoons unsalted butter, plus more for greasing the pan
1 large eggplant (about 1 pound)
Salt
2 medium zucchini (about 1 pound)
6 medium ripe tomatoes (about 1½ pounds)
2 large handfuls of basil leaves
Olive oil (the oil from Confit Tomatoes, page 182, would be fantastic here)
1 to 2 cups Salmoriglio (page 186)

Preheat the oven to 450 degrees. Rub a 10-inch round cake pan with the split garlic clove, then grease it with butter.

Using a mandoline or a sharp knife, slice the eggplant into thin rounds, approximately ⅛ inch thick. Place the slices in a large bowl and season with salt. Slice the zucchini to the same thickness and add them to the bowl, along with the sliced garlic. Salt will draw out the vegetables' water as they sit.

Using a bread knife, slice the tomatoes horizontally into ⅛-inch-thick rounds, trying not to squash the tomatoes. Lay the slices out on the cutting board and sprinkle with salt.

Pour off any water that has been released from the zucchini and eggplant.

Stack a few zucchini and eggplant slices in one hand and, with your other hand, insert a few tomato slices and basil leaves here and there. Doing this is somewhat like threading a kabob without a stick. Once you have a full hand of vegetables, place the stack on its side against one side of your prepared pan. Continue making stacks of the remaining vegetables and basil and laying them on their sides in the dish, working from the outside in and packing the vegetables tightly into the dish so they spiral toward the dish's center and stand upright.

Top the tian with the remaining butter, diced into smaller bits. Drizzle the top with olive oil, about 1 to 2 tablespoons, and bake until the vegetables completely soften and brown on top, about 1 hour.

(Continued)

Remove the tian from the oven and, while it's still piping hot, generously brush the top with the salmoriglio until it is well lacquered. Let the tian cool until it's just warm or room temperature, at least 45 minutes, before serving.

Salmoriglio

Salmorigio is an herby Sicilian marinade that gives a boost to anything off the grill or any freshly blanched vegetables, as well as the tian. This recipe calls for marjoram, but other soft herbs (basil, mint, or fennel fronds) will work. Add the lemon juice just before serving to stop the herbs from turning swampy.

Makes 1 cup

½ garlic clove
½ cup marjoram leaves
Salt
Olive oil
Juice of ½ lemon

Using a mortar and pestle, crush the garlic, herb leaves, and a good pinch of salt together to form a paste, about 5 minutes of good bashing. Mix in ½ cup olive oil and then finish with a squeeze of lemon. Season with salt until it tastes flavorful and herbaceous.

Tomatoes Farci

Few plates will leave a Côte d'Azur kitchen without a vegetable stuffed with rice, ground pork, and garlicky breadcrumbs. Zucchini, eggplants, tomatoes, and peppers are all routinely rounded out with a filling.

These rice-and-chard-stuffed tomatoes go particularly well with slow-cooked lamb (page 224). Any leftovers will make a fine lunch the following day with a salad of butterhead lettuces.

Serves 6

6 large beefsteak tomatoes or large heirlooms
2 garlic cloves, slivered
Salt and freshly ground black pepper
Olive oil
1 cup basmati rice
1 bunch rainbow or Swiss chard (about ¾ pound), trimmed and washed
2 teaspoon cumin seeds
½ cup Taggiasca olives, drained, pitted, and roughly chopped

Preheat the oven to 400 degrees. Slice the top ½ inch off the tomatoes and set these hats aside. Scoop out and discard the seeds and pulp from each tomato. Lay a sliver of garlic in each hollowed-out cavity and season with salt and pepper, plus a drizzle of olive oil.

Place the tomatoes in a baking dish and bake until slightly softened, 10 to 12 minutes. Remove the tomatoes from the oven and let cool.

Add the rice to a medium pot and cover generously with cold water. Bring to a boil over high heat, then reduce the heat to a simmer and cook until the grains are just starting to become tender, 8 to 10 minutes. Drain and cool the rice. (If the rice seems at all overcooked, spread the grains out on a baking sheet to cool them quickly.)

Meanwhile, bring a wide pot of salted water to a boil over high heat. Once rumbling, add the chard and blanch until the stems just soften, about 5 minutes. Drain in a colander, dry thoroughly, and finely chop.

Warm 2 tablespoons olive oil in a large pot over medium heat, add the remaining garlic slivers and the cumin, and warm just until aromatic, about 1 minute. Add the chopped chard, parcooked rice, and olives, stirring to combine, and cook for a few minutes to blend the flavors, then taste and add salt as needed. If the parcooked tomatoes released any juices, add them to the rice mix for good measure. Remove from the heat.

Preheat the oven to 500 degrees. Stuff the tomatoes with the rice mixture and then top each one with its cap. Drizzle with olive oil, about 1 to 2 teaspoons per tomato, and season with salt.

Bake on the oven's uppermost rack until the tomatoes take on some color, about 12 minutes. Serve warm or at room temperature.

Potatoes

with King Rosé, Bay, and Olives

Use waxy potatoes that can stand up to a long roast and high temperature for this. To peel or not to peel is entirely up to you. We like these potatoes with their skins on (especially if they are young), but they will be delicious either way.

Serves 4 to 6

3 pounds thin-skinned potatoes, such as Yukon Golds
Salt and freshly ground black pepper
Olive oil (about 1 cup)
3 shallots, thinly sliced
3 garlic cloves, finely chopped
Needles from 6 sprigs of rosemary, finely chopped
Leaves from a large handful of thyme branches
1½ to 1¾ cups King rosé or similar dry rosé, like Bandol
4 to 6 fresh bay leaves
6 tablespoons Taggiasca olives, drained, pitted, and roughly torn

Preheat the oven to 450 degrees. Roughly chop the potatoes on the bias into dice approximately the shape of peach pits (an angled dice gives more surface area for crisping).

Place the potatoes in a large bowl and season generously with salt and pepper and with about ½ cup olive oil, tossing to coat. Add the shallots, garlic, rosemary, and thyme and tumble everything together, coating the potatoes evenly. Spread the potatoes out in a large roasting pan in a single uncrowded layer and splash in a bit more than 1½ cups wine. Cover the pan with aluminum foil and crimp the edges to seal.

Roast in the oven until the largest piece of potato is tender to a knife's poke, 20 to 25 minutes.

Carefully remove the foil and stir in the bay leaves and a generous drizzle of oil, 2 to 3 tablespoons. Spread the potatoes out again and return to the oven until they are a nice, golden brown, about 30 minutes more; as the potatoes roast, toss and crush them with the back of a spoon every 10 minutes or so. If the pan looks at all dry, add some extra oil.

Once the potatoes are golden brown and quite crisp, mix in the olives and roast for a final 10 minutes. Season with salt and serve warm.

Honeynut Squash Gratin

This is another Sade recipe, one of our original beloved chefs. Always delicious, it's especially satisfying during the holidays, served hot from the oven.

Serve this with grilled quail (see page 281), grilled beef (see page 207), or roasted pork chops (see page 220).

Serves 6

3 cups heavy cream
20 large sage leaves
A nub of nutmeg
4 garlic cloves
8 whole black peppercorns
3 honeynut squash or 1 large butternut squash (2 to 3 pounds total), peeled, halved, and seeds and membranes removed
Salt and freshly ground black pepper
½ cup crème fraîche
1 to 2 tablespoons unsalted butter for greasing the pan
A small piece of Parmesan cheese for grating
Olive oil

Preheat the oven to 400 degrees. Pour the cream into a small pot, add 5 of the sage leaves, and grate in a scant ½ teaspoon of nutmeg, using a Microplane. Smash 3 of the garlic cloves and add them to the pot, along with the peppercorns. Bring the cream to a gentle simmer over medium-low heat and cook, stirring frequently to prevent the cream from boiling over, until it thickens slightly and picks up the scent from the aromatics, about 20 minutes. Remove cream from the heat and let cool.

Using a mandoline or a sharp knife, slice the squash crosswise into paper-thin slivers, ⅛ inch thick or less. Finely slice half the remaining sage leaves crosswise into a chiffonade (thin strips).

Place the squash in a large deep bowl and season with salt and pepper. Add the sage and crème fraîche and toss well. Set a sieve over the bowl and pour in the infused cream; press on the trapped aromatics to extract all their flavor and then discard. Toss to combine.

Halve the remaining garlic clove and rub the inside of a medium baking dish with the cut side of the garlic, then generously grease it with the butter. Lift the squash out of its cream and pack it into the dish, arranging the slices in layers, taking care to fill the dish's corners. Pour over enough of the cream to submerge the squash. Scatter the remaining whole sage leaves evenly over the top. Dust the gratin very lightly with grated nutmeg. Finish with a generous drizzle of olive oil and a generous dusting of grated Parmesan, covering the top.

Cover the dish tightly with aluminum foil, crimping the edges, and bake in the oven until the squash slices in the center of the gratin are easily pierced with the tip of a knife, about 45 minutes.

Uncover the dish and bake until the cream caramelizes and a crisp, golden crust forms on the top of the gratin, 40 to 60 minutes more. Remove from the oven and let settle for 10 to 15 minutes before serving.

Wax Beans
with Anchovy and Basil

In the classic Italian "ripassata" approach of cooking something twice, we first boil these wax beans until they are properly soft (no squeak) and then cook them again until they turn creamy. Salty and intense, they are best eaten at room temperature, either on their own or with just about anything.

After the beans are blanched, we quickly split them lengthwise to make them finer.

Serves 4

Salt
1½ pounds mixed green and yellow wax beans, topped and tailed
Olive oil
4 garlic cloves, thinly sliced
2 cups packed basil leaves
20 anchovy fillets (about ⅓ cup), rinsed
Freshly ground black pepper

Bring a large pot of well-salted water to a rumbling boil over high heat. Add the beans and cook until they are so soft they no longer squeak when bitten into, about 10 minutes.

Drain the beans in a colander and let them steam-dry for a moment. Once they've cooled slightly, split them in half along their natural seams.

Warm ¾ cup olive oil with the sliced garlic in a wide heavy pot over low heat. Once the garlic is sticky but before it browns, about 3 minutes, add half the basil, the anchovies, and some pepper and stir until the anchovies just melt into the oil and the basil's scent blooms, less than a minute. Add the drained beans and stir to coat. Continue cooking over low heat, stirring now and again, until the beans are custardy, within about 15 minutes.

Stir in the remaining basil leaves and cook just to set their color, 2 to 3 minutes. Remove the pot from the heat. The beans will only get better as they rest and cool to room temperature. Allow the beans to cool a little to room temperature, before finishing with a final drizzle of olive oil.

Smashed Pumpkin

When pumpkin is cooked slowly, its natural sugars intensify. For a pasta filling (see page 157), we make it very smooth, but if serving it with roasted pork chops and some tapenade (see page 30) we like to keep it a little chunkier.

Serves 6

Olive oil
2 garlic cloves, halved
½ cup sage leaves
3 to 4 pounds honey nut squash or butternut squash, peeled, halved, and seeds removed
Salt

Cut the squash into 1-inch cubes. Warm ½ cup olive oil in a wide heavy pot over medium heat and add the garlic and sage. Once their scents bloom but before either browns, about 2 minutes, stir in the squash, coating all the pieces in oil. Season generously with salt, reduce the heat to low, partially cover the pot, and slowly cook, stirring now and again, until the squash is very tender, about 1 hour and 15 minutes; if necessary, add splashes of water to prevent sticking and scorching. Once the liquid has cooked off and the largest squash cube is completely soft and smashes easily, remove from the heat.

Mash everything to a more-or-less smooth puree. Season with salt and stir in 2 tablespoons olive oil. (If using this for a pasta filling, transfer the smash to a sieve set over a bowl so excess moisture will drip out as it cools to room temperature.)

Serve warm.

Confit Chanterelles

Chanterelle season is fleeting, so we preserve some of these golden mushrooms and cherish whatever we get in for a little longer than nature intended.

We've included measurements, but just as with the Confit Tomatoes (page 182), the recipe doesn't really need them: Just preserve as many chanterelles as you can by submerging them in oil and gently warming them until they no longer squeak when bitten into. Serve these for breakfast with a fried egg and crisp sage leaves. Or toss the mushrooms and some of their oil into pasta, or spoon them onto toast, or . . .

The resulting oil is as precious as the mushrooms themselves. Use both with abandon (see page 69).

Serves 4
(with lots of precious mushroom oil)

4 cups chanterelles, cleaned and dried, ends discarded
A small handful of thyme branches
4 garlic cloves, bashed open in their skins
Salt
Olive oil (at least 4 cups)

Preheat the oven to 250 degrees. Place the mushrooms in an ovenproof pot that is wide enough to hold them in a snug single layer and deep enough to hold the oil bath comfortably; if necessary, use two pots. Add the thyme and garlic cloves to the pot (leaving them in their skins encourages a slow oozing). Season with a pinch of salt, but tread lightly: there's more to come. Pour in enough olive oil to submerge the mushrooms.

Cook the chanterelles low and slow in the oven until they soften, about 45 minutes. Remove a mushroom and taste if it is cool enough to handle; if there is any squeak, keep the confit going. Once the mushrooms have passed the test, remove from the oven and allow them to cool completely in their oil. This final step is vital and allows the chanterelles time to bloom. As they cool, season with salt to taste.

Submerged in the oil, tightly sealed, the mushrooms keep for about 2 weeks in the fridge.

Grilled and Marinated Fennel

Marinating fennel with its fronds and some seeds makes it extra fennel-y. We serve this with fish and pork.

Serves 6

4 fennel bulbs, stalks and fronds attached
Salt
Olive oil (at least 1 cup)
Finely grated zest of 4 lemons
2 teaspoons fennel seeds, lightly crushed
½ garlic clove, crushed

Remove the fennel fronds from the stalks and and finely chop them; set aside. Cut the stalks off the bulbs, then remove the bulbs' tough outermost layers and discard both the stalks and outer layers (or reserve them for the stockpot). Halve the bulbs lengthwise, root end to tip, then slice each half lengthwise into quarters.

Bring a large pot of heavily salted water to a boil over high heat. Add the fennel wedges and cook until tender, about 5 to 7 minutes. Drain in a colander and allow the fennel to steam-dry.

SET UP A HOT FIRE IN A GRILL. AS IT WARMS, PREPARE THE MARINADE: Combine the chopped fennel fronds, 1 cup olive oil, the lemon zest, crushed fennel seeds, garlic, and a pinch of salt in a large bowl.

When the grill is white-hot, use tongs to arrange the fennel wedges on the grate, flat sides down. Once grill marks have formed, 1 minute or less, flip the wedges and mark the second flat side, another minute or so. Pull the fennel off the grill and add it to the marinade. Toss, taste, and adjust the seasoning with more salt and/or olive oil as needed; this should taste bright. Let the fennel wedges marinate for at least 10 minutes.

Serve the fennel warm or at room temperature.

Potatoes
with Lentils, Chicories, and Anchoïade

A potato salad for all your grilled beef, fish, or bird needs.

Serves 4 to 6

Salt
1 pound thin-skinned waxy potatoes, such as Yukon Gold
1¼ cups cooked lentils (see page 20), held in their cooking liquor
1 lemon, halved
1 large head Treviso radicchio
¾ cup finely chopped parsley
3 tablespoons Anchoïade (page 23), plus more as needed
Freshly ground black pepper
Olive oil

Bring a medium pot of salted water to a boil over high heat. As the water comes up, peel the potatoes. Once the water is rumbling, add the potatoes to the pot and cook until the largest one is easily pierced with the tip of a knife, about 15 minutes.

Drain the potatoes and cut into pieces roughly the size of ½-inch cubes. Add the potatoes to a wide bowl. With a slotted spoon, drain the lentils and scatter them over the potatoes. Season with salt and a squeeze of lemon juice and mix to combine, then taste and adjust the seasoning as needed. (It's important to season potatoes and lentils while they're hot and at their most absorbent.) When they have cooled slightly, 5 to 10 minutes, taste and season again as necessary. Set aside.

Slice the top 2 inches off the Treviso head and throw the leafy tips into the bowl with the potatoes. Very finely slice the rest of the head, down to the root end. Add to the salad bowl, along with the parsley, and fold in the anchoïade and lots of pepper. Wait a few minutes, then taste and season with more salt, olive oil if needed, and pepper and lemon juice to taste. You may need to season once or twice more before serving—lentils and potatoes are sponges, and their seasoning mellows as it settles into place.

Roasted Treviso
with Vinegar, Sage, and Parmesan

We're always looking for vehicles to set over mounds of soft polenta laced with lots of butter and Parmesan. These roasted Treviso halves, cut with a dash of vinegar and rounded out with crisped sage and Parmesan, are one option. The recipe is adapted from Lidia Bastianich (a copy of her cookbook *Lidia's Kitchen* sits on the shelf above our pass).

Treviso is favored at King, but endive, red radicchio, Tardive, or any other chicory that holds up when roasted does the trick.

Serves 4 to 6

2 heads Treviso or other radicchio
Salt and freshly ground black pepper
Olive oil
1 garlic clove, slivered
16 sage leaves, stems removed
⅓ cup red wine vinegar
⅓ cup grated Parmesan cheese

Preheat the oven to 350 degrees. Remove any tatty outer leaves from the radicchio and trim away any browned bits from the root ends. Halve or quarter each one, depending on its size; we like these wedges about 2 inches wide at their thickest point. Season them all over with salt and pepper.

Choose an ovenproof skillet that is wide enough to hold the radicchio comfortably in a single layer. Pour ⅓ cup of olive oil into the pan and warm it over medium heat. Once it is hot, lay in the wedges flat sides down—do not overcrowd the pan!—and sear, turning as necessary, until golden brown and caramelized on all sides, about 3 minutes per side.

Turn off the heat and squidge all the radicchio into one side of the pan. Add the garlic and sage; they should immediately sizzle (if necessary, add a little extra olive oil to ensure they do). Once the aromatics fry and deepen in color, but do not brown, drape the leaves over the radicchio, distributing them evenly.

Return the pan to medium heat and spread out the Treviso wedges. Once the pan is hot, after a minute or so, splash in the vinegar and sprinkle over the Parmesan. Roast on the oven's top rack until the cheese melts and browns in spots, about 25 minutes. (The burnt, crispy pieces of Parm on the pan's bottom are the best bits.)

Remove from the oven and serve warm.

Ceci and Cavolo Inzimino

An Italian contorno that combines two of our favorite things: perfectly prepared beans and cooked greens. A cima puree, essentially more blanched greens blended with olive oil until silky, holds everything together while staying on brand. The combination tastes creamy, vital, and very Italian.

It's important to use home-cooked chickpeas and heavily blanched cavolo so the cooking liquor from both can be added as needed when you bring everything together.

Serves 4 to 6

Salt
2 bunches Tuscan or lacinato kale (about 1½ pounds), stems discarded
4 garlic cloves, one left whole, the others thinly sliced
Olive oil
2 good pinches crushed dried red chili, preferably Calabrian
2½ cups drained cooked chickpeas (see page 15)
1 cup Cima Puree (page 13), plus more if needed

Bring a medium pot of salted water, with a clove of garlic, to a boil over high heat. When rumbling, add the kale and boil until completely soft, about 15 minutes (definitely longer than you might think!). Meanwhile, set a colander in the sink.

Transfer the soft greens to the colander and press on them to release all their water. Once they are cool enough to handle, wring the leaves dry, then use a kitchen towel to blot them bone-dry. Thinly slice the kale and set aside.

Add ½ cup olive oil to a medium heavy pot set over low heat, then add the sliced garlic, chili, and a generous pinch of salt and cook until the garlic softens and turns sticky but doesn't color, less than a minute. Add the kale, stirring to coat all the greens, and braise gently until they have no bite whatsoever, about 10 minutes.

Stir in the chickpeas and cook, stirring gently, until the flavors meld, about 5 minutes. Add the cima puree and warm it through, a minute or two. Turn off the heat, taste for salt, and adjust as needed.

Drizzle generously with olive oil and serve warm or at room temperature.

Tortino di Indivia e Alici

At King, we've reinterpreted this Italian endive and anchovy bake as an accompaniment for boiled ox and beef tongue (page 212) and roasted birds. But with just a salad, it will serve very nicely as the main event too. With layers of baked endive, breadcrumbs, and anchovy, perfumed with rosemary, it warms and impresses in winter.

Audrey Falk, a long-standing (now ex) sous chef, developed this recipe. Over to you, Auds . . .

We have Rome's Jewish community to thank for some of the Eternal City's most beloved dishes. Carciofi alla Giudia, anyone? Centuries ago, Jewish cooks' culinary ingenuity combated limited resources and transformed humble ingredients into delicacies for the ages. This is one such recipe. We like the look of pink endive for this, but if white is what is on hand, use that instead.

Lastly, if you want to introduce some acidity, splash some wine into the pot when the endive starts to cook and then increase the heat to high, quickly driving off the alcohol. Then reduce the heat and continue as instructed.

—Audrey Falk

Serves 6

12 ounces day-old white country bread, such as ciabatta
Olive oil (at least 1¾ cups)
Salt
2 to 3 tablespoons finely chopped rosemary needles
Butter for greasing the baking dish
20 anchovy fillets, rinsed
4 large garlic cloves, thinly sliced
12 endives (about 4 pounds), tatty outer leaves and root ends discarded
Freshly ground black pepper
A few tablespoons of dry white wine (optional)

To make the breadcrumbs, remove the loaf's crust and tear the interior into bite-sized pieces. Spread the bread on a baking sheet and set aside to dry until the edges harden slightly, about 1 hour.

Preheat the oven to 375 degrees. Toss the bread with enough olive oil to coat generously, about 6 tablespoons. Season with a generous pinch of salt and spread the bread out on the baking sheet. Bake in the oven until golden brown, about 15 minutes. Remove the bread from the oven and let cool to room temperature. Increase the oven temperature to 400 degrees.

Add the bread and about 1 tablespoon of the chopped rosemary to a food processor

(Continued)

(if necessary, work in batches) and pulse the bread to pebble-sized crumbs; inconsistency is fine as long as most bits are small. Do not run the blade, or your breadcrumbs will turn to dust!

Slice the endives on the diagonal into ¼-inch-wide slivers.

Generously grease a deep medium baking dish (at least 2 inches high) with butter. Chop 4 of the anchovies and add to a medium saucepan, along with 6 tablespoons olive oil, the garlic, and the remaining chopped rosemary. Cook gently over medium-low heat to infuse the oil, about 2 minutes. Once the garlic bubbles and its scent blooms, but before it browns, stir in the sliced endive and season with a pinch each of salt and pepper. Increase the heat to medium and cook, stirring occasionally, just until the endive softens, about 4 minutes. Add 2 more tablespoons olive oil and continue cooking until the endive is tender but retains some bite, about 10 minutes. Season lightly with salt again, but remember that there are many anchovies coming. Remove from the heat.

With a slotted spoon, transfer the cooked endive to the prepared baking dish, leaving the cooking juices behind in the pan (these can be discarded). Spread the endive out evenly in the dish and top with the breadcrumbs, scattering them over the endive in a thick blanket. Gently press down, compressing the endive, and drizzle over more olive oil, about 2 tablespoons.

Split the remaining fillets lengthwise in half and lattice the anchovies across the top (like the Pissaladière on page 76) spacing the lines at 1-inch intervals. Or spell out KING if you wish! Drizzle over another tablespoon of olive oil.

Bake on the oven's top rack until the crumbs are golden and the edges are bubbling and crisp, about 20 minutes. Serve warm or at room temperature.

CHAPTER 9

Meat

There are endless directions we take meat at King, but all of them begin with a good cut. Whether we're grilling, roasting, braising, or poaching; whether it's beef, pork, or lamb, flavor begins in the field.

At King, steak is always on the menu, and on most mornings, someone is breaking down a large cut of beef in the kitchen. But for cooking at home, we typically ask the butcher to cut steaks that are at least 2 inches thick. Thickness goes a long way in developing a proper crust and rosy center. If you are feeding many, T-bones, porterhouses, or Fiorentinas are ideal. They cook unevenly and so, after carving, provide each guest with a slice at the desired level of doneness.

Hanger steak, a King classic, is often called "butcher's cut." It is particularly flavorful and tender, without being too lean. We grill it in the Tuscan style—charring it heavily and then resting it whole over rosemary branches doused with olive oil. As the meat relaxes and aromatic juices puddle, it absorbs the herb's woody flavor and the olive oil's fragrance.

When it comes to pork chops, the fattier the better. And, whenever possible, use bone-in chops.

The techniques we use for grilling or roasting beef, pork, and lamb are simple and forgiving, but the meat should always be high quality and the cuts must be fully tempered. If meat is brought to room temperature before cooking, the heat will be conducted evenly and the inside will blush.

When we grill, especially smaller cuts, we want to develop as much char as possible in a short period, meaning we go fast and hard to sear the meat without overcooking. But when we're roasting—this is typically reserved for larger pieces—we employ a gentler approach, to slowly develop color on the exterior.

When we're pan-roasting, we brown every side (uneven ends included) to build up a crust that envelops the whole.

And before we move any cut off the heat, no matter how it's been prepared, we ask ourselves, "Is this cooked?" The answer should always be, "No!" Resting meat is essential and considered part of the "cook." The residual heat will continue to transform meat long after it's removed from the heat. This holds true even with a braise, though braising is the most forgiving technique of all.

The braises in this chapter run the gamut. Tongue, for example, is simply boiled until tender and then sliced. The resulting broth is as savory as the meat itself. Pork belly gets rolled and made spoon-soft, thanks to a good pour of wine and a lardo rub. While perhaps more laborious, these dishes are also foolproof—ideal for ambitious cooks starting out.

Finally, slice all meat against the grain. And if a cut is rosy within, try to show off its contrasting colors with chunky, angular slices.

Tuscan Grilled Hanger Steak

Grilled hanger steak is on King's menu every night. And each night we follow the Tuscan technique of grilling it, over very high heat, and then resting it, for just as long, over rosemary branches and olive oil. Make sure to bring the meat to room temperature and heavily season it before laying it on the very hottest grill.

The grid on pages 208–209 shows how hanger steak can be served with almost anything. Be sure to always spoon over the rosemary-infused resting juices.

Serves 2 (scales up easily)

2 hanger steaks (about 1 pound total)
Salt and freshly ground black pepper
5 to 7 large rosemary branches
Olive oil (at least ½ cup)

Remove the steaks from the fridge an hour before cooking so they can come to room temperature. (Hangers, no matter their size, are a similar thickness, so regardless of how many people you're feeding, the tempering time will always be the same.) Heavily season both sides of the meat with salt and pepper.

Set up a fiery-hot grill. As it heats, grab a shallow bowl that's large enough to hold both steaks. Lay in the rosemary branches to make a bed for the steaks and pour over enough olive oil to pool around the branches, ½ to 1 cup.

When the grill is hot, clean the grates with a sturdy grill brush (we do not oil the grill or meat prior to cooking). Check that the grill is sufficiently hot by holding your palm about 2 inches above the grate: If your palm immediately feels uncomfortably hot, lay the steaks down on the hottest portion. If the heat is bearable, wait a few more minutes.

Once the steaks have hit the grill, do not move them until very strong grill marks have set in, about 3 minutes. Flip, using tongs, and sear the other side until solid grill marks appear, 2 to 3 minutes more. When the steaks' second side has charred, poke the top to feel for tension, and pull the charred steaks off the grill when they are still soft to the poke. This test will yield a rare to medium-rare result—we never cook steak beyond medium-rare. Transfer the meat to the prepared bowl and spoon some of the scented olive oil over the top. Give both steaks a rest on the rosemary branches; they should sit for at least as long as they cooked.

To serve, slice the steaks against the grain into chunky ¾-inch-wide pieces (pages 208–209). Season their rosy interiors with salt and spoon over the resting juices.

Grilled Hanger Steak, Soft Polenta (page 207) and Roasted Treviso (page 198)

Grilled Hanger Steak, Ceci and Cavolo Inzimino (page 201) and Cavolo Nero Puree (page 13)

Grilled Hanger Steak, tomatoes and borlotti beans (page 15), and Horseradish Cream (page 29)

Grilled Hanger Steak, Crema di Carciofi (page 219), and Artichokes Sott'olio (page 174)

Grilled Hanger Steak, Smashed Pumpkin (page 191), and a Grilled Holland Chili (page 36)

Grilled Hanger Steak, Potatoes with Lentils, Chicories, and Anchoïade (page 197)

Grilled Hanger Steak, arugula, and Salsa di Noci with Pepperoncini (page 32)

Grilled Hanger Steak, boiled vegetables, and a ladle of Bagna Cauda (page 24)

Tagliata di Manzo

We offer tagliata di manzo—Italian for thinly sliced, seared large cuts of beef—on hot, busy nights. As the Italians do, we serve this at room temperature. Tomatoes, which roast alongside the steak until jammy, are spooned all around at the end.

This dish is ideal for large parties, as it holds beautifully and scales up well. Generally, we prefer to use very large cuts of steaks for this recipe (sometimes as much as 7 pounds), so if you're serving a big group, do the same if you can.

Serve this with spinach and Ligurian Olive Sauce (page 30), Tian (page 185), Braised Artichokes (page 178), or Wax Beans with Anchovy and Basil (page 190).

Serves 4 to 6

2 to 3 pounds strip steak, ideally 1 large steak
Salt and freshly ground black pepper
Olive oil
2 very large heirloom tomatoes (about 1½ pounds total), cored
3 rosemary branches

Remove the steak from the fridge an hour before cooking so it can come up to room temperature. Season generously with plenty of salt and a hefty amount of pepper, using enough to form a crust all around the meat.

Preheat the oven to 450 degrees. Set a large cast-iron or other heavy ovenproof skillet over medium heat and add 1½ tablespoons olive oil. When the pan gently smokes lay in the steak (if one side has a fat cap, cook that side first). Be mindful of the temperature while searing, as you may need to adjust the heat to ensure that the steak colors evenly and steadily without scorching. Once the first side is golden brown, about 3 to 5 minutes, flip and sear on the other side for 3 to 5 minutes more. Then, using tongs to hold the steak upright in the pan, sear the narrower edges. Once one edge browns, 1 to 2 minutes, move on to the others. For the arched side, hold the steak in place with tongs to color the curve evenly.

Lay the steak back down into the pan and turn off the heat. Discard all but 1 tablespoon of the rendered fat. Using your hands, tear the tomatoes into quarters, ripping them directly over the pan; make sure to capture everything in the pan: seeds, juice, pulp, etc.

Arrange the tomato quarters around the steak and lay the rosemary branches over the beef. Season everything with 2 to 3 tablespoons olive oil and a sprinkle of salt and pepper. Place the pan in the oven and roast until the steak is medium-rare (the way we like it), 10 to 12 minutes. To check, insert a cake tester or metal skewer into the center of the meat for 10 seconds, then remove it and hold the tip against your bottom lip: It should feel just warm. If using a thermometer, the center should register between 130 and 140 degrees.

Remove from the oven and let the steak rest in the pan for 10 minutes. As it sits, turn it often so every side gets a moment in the pan juices. And as you go, squish the tomatoes with the back of a spoon to release their juices into the pan and baste the steak with the oily juices.

Transfer the steak to a cutting board and slice against the grain as thin as you can, ½ inch thick or less.

To serve, spoon some of the pan juices onto a warm serving platter and set the slices of steak over them. Finish by spooning over more tomato juices plus the roasted tomatoes and a drizzle of olive oil.

Poached Ox Tongue

Italians are never wrong about the classics, and poached ox tongue is just that. It's a cornerstone of a Piedmontese bollito misto, the meaty feast where tongue boils in a pot with guinea hen and brisket before arriving at the table with the warm, steaming broth for ladling and lots of sauces for dressing up the plates.

We like to simplify that meal and serve just boiled tongue with Lentils (page 20), Horseradish Cream (page 29), and Dragoncella (page 26). Sometimes, we simplify even further and serve the sliced tongue with just boiled romanesco and soft-set eggs. While most of the work is hands-off, you will need to plan in advance and give the tongue at least 4 days in the brine before its few hours of simmering.

Serves 6

1 ox tongue (3 to 4 pounds), skin on
Salt
About 4 quarts Master Brine (recipe follows)
2 bay leaves
½ tablespoon whole black peppercorns
2 or 3 juniper berries
Olive oil

Choose a large container or pot that will comfortably hold the tongue and the brine. Add the tongue and pour in enough of the brine to fully submerge. Cover and refrigerate for at least 4 days (a few days longer only adds flavor and may shorten the cooking time).

Remove the tongue from the brine (discard the brine) and place it in a clean tall pot. Cover with cold water, adding enough to submerge it by 3 inches. Add 1 tablespoon salt, the bay leaves, peppercorns, and juniper berries. Cover with a cartouche (see page 15) and set a plate or small pan lid on top to keep the tongue from bobbing up. Turn the heat to medium-high and bring the water to an active simmer. Reduce the heat to medium-low and gently poach the tongue until tender, about 3 hours. Cooking tongue is a forgiving process that needs little attention. Still, every now and then, check and taste the broth (more for indulgence than anything else); top up with water if the level gets low and check that the tongue is submerged throughout. Taste the broth toward the end of the cooking time: If it is lacking flavor, add salt until the sips are delicious.

The tongue will give little indication that it's done other than feeling somewhat bouncier to the squeeze. If tongue is undercooked, it will be very difficult to peel. If that's the case after you've removed it, return it to the pot and simmer for 20 or so more minutes before trying again. Turn off the heat and transfer the tongue to a cutting board.

To peel it, score an incision down its centerline and use your fingers to peel away the tough skin; discard. Cut the tongue into ¼-inch-thick slices and fan them out on a platter. Spoon a few tablespoons of the warm broth over to just moisten the slices and serve. Reserve the remaining broth for another use.

(Continued)

Master Brine

There is really only one recipe for brine, and it belongs to the great Fergus Henderson, Britain's renowned nose-to-tail chef. His deeply flavorful version transforms ox tongue in 4 to 7 days. In that same amount of time, it works magic on brisket, pork belly, veal shin . . .

Makes 6 quarts

Salt
2 cups granulated sugar
12 juniper berries
12 whole cloves
12 whole black peppercorns
3 bay leaves

Combine 1¼ cups of salt and all the remaining ingredients with 4 quarts of water in a large pot set over medium-high heat, bring to a boil, and boil until the salt and sugar dissolve, 5 to 6 minutes. Transfer the brine to a heatproof container, one that is large enough to hold both the brine and your cut of choice, and let cool completely (you do not want to start poaching the meat just yet!).

Add your meat, weighting it down with a plate to keep it submerged if necessary. Cover the pot and place it in the fridge to hibernate until it is time to cook. Generally the timing will depend on a cut's size and density.

Rolled Pork Belly
with Fennel, Whipped Lardo, and White Wine

Pork belly, rolled and slathered in lardo, does nicely when braised with fennel and white wine. The resulting texture may be divisive to porchetta devotees, as it is soft and tender, without any of the crisp-crunch of a classic porchetta. But we love this gently cooked belly, and we serve it, most often, with plenty of its sweet braising juices spooned over and the fennel wedges alongside as well. Cannellini beans or lentils (see page 20) also do well with this belly.

Do your best to find a cut of belly with a ½-inch fat cap or something close to it. Then ask your butcher to remove the cap (or do it yourself with a long, sharp knife) to make the lardo. Leftover lardo is wonderful on grilled steaks (see page 207). Since it is all fat, it keeps for ages in the refrigerator.

Once seasoned and rolled, the belly should rest for at least a day in the fridge. Although you could cook it right away, the flavors won't be quite as developed or delicious.

Serves 6 to 8

One 3- to 4-pound pork belly with a ½-inch-thick fat cap, cap removed and reserved (you can ask the butcher to do this)
2 tablespoons fennel seeds, coarsely smashed
Finely grated zest of 3 lemons
4 fennel bulbs with bushy stalks, fronds removed and roughly chopped
1 tablespoon whole black peppercorns, coarsely crushed
Salt
Olive oil
A head of garlic, halved across its equator
1 bottle (750 ml) Soave or similar dry white wine

SPECIAL EQUIPMENT: Kitchen twine

To make the whipped lardo, cut the belly's fat cap into ½-inch cubes; you will need at least 1 cup for this recipe. (The rest can be frozen or spread on toast or potatoes.) Combine the fat, fennel seeds, lemon zest, chopped fennel fronds, and half the peppercorns in a food processor and whiz until a speckled paste the consistency of whipped butter forms. Set the lardo aside at room temperature (it holds sealed in the fridge forever, but it must be at room temperature to spread easily).

Season both sides of the pork belly evenly and heavily with salt. Lay it on your work surface so the side where the fat cap once sat faces down. Spread the lardo across the belly, leaving a 1-inch border without lardo along one of the long sides. Lift up the other long side and roll it up and around the belly, forming a cigar-in-process, and continue rolling until the cigar is shaped, then turn it seam down on the work surface. Secure the roll with kitchen twine, tying tight loops around it at 2-inch intervals.

(Continued)

Finely crush the remaining black peppercorns. Season the belly on all sides with salt (go lightly this time) and the crushed pepper. Let the belly sit, uncovered, in the fridge overnight. Refrigerated, it will hold for up to 3 days.

Remove the belly from the fridge at least an hour before cooking so it can come to room temperature. Preheat the oven to 400 degrees.

Heat 2 tablespoons olive oil in a wide heavy pot over medium heat until very hot but not smoking. Lay the belly in the pot and brown on the first side, gently and steadily, about 5 minutes. Lower the heat to medium and brown the belly on the remaining sides, rolling and browning it until a chestnut-colored crust has set in all the way around, about 20 minutes. Turn off the heat and transfer the seared belly to a rimmed tray.

Meanwhile, as the belly browns, cut off the fennel stalks and discard (or save for a stockpot). Halve the bulbs tip to root and slice the fennel halves into 1½-inch-wide wedges.

Pour off the excess fat from the pot and discard (or save it for another use); there should be a thin coating of fat over the pot's bottom. Wipe out any black or burnt flecks, leaving the tasty golden bits intact. Put the pot back over medium heat and add a splash of olive oil, about a tablespoon. Add the fennel wedges and the split garlic head, setting it cut side down in the pot. Cook until the garlic and fennel wedges soften but do not color, about 5 minutes. Return the seared belly to the pot, nestling it into the fennel. After a minute or so, add the wine, stirring to deglaze the pot, and bring to a simmer. Turn off the heat and cover the belly with a cartouche (see page 15). Seal the pot with a lid or with aluminum foil, crimping it all around.

Braise the belly in the oven until it holds a dent when pressed with a spoon, 2 to 2½ hours. It shouldn't be pulled-pork soft, but it should be mighty tender. Remove the pot from the oven and let the belly cool slightly in its juices, at least 15 minutes.

Move the belly to a cutting board and cut away the string. Using a sharp knife, gingerly slice the roll into 1- to 2-inch-thick rounds. The belly's tenderness means this can get messy; proceed with care.

Season the braising juices with salt to taste. Serve the belly slices in shallow bowls with some of the warm brothy juices and the braised fennel and finish with a drizzle of olive oil.

Pork Loin
with Crema di Carciofi

Vitello tonnato—the classic cold veal dish from the Piedmont region—inspired this spring starter. But it was just a starting point, because no tuna is called for, as it is in the original. The thinly sliced pork is served at room temperature and lavishly garnished with artichokes, our twist.

Here artichokes come two ways: sott'olio and in a crema. Together they complement the slices of rose-pink pork loin.

When planning to make this recipe, prepare a double recipe of Artichokes Sott'olio (page 174). One portion will be used for the crema and the second will go onto the plates to finish them.

Serves 4 to 6

FOR THE PORK

One 2-pound pork loin, silver skin removed
Salt and freshly ground black pepper
Olive oil
2 thyme branches
1 rosemary branch
4 sage leaves
1 cup dry white wine

FOR THE FINISH

½ cup Crema di Carciofi (recipe follows)
8 to 12 Artichokes Sott'olio (page 174)
1 tablespoon finely chopped parsley
Salt
Olive oil

Heavily season the pork loin on all sides with salt and pepper. Let the loin rest on the counter for an hour so it comes up to room temperature. Preheat the oven to 400 degrees.

Set a large ovenproof frying pan over high heat and add 2 tablespoons olive oil. Lay the loin in the pan and cook until a nice golden sear develops on the first side, 2 to 3 minutes. Turn the heat down to medium and sear the remaining sides, turning the pork with tongs as necessary, until chestnut brown all around, about 2 to 3 minutes per side. If the pan looks at all dry, add some more oil.

Turn off the heat and throw the thyme, rosemary, and sage into the pan. Give them a moment to sizzle and bloom, and when the herbs have crisped but not browned, deglaze the pan with the white wine.

Transfer the pan to the oven and roast until the pork loin's internal temperature reads 138 degrees, about 10 minutes. If you don't have a thermometer, insert a metal skewer or cake tester into the middle of the loin for a few seconds, then remove and gently press it to your bottom lip—it should be warm but not burning hot; the pork will continue to cook as it rests out of the oven, but the loin's center should still blush when sliced. Remove the pan from the oven and let the pork cool to room temperature, about 30 minutes; as it cools, rotate the loin now and then so the pan's residual heat penetrates it evenly.

When the pork is at room temperature, and not a moment before, transfer it to a cutting board (keep the pan nearby); it is much harder, maybe even impossible, to get thin slices if the pork has not cooled completely. Cut the pork into slices as thin as possible; aim for ⅛ inch thick or less.

Arrange the pork slices on a platter and pour all the accumulated juices from the cutting board into the frying pan. Stir the drippings together and taste: They should be delicious and neither overly salty nor sticky. If necessary, thin them with a splash of cold water and stir to combine.

To serve, spoon some of the juices (these should be at room temperature) onto individual plates. Fan about 6 or so slices of the pork over the resting juices on each plate and then drizzle a little more of the juices over the meat. Dot about 2 tablespoons of artichoke crema around each serving, taking care not to cover up the pork, as its rosiness is the draw! Drain the artichokes sott'olio and fan out the leaves with your fingers. Place a couple of artichokes on each plate and finish with a sprinkle of chopped parsley, a little salt, and a drizzle of olive oil.

Crema di Carciofi

Excellent with grilled meat or fish, this is also tasty tossed with fresh pasta.

Makes 2 cups

3 cups packed parsley leaves, roughly chopped
1 batch Artichokes Sott'olio (page 174), drained
Olive oil
Finely grated zest of 1 lemon
Salt

Blitz the parsley in a food processor until a coarse bright green paste forms. Add the artichokes and, with the blade running, stream in ½ cup olive oil, whizzing until smooth. Blitz in the lemon zest. Season with salt until it tastes delicious.

Pork Chops Roasted with Cherries, Thyme, and Prosciutto

Unlike almost every other recipe in this book, this one is designed to feed only two. It can, of course, be scaled up, but we rather like that the dish can be made in one pan, relatively quickly, and without turning on the oven.

The cherries can be substituted with fresh figs, or with prunes soaked in some Armagnac (in which case, omit the rosé). The chop can also be finished with dollops of Quince Preserves (page 38) instead of the fresh fruit.

Serves 2

Two 10- to 12-ounce bone-in pork chops, about 1½ inches thick
Salt and freshly ground black pepper
Olive oil
2 tablespoons thyme leaves
1½ cups cherries, halved and pitted
½ cup King's or Bandol rosé, or a similar wine
4 thin slices lardo, prosciutto, or speck

Remove the chops from the fridge at least 1 hour before cooking so they can come to room temperature. Season them all over with salt and pepper.

Set a large skillet over medium heat and add 1 tablespoon olive oil to the pan. Once it is hot, use tongs to place each pork chop into the pan so its fat-covered arch faces down and render this fat cap by rocking and holding the chop in place with the tongs so the fat browns evenly, about 2 minutes. Lower the heat if there is any scorching.

Once the fat caps have rendered, lay them down in the pan so they sizzle in the drippings and, keeping the temperature steady, sear on the first side until nut brown, about 5 minutes. Flip the chops and sear the other side until nicely browned, about 5 minutes more.

Pour off all but a thin layer of fat from the pan. Quickly add the thyme to the pan, and when the leaves crackle and their scent blooms, add the cherries and a sprinkle of salt. Roll the fruit around in the pan, then pour in the rosé and add a drizzle of olive oil, about 1 tablespoon. Cook the cherries for a couple of minutes while the alcohol cooks off, about 5 minutes. Turn off the heat and arrange the chops so their arched fat caps face up (resting this way keeps them succulent). Drape the lardo over the chops to melt over the pork. Let the chops rest for 5 to 7 minutes and then poke the center: It should feel fleshy but not soft.

Serve the pork chops with the cherries and pan juices, draping whatever is left of the lardo over the top. Finish with a drizzle of olive oil.

Daube D'agneau
with Panisse

Daube is a traditional French braise from northern Provence that is most often made with beef or lamb; typically it calls for inexpensive cuts that braise well. Its charms lie in the variations that exist from kitchen to kitchen, as, ultimately, these are simply homey dishes.

As for its name, it refers to the *daubière*, the pot that the region's braises were traditionally cooked in. Made of terra-cotta, these are ideal vehicles for slow, gentle cooking. But at King, we use regular pots and carefully monitor the heat to ensure that nothing is seared too hard and no flavoring becomes too harsh.

We add artichokes and baby carrots to the daube for a lamby spring fling. For the accompanying panisse, make the batter a day or two ahead and fry the ribbons off (or, if it's easier, sear them in a pan) while the lamb rests.

Serves 6

FOR THE BRAISE

6 to 8 pounds bone-in lamb necks or lamb shoulder
Salt and freshly ground black pepper
Olive oil
2 large shallots, thinly sliced
4 to 6 tender inner celery ribs, minced
3 garlic cloves, thinly sliced
2 large heirloom tomatoes (about 1 pound each), cored
A handful of whole parsley sprigs
2 to 3 rosemary branches
3 to 4 thyme branches
2 bay leaves
12 baby artichokes, trimmed, chokes removed, and held in lemon water (see page 110)
10 to 12 whole baby carrots or 5 or 6 thin medium carrots, halved lengthwise
4 cups chicken stock, homemade (see page 35) or store-bought, plus more as needed
Half a bottle (750 ml) Marsanne and Roussanne, or similar low-acid dry white wine

FOR SERVING

1 batch Panisse (page 70)

SPECIAL EQUIPMENT: Kitchen twine

Remove the lamb from the fridge at least an hour before cooking so it can come to room temperature. Pat it dry and season generously all over with salt and pepper. Preheat the oven to 350 degrees.

Warm about 2 tablespoons of olive oil in a large Dutch oven over medium heat. When the oil just starts to waft smoke, working in batches, add the lamb and brown it on all sides until a deep golden crust forms, about 15 minutes; monitor the heat so that the pot doesn't scorch, and give this process time so the meat colors evenly and steadily. Transfer the browned meat to a baking sheet and set aside.

Discard all but 1 tablespoon of the fat from the pot and add a fresh tablespoon of olive oil. Set back over medium heat, stir in the shallots and celery, and season with salt and pepper. Once the vegetables soften, about 5 minutes, add the garlic and immediately reduce the heat so its scent blooms but the slices don't color, about 30 seconds. Tear in the tomatoes, ripping them over the pot so as not to lose any precious juice; rough chunks about the size of a walnut are ideal. Cook until the tomatoes soften, about 3 minutes.

MEANWHILE, MAKE A BOUQUET GARNI: Pull off 5 or so thick stalks from the parsley sprigs, bundle them up with the rosemary, thyme, and bay leaves, and tie together with kitchen twine, making a couple of loops around the bundle so it is snug and tightly bound. Add it and the artichokes to the pot, stirring to coat the artichokes with the vegetables. Nestle the browned lamb pieces into the pot, smudging the aromatics into all the nooks and crannies. Scatter the carrots all around the meat, then pour in the chicken stock and wine, adding enough to submerge everything by at least two-thirds. Increase the heat to medium-high and bring the liquid to a simmer. Cover with a cartouche (see page 15) and then cover with the pot's lid.

Transfer the pot to the oven and cook until the meat is falling off the bone, 2½ to 3 hours. Remove the pot from the oven and let the lamb rest for at least 30 minutes. Finely chop a generous handful of the parsley leaves and set aside.

While the daube rests, fry the panisse according to the directions on page 70; hold the finished batches on a baking sheet in a warm oven (about 300 degrees). It's also possible to sear the panisse in a very hot cast-iron skillet: Set the pan over high heat and add 2 to 3 tablespoons olive oil. When the oil begins to smoke, carefully add the panisse ribbons to the hot oil, working in batches to avoid overcrowding the pan. Sear the panisse for 2 to 3 minutes, or until they color evenly on the first side. Using a fish spatula, flip them and sear on the other side. Remove from the pan, blot on a paper towel to remove excess oil, and hold in a warm oven until ready to serve.

Serve the lamb on a warm platter or dole out helpings straight from the pot, juices and all. Either way, garnish with the chopped parsley and serve the panisse, piled high like a failed game of Jenga, on another platter.

Roast Leg of Lamb
with Braised Lettuce and Peas

This meal has Easter lunch written all over it.

You can cook the lamb ahead and serve it at room temperature, so you can focus on cooking the peas, which must be done at the last minute to keep them vibrant.

Serves 8 to 10

One 5-pound bone-in leg of lamb
Salt and freshly ground black pepper
6 garlic cloves, smashed
A few rosemary branches (about 5)
Grated zest of 1 lemon
Olive oil
Braised Lettuce and Peas (page 180)

Place the lamb in a roasting pan that holds it snugly and season heavily with salt and pepper. Let the leg rest at room temperature for 3 to 4 hours, or, better yet, rest it overnight, covered, in the fridge. If it's been held in the fridge, remove the leg at least 2 hours before cooking so it can come to room temperature.

Preheat the oven to 400 degrees. Place the garlic in a small bowl. Strip the rosemary needles off their branches, roughly chop them, and add to the garlic. Add the lemon zest to the bowl and stir in about ½ cup olive oil. Rub the marinade all over the lamb, coating it evenly.

Roast the leg in the oven for 70 to 80 minutes. To test the lamb, insert a metal skewer or a cake tester into its thickest part for 10 seconds, then remove it; it should feel warm when held against your lower lip. If using a thermometer, the internal temperature, near the bone, should be 120 degrees for a blushing-pink interior. Remove the leg from the oven and let it rest for at least 20 minutes.

Place the lamb on a carving board and thinly slice it at an angle relative to the bone. Transfer the meat to a platter and pour over any juices, then spoon the drippings from the roasting pan. Your guests can choose slices cooked to their preference.

Serve the lamb warm or at room temperature with the lettuce and peas.

Pot-au-Feu

Pot-au-feu is a meaty feast. Classically it consists of brisket, veal shank, chicken, and marrow bones. All of these are poached in veal broth until they are richly perfumed and falling apart. As the cuts rest out of the poaching liquid, vegetables take a turn in the simmering broth, cooking until just tender. The meats are served at the table so that guests can assemble their own bowls, ladling the steaming broth onto their choice of meats and vegetables. We serve ours with sauces like Horseradish Cream (page 29) and Dragoncella (a riff on the classic sauce ravigotte) and, of course, mustard and bowls of warm lentils.

Veal—bones and shanks—is essential to the flavor of pot-au-feu. It may be a special order from your butcher, but if you can't find it, chicken bones can be used instead.

As with any celebratory French recipe, you should plan ahead and shop about two days in advance. You'll need to make the broth at least one day before cooking the meat.

Serves 8 to 10

FOR THE BROTH

4 pounds veal or chicken bones
Salt and freshly ground black pepper
A large handful of thyme sprigs
A large handful of parsley sprigs
2 tablespoons whole white peppercorns
2 tablespoons whole black peppercorns
8 large celery ribs from the outside of a bunch, roughly chopped
2 medium carrots, peeled and coarsely chopped
2 white onions, coarsely chopped
2 heads of garlic, halved across their equators

FOR THE MEATS

A 4-pound brisket
Salt
5 pieces veal shanks (osso buco; about 5 pounds), about 2 inches long
1 whole chicken (about 4 pounds)
10 beef marrow bones, about 1½ inches long

FOR THE BOUQUET GARNI

1 leek
5 parsley stalks
5 sprigs of thyme

FOR THE VEGETABLES

6 large leeks
5 pounds small Yukon Gold potatoes or other small potatoes
2 bunches small carrots, trimmed
2 heads Savoy cabbage, outer leaves removed and cut into 6 wedges each
2 bunches turnips (about 18 to 20), tops left on if nice, and cut in half
1 celery heart, cut on the bias into 3-inch lengths

FOR SERVING

Horseradish Cream (page 29)
Dragoncella (page 26)
Lentils (page 20)
Cornichons
Baguettes

SPECIAL EQUIPMENT:
A very large stock pot (about 20 quarts), two large pots (about 12 quarts); two roasting pans; and kitchen twine

At least a day before you intend to serve the pot-au-feu, prepare the broth: Preheat the oven to 450 degrees. Season the bones all over with salt and pepper. Lay them in a single layer on a baking sheet or two and roast until aromatic and richly caramelized, about 2 hours.

Pour off all the rendered fat from the bones and transfer the roasted bones and any crusty bits from the baking sheet(s) to a very large stock pot.

Add the thyme, parsley, peppercorns (both white and black), celery, carrots, onions, and split garlic heads to the pot with the bones and cover with enough cold water to submerge everything (about 12 quarts or so). Slowly bring the broth to a simmer over medium-high heat, then reduce the heat slightly and gently simmer the broth for about 3 hours, until richly flavored and meaty tasting.

MEANWHILE, PREPARE THE BRISKET: Trim away its excess fat and any silver skin. Season evenly and generously with salt, transfer to a tray, and refrigerate it, loosely covered, overnight.

When the broth is ready, strain it through a sieve into a large pot and press on all the vegetables and aromatics to extract the last of their flavor, then discard. Taste the broth and season gently with salt (the broth will take on the salt from the seasoned meats cooked in it later). Let cool completely, then cover and refrigerate. This can be done up to 3 days in advance.

On the day of your feast, remove the brisket, veal shanks, and chicken from the fridge. Season the chicken and shanks with salt.

Remove the broth from the fridge and skim away any fat that's risen to the surface. Set the pot over low heat and bring to a simmer. Meanwhile, make a bouquet garni with the leek, parsley, and thyme (see page 223), and add it to the pot.

Once the broth is at a simmer, add the seasoned brisket and simmer for 2 hours. Add the veal shanks and chicken to the pot and continue simmering until all the meats are tender, about 1 hour. The brisket ahould be tender, and you should be able to pull one of the chicken's drumsticks off after a delicate wiggle; the meat from the veal shanks should come away from the bone easily. Turn off the heat and let everything stand in the pot for 10 minutes.

Using tongs and a slotted spoon, remove the brisket, shanks, and chicken from the pot, placing them on a cutting board.

Carve the brisket across the grain into ½-inch-wide pieces using a sharp knife. Remove the skin from the chicken and discard. Separate the legs, thighs, and wings from the chicken carcass by slicing through their joints. Then slice away the breasts, leaving them on the bone or off (carver's choice). Reserve the chicken carcass for a future stockpot or discard. Finally, trim off any tough meat from the outside of the veal shanks and discard. Tear its tender meat into bite-sized pieces.

(Continued)

To prepare the marrow bones, trim off any meat around the outside. Generously salt each one evenly all over. Cut away the dark green tops of 2 of the leeks and split them lengthwise in half. Cut away the root ends and then separate the loose layers, discarding any that aren't pliable. Clean all the leek leaves thoroughly, dunking them in a large bowl of water and shaking off any lingering grit. Once they are squeaky-clean, dry the leaves.

Place one leek leaf on a cutting board and lay another across its center to form an X. Place a marrow bone at the X's center and lift the flaps of leek up and over the bone, wrapping it up snugly. Tie the parcel closed with kitchen twine to prevent the bone from slipping out. Repeat with the remaining leek leaves and marrow bones.

Evenly divide the broth between two 12-quart pots. Taste the broth for seasoning and adjust accordingly with salt: It should taste savory and robust. Return all the meats to one pot to keep warm, but do not heat the broth.

Add 4 cups water to the second pot of broth and taste for salt. Bring the broth to a simmer and add the wrapped marrow bones and potatoes. Simmer over low heat for 5 minutes, then add the rest of the vegetables in order of the time they will take to cook: carrots and cabbage, followed by the turnips, the remaining leeks, and the celery. Simmer until everything gives easily to the poke of a knife, about 15 minutes from dropping in the celery.

Bring the pot of broth with the sliced meats to a simmer.

Come to the table with both pots. Invite everyone to dig in and build their own bowl of poached vegetables, meats, and, finally, a ladleful or more of the broth. Put bowls of the horseradish cream, dragoncella, lentils, cornichons, and warm baguettes on the table as accompaniments.

CHAPTER 10

Fish

THE HARDEST PART OF COOKING SEAFOOD IS FINDING A GOOD SOURCE. GETTING YOUR hands on impeccably fresh fish is not easy, but it makes all the difference. Our advice: Seek out a trusted fishmonger, become a loyal customer, and always offer to take home spare fish heads, bones, and shells. These are critical for fish stocks, a luxury in any kitchen, and fishmongers are often happy to share this trim.

It's important to fill your net only with fish that smells of the sea. The flesh should be firm and the belly should be brilliantly white. If you are buying whole fish (always preferred, as these are more flavorful and add a sense of occasion), the gills should be ruddy red (not milky!), and the eyes should be bright and clear. For fillets, get the thickest cuts available—2 inches plus, if possible. Once grilled, roasted, or poached, your fillets should rest much like a steak so the juices settle and the center steams through. And always get fish with the skin on—it crisps up when grilled, and when you are poaching or steaming, it provides an extra barrier to keep everything juicy.

King's seafood dishes are inspired by the classics found along the Mediterranean coastline: the mighty Provençal bouillabaisse (loaded with rockfish and rascasse); salt-baked turbots, red mullet, and sea bass; tiny Venetian clams steamed with garlic and white wine. . . .

But New York is on the Atlantic, so we've adapted to our coastline, and for firm, white, meaty fish, we order monkfish, skate, striped bass, and John Dory. Each can take an extended cook, and because of their mild flavor, they pair well with punchy sauces and dressings.

When we want something richer, we turn to oily catches like Boston mackerel and trout. Their season falls in warmer months, so we keep these preparations light and serve them whole, either grilled (see page 231) or salt-baked (see page 247). On the table, they come all but nude so little distracts from the meat's delicate flavor. Still, for every rule there is an exception, and, when we sauce fattier fillets, we like to either match the richness with round and creamy sauces (see pages 236 and 253) or head in the opposite direction and cut through the richness with potent, herby drizzles (see page 245) or bright salads (see pages 243 and 247).

If there is a single recipe to master, we believe it would be whole grilled fish (see page 231). It can go into a million directions, depending on what it is paired with, and nothing is more satisfying to eat or cook. That is why we grill fish throughout the year and, for the simplest approach, stuff them with lemon rounds and herbs before giving them time over a crackling-hot grill. On your grill at home, always pursue a deep char, and do not shy away from color! Then, off the heat, after a moment's rest, douse the fish with olive oil, give it a generous squeeze of lemon, and scatter over some fresh herbs.

Grilled Mackerel

Mackerel is one of the very best things to grill. Its fattiness keeps the meat moist while ensuring that the skin gets very crisp. Choose fish that's the right size for you—we like one per person.

Serves 1 (scales up effortlessly)

1 whole mackerel (about 1 pound),
cleaned and gutted
Salt
A lemon wedge

Let the mackerel come to room temperature while you set up a very hot fire in the grill. When it is blistering hot—the palm of your hand held about 2 inches above the grate should immediately feel uncomfortable—generously salt the fish, seasoning its cavity and skin evenly.

Lay the fish on the grill and leave it undisturbed for at least a minute or two. Peek inside as it cooks: When the flesh closest to the grill turns pinkish-white, get ready to flip it, but don't take any action until strong grill marks crisp the skin, 5 to 6 minutes. Flip and grill the other side; again, do not move it. It is ready when the flesh within the cavity looks pale and evenly colored throughout and the skin is very crisp, 5 to 6 minutes longer; pay special attention to the meat by the spine when checking to ensure it is cooked.

Remove the mackerel from the grill and let it rest for a few minutes before serving with the lemon wedge.

Grilled Mackerel, Salsa Verde (page 33)

Grilled Mackerel, Lentils (page 20),
Salsa Siciliana (page 32)

Grilled Mackerel, Winter Leaves in Lucy's Dressing
with Blood Orange, Olives, and Almonds (page 98)

Grilled Mackerel with
Grilled and Marinated Fennel (page 195)

Grilled Mackerel, Boiled Baby Zucchini (page 181), and Salsa Mandorla (page 31)

Grilled Mackerel, Smashed Cannellini Beans (page 18), chopped Holland Chilies (page 36), wild oregano, and arugula

Grilled Mackerel, Confit Tomatoes (page 182), torn olives, and marjoram

Grilled Mackerel, Chickpeas (see page 15), and Boiled-Lemon and Caper Sauce (page 25)

Grilled Scallops

Grilled scallops should be cooked to medium-rare and sport strong grill marks. They are very versatile and can be served with anything from our grid for mackerel (see pages 232–233). Or serve them with any of the following: Lentils (page 20) with Ligurian Olive Sauce (page 30); Confit Tomatoes (page 182) and torn basil leaves; Fennel, Sungold Tomatoes, and Bottarga Dressing (page 243); Ceci and Cavolo Inzimino (page 201) with Grilled Holland Chilies (page 36).

Essentially, dress these however you fancy. Just a lemon wedge would be fine too. . . .

Serves 4

12 large sea scallops (about 1½ pounds)
Salt
Olive oil
1 to 2 lemons, cut into wedges

Set up a very hot fire in a grill. As it heats up, season the scallops on both sides with salt and a drizzle of olive oil.

When the grate is scalding—the palm of your hand held about 2 inches from the grate should immediately feel uncomfortable—lay the scallops on the grate. By the time the last scallops are in place, the first may be ready to flip. After about 1½ minutes on the grill, check for solid grill marks on the first few scallops. Once these appear, flip the scallops in the same order they were placed onto the grate. Cook on the second side for slightly less time so the middle stays glassy and rare, about 1 minute.

Remove the scallops from the grill (first on, first off) and place them on a plate with their most heavily charred side up. Drizzle with olive oil and serve with lemon wedges.

Confit Monkfish

Cooking thick tranches of meaty white fish, like monkfish, turbot, or halibut, in warm olive oil shows them at their most succulent and tender. When possible, poach the fish bone-in as it adds extra flavor and keeps it even juicier.

As with other simple fish preparations, the possibilities for this plate are infinite. Serve with cooked ceci or cocos blancs (see page 15) and blanched greens (see page 12) with Salsa Verde (page 33), an heirloom tomato salad with French Tapenade (page 26); or Potatoes with King Rosé, Bay, and Olives (page 188) and Confit Chanterelles (see page 192).

Serves 4

Four 8-ounce monkfish tranche, bone-in
Olive oil (at least 4 cups)
¼ cup thyme leaves
6 whole black peppercorns
1 garlic clove, crushed
Salt
2 lemons

Remove the fish from the fridge about 20 minutes before cooking so it can come to room temperature. Combine 2 cups olive oil, the thyme, peppercorns, garlic, and a few generous pinches of salt in a wide pot that's large enough to hold the fish in a single layer and deep enough to comfortably keep them submerged in the oil. With a vegetable peeler, remove the zest from the lemons in strips and add to the pot.

Lay the fish in the pot, adding more oil as needed for submerging, and set over very low heat. Bring the oil to a very gentle simmer, about 3 to 5 minutes; it's important the oil comes to a simmer slowly so the aromatics release their flavor and infuse the oil as the fish warms through. Continue to cook the monkfish at a very low simmer for 7 to 10 minutes, or until there's no resistance at the thickest point of a tranche when poked with the tip of a knife. Or, if you're using boneless fillets, check on doneness after 5 minutes or less. Remove the pot from the heat and allow the monkfish to rest in the warm oil for a couple of minutes.

Use a fish spatula to lift the fish out of their oil, letting the excess oil drain away, and place on warm plates, with a dribble of the poaching oil on top.

Steamed Clams

with Tarragon and Crème Fraîche

We owe this one to Elizabeth David, whose recipe for mussels with cream and tarragon we've lovingly adapted. Our recipe calls for clams rather than mussels, and we use an Italian loaf rather than a French baguette for the croutons, but we've stayed true on other fronts.

Take seriously the step of whisking the crème fraîche into a bit of the warm clam liquor. And do use homemade chicken stock here—Elizabeth deserves no less.

Serves 4

2 cups torn white Italian country bread, such as ciabatta (crust removed, bread torn into rough croutons about 1½ inches across)
Olive oil
Salt
2 garlic cloves, thinly sliced
3 pounds medium clams (about 36), rinsed and soaked
2 cups chicken stock, homemade (see page 35)
¼ cup tarragon leaves, coarsely chopped
3 tablespoons crème fraîche
½ lemon

Preheat the oven to 300 degrees. Toss the torn bread with 2 to 3 tablespoons olive oil and a pinch of salt. Spread the bread out on a baking sheet and bake in the oven until crisp but not browned, around 30 minutes. Drying these pieces out slowly is critical. Remove from the oven and let cool completely.

Use a wide heavy pot that will accommodate all the clams. Set the pot over medium heat, add a tablespoon or so of olive oil and the garlic, and warm the garlic in the oil until sticky but not browned, about 3 minutes. Quickly stir in the clams, coating them in the garlic oil, and spread them out. Add the chicken stock, cover the pot with a lid, and steam until the clam shells just open, 4 to 5 minutes. Turn off the heat and stir in the tarragon.

Transfer a ladle or two of the clam juices to a medium bowl and quickly whisk in the crème fraîche until combined. Add the mixture to the pot, swirling to thoroughly combine. Taste and add a squeeze of lemon juice and, if necessary, some salt.

Place the croutons in warm shallow serving bowls. Ladle over the hot clams and enough of the liquor so it pools around the bottom third of the croutons. Drizzle with olive oil.

Mussels en Papillote

This mussel recipe comes from Nice, and the North African influences on the city's cuisine are evident in the fresh ginger and garlic (plus basil) that perfume the mussels as they steam open within their parcels.

Serves 4

2 pounds ripe heirloom tomatoes
4 garlic cloves
Olive oil
A 2-inch knob of ginger, peeled and finely julienned
2 pinches crumbled dried red chili
Salt
4 pounds mussels, preferably from Prince Edward Island, rinsed and debearded
2 cups Vermentino or similar dry white wine
2 tablespoons unsalted butter, cut into 4 pieces
A generous handful of basil leaves
A baguette

SPECIAL EQUIPMENT: Parchment paper; kitchen twine

Bring a large pot of salted water to a boil over high heat. Meanwhile, score the top and bottom of each tomato with an X mark and set up a large ice bath. When the water is rumbling, drop in the tomatoes and tamp them down with a small lid or a plate to keep them submerged. Count to 10 before removing the weight; the skins should be peeling away at the X marks. Scoop out the tomatoes with a slotted spoon and drop them into the ice bath.

When the tomatoes are cool enough to handle, remove them from the ice bath and peel away and discard the skins.

Set a sieve over a medium bowl. Halve the tomatoes across their equators. Squeeze each half tomato over the sieve so its pulp and seeds shoot into the sieve. Set the squeezed tomatoes aside and press on the captured seeds to extract as much juice as possible, then discard the seeds. Tear the squeezed tomatoes into pieces the size of a plump mussel, working over the bowl of tomato juices so as not to lose a single bit of juice, and then dropping the tomates into the bowl; discard their cores.

Mince one of the garlic cloves and add it to a large heavy pot, along with about 2 tablespoons olive oil, the ginger, chili, and a pinch of salt, and warm over medium heat until the garlic starts bubbling, about a minute. Pour in the tomatoes with all their juices, swirl everything together, and season with salt. Bring to a simmer and simmer until the flavors meld, about 5 minutes. Remove from the heat and let the tomato mixture cool to room temperature.

(Continued)

Meanwhile, preheat the oven to 500 degrees and place a baking sheet on the oven's center rack to preheat; set another rack in the upper part of the oven. Cut eight 12-by-15-inch rectangles of parchment paper. Cut four 5-inch-long pieces of kitchen twine.

Lay one sheet of parchment crosswise over another sheet to form an X and lay the sheets in a shallow soup bowl. Repeat with the remaining sheets in three more bowls. (The bowls will prevent the juices from running out when you assemble the parcels.)

Place ¼ cup of the tomato mixture in the center of each parcel. Add one-quarter of the mussels and ½ cup of the white wine to each parcel and distribute the remaining tomato mixture among the parcels. Top each with a few basil leaves, a drizzle of olive oil, and a piece of the butter. Bring the corners of the parchment paper up and around the mussels in each parcel, cinch the paper together, and tie firmly closed with a piece of twine.

Snap the baguette in half crosswise. Using a pointy tip, slice each piece lengthwise in half to get 4 large pieces. Place the bread on a baking sheet, cut side up, and season the cut sides with olive oil and salt.

To cook the parcels, place them on the hot baking sheet and roast for 10 minutes. Meanwhile, halfway through the fish's cook time, toast the bread on the oven's top rack until golden and crisp. Once the mussels have cooked for 10 minutes, peek inside one of the parcels by untying it: If all the mussels are open, remove the parcels and the toasted bread from the oven. If not, cook them until the stubborn shells open. Slice a garlic clove in half and rub it over the cut side of the toasted bread.

Serve the steamy parcels in shallow bowls, with the warm, garlicky baguette halves on the bowls' sides.

Sea Bass

with Leeks, Anchovy, and Vermouth

We love the intensity of fish cooked with vermouth, bay, and anchovy. As the vermouth reduces and the bay does its thing, the anchovy balances out the sweet herbal notes.

Make this in the spring, when young, tender leeks are available. If larger ones are all you can get, use just the delicate white parts.

This dish is very good served as is or, if you want something more, with warm lentils (see page 20), flageolets (see page 15), or with blanched spinach (see page 12).

Serves 4

Four 6-ounce sea bass fillets, skin on
8 baby leeks or 4 medium ones (or 2 large!), rinsed
Olive oil
Salt and freshly ground black pepper
4 fresh or dried bay leaves
10 to 12 anchovy fillets
1½ tablespoons unsalted butter, cut into pieces
¾ cup vermouth, preferably Dolin Dry

Remove the fish from the fridge at least 20 minutes before cooking so it can come to room temperature. Preheat the oven to 450 degrees.

If you've scored young leeks, nip off just their roots, give them a rinse, and use them whole. If you have larger ones, trim off their roots and then halve them lengthwise, without slicing through their last few outer layers, so they open like a book. Run each of the split leeks under cold water to remove any sand or grit. If your leeks are much longer than 10 inches, trim them down to equal lengths that fit within a large pan (the dark green tops should head to a stockpot for another use).

Set a heavy ovenproof 12-inch skillet over medium heat and add ¼ cup olive oil. Pat the fish dry with paper towels to ensure crispy skin. Season both sides of each fillet with salt and pepper. When the pan begins to waft with smoke, reduce the heat to low and add the fillets skin side down. (If necessary, work in batches so as not to overcrowd the pan.) Sear until skins turn acorn brown, about 4 minutes; jiggle the pan every now and then to ensure the fillets don't stick.

Using a fish spatula, transfer the fish to a plate, skin side up. Add the leeks to the hot pan, cut side down if using larger ones, or just tumble them in if small and whole. Cook until they are golden and start to soften, about 4 minutes. Turn off the heat and spoon off enough oil so there's only about 2 tablespoons left in the pan.

Immediately add the bay leaves and let them crackle in the hot oil for a minute. Then scooch the bay leaves to the side and return the fish to the pan, skin side up, arranging the fillets around the leeks. Lay a fried bay leaf and 2 anchovies on top of each fillet and scatter the remaining anchovies and the bits of butter all around the pan.

Place the pan back over low heat, and once the butter foams, splash in the vermouth. Drizzle the fish with 1 tablespoon or so of olive oil and then move the pan to the oven. Roast until the sea bass is cooked through, about 6 minutes or so, but this will depend on the thickness of the fillets. To check, poke each one with a sharp knife (or cake tester), and if there's no resistance at the center, it is ready. Check that the leeks are also tender by poking and feeling for give. If the leeks need more time but the fish is done, transfer the fish to a plate and continue roasting the leeks until they're fully soft. Remove the pan from the oven and baste the fish with the anchovy-butter drippings.

Serve the sea bass skin side up with the leeks draped on top and finish with some roasting juices from the pan.

Poached Striped Bass

with Fennel, Sungold Tomatoes, and Bottarga Dressing

Wild striped bass can be hard to find on the East Coast, but when it is available in summer, this is our favorite preparation: poached and served with a luxuriously dressed fennel salad. Bass's delicate flavor and firm texture lend it nicely to poaching, but we've also happily used red snapper and halibut in this recipe.

Seeing as the bottarga and sweet tomato dressing for the salad are quite intense, we keep the poaching liquid on the neutral side. It easily simmers away as the other ingredients come together. If you like, it can be made a day in advance.

Serves 4

Four 6-ounce wild striped bass fillets, skin on

FOR THE COURT BOUILLON

1 fennel bulb, stalks removed and roughly chopped, bulb quartered
2 garlic cloves
4 whole black peppercorns
A small handful of thyme sprigs
2 bay leaves
2 to 3 outer ribs of celery, roughly chopped
Salt

FOR THE SALAD

2 fennel bulbs, stalks removed, and bulbs halved lengthwise
Salt
2 cups Sungold tomatoes, halved across their equators
Olive oil
½ lemon
¼ cup Whipped Bottarga with Tomato Juice (page 34), made with the juices reserved from the Sungold tomatoes (see method below)
A piece of bottarga di muggine, thin skin peeled away

Remove the fish from the fridge at least 20 minutes before cooking so it can come up to room temperature.

MEANWHILE, MAKE THE COURT BOUILLON: Combine the fennel, garlic, peppercorns, thyme, bay leaves, and celery in a medium pot and cover with enough cold water to submerge the vegetables by about 4 inches. Season lightly with salt, slowly bring the water to a simmer, and simmer until fragrant and delicate, about 20 minutes. If sips lack intensity, simmer for longer, tasting every few minutes, until the flavors of the aromatics are present and the broth is delicious.

WHILE THE COURT BOUILLON SIMMERS, PREPARE THE FENNEL FOR THE SALAD: Thinly slice the halved fennel crosswise into ¼-inch-thick crescents. Place these in a medium bowl, season with salt, set aside to tenderize for a few minutes.

(Continued)

Set a sieve over a small bowl. Pinch each halved tomato over the sieve, squeezing its belly and seeds into the sieve, and reserve the pinched tomatoes. Press on the captured seeds to extract as much juice as possible, then discard the seeds. Add the pinched tomatoes to the bowl with the fennel and mix to combine.

Once the bouillon is ready, set a strainer over a large wide pot that is roomy enough to comfortably hold all the fish in a single layer. Pour the bouillon through the strainer into the pot and discard the aromatics.

Season the fish with salt and add the fillets skin side down to the warm bouillon. Set the pot over very low heat, bring the liquid to a gentle simmer, and poach until the fish is just tender at its thickest point, 5 to 7 minutes. Turn off the heat and let the fillets rest in the pot to finish cooking through, 1 to 2 minutes. Any longer and they are likely to overcook.

Carefully remove the fillets with a fish spatula and arrange on a warm platter and discard the cooking liquor.

To serve, add about 1 tablespoon of olive oil and a squeeze of fresh lemon juice to the fennel-tomato jumble. Toss in a few tablespoons of the whipped bottarga dressing (a little goes a long way, so start lightly). Mix until everything is just covered with the dressing, toss, taste, and adjust with more dressing, salt, and/or lemon juice as needed.

Peel away and discard the fish's skin and place the fillets on a platter with a mound of dressed salad. Grate over the bottarga di muggine.

Poisson en Papillote

We served this dish when we first "popped-up" in London for a week.

But be careful of open flames on the table when serving it—we very nearly set fire to the restaurant when one guest accidentally opened their parcel over a candle.

Serves 4

FOR THE TARRAGON BUTTER

7 tablespoons unsalted butter, at room temperature
⅔ cup tarragon leaves, finely chopped
Salt
½ garlic clove

FOR THE PARCELS

Salt
2 fennel bulbs, stalks removed and tough outer layers discarded
Four 3-ounce red mullet, snapper, or sea bass fillets
Four 2-ounce monkfish fillets
8 large mussels, rinsed and debearded
8 littleneck or Manila clams, cleaned and soaked
1 cup fish stock or water
1½ tablespoons pastis, Pernod, or dry white wine

SPECIAL EQUIPMENT:
Parchment paper; kitchen twine

To make the tarragon butter, combine the butter, tarragon, a pinch of salt, and a couple of gratings of garlic (start with no more than a quarter clove run over a Microplane) in a small food processor or blender and process until the butter is speckled green and completely smooth. Taste for salt and garlic, whizzing in more of either or both if needed. Set aside. If you like, the tarragon butter can be made 1 or 2 days in advance, wrapped well, and held in the fridge (any longer, and the tarragon fades). Bring the butter to room temperature before using.

Preheat the oven to 450 degrees. Cut eight 12-by-15-inch rectangles of parchment paper. Cut four pieces of kitchen twine about 5 inches long.

Bring a medium pot of salted water to a boil over high heat. Halve each fennel bulb tip to root, and then cut each half into 3 equal wedges. Once the water is at a rumble, add the fennel wedges and cook until their outer layers soften but the centers remain a bit firm, about 3 minutes or so. Drain and set the fennel aside to fully cool.

When ready to assemble the parcels, season both sides of each piece of red mullet and monkfish with salt. Cross two rectangles of parchment to make an X. Add a blob of tarragon

(Continued)

butter, about 1 tablespoon, to the center of the parchment, and, with the back of a spoon, smudge it out, making a ¼-inch-thick bed for the fish. Place a piece of red mullet on top and then top it with a piece of monkfish. Add 3 fennel wedges and one-quarter each of the mussels and clams, setting them over and around the fillets. With one hand, gather the parchment up and around the fish, forming an open pouch, and then pour in ¼ cup of the fish broth and about a teaspoon of the pastis. Finish with a second blob of tarragon butter, about the same size as the first. Twist the parchment parcel shut, making it airtight, and then secure it firmly with a piece of the twine. Assemble the remaining parcels by repeating the process with the remaining parchment squares, ingredients, and string.

Place the tied parcels on a baking sheet and bake in the oven until your kitchen is aromatic and the shells have mostly opened when you gently prod a parcel, about 15 minutes. Remove the pan from the oven and allow the parcels to rest so that the mussels and fish finish steaming in the residual heat, about 5 minutes. Check on doneness by peeking inside one parcel: The shellfish should be open and the fish should flake when pressed. If the parcels need more time, return them to the oven and then check again after a few minutes.

To serve, place the parcels in bowls and let guests open their own—that first plume of steam is delicious—and eat straight from the paper. Place a few bowls around the table for the spent shells.

Salt-Baked Trout
with Cucumber, Purslane, and Lentils

Baking whole fish in salt is possibly our favorite preparation. The fish steam and then rest within their salt crust, and the outcome is exceptionally succulent. It's always very festive—guests love to see when one is paraded through the dining room and unearthed tableside!

Buy only whole fish with the scales still on; they act as a barrier against the salt and help protect the fish's delicate flesh. This said, do ask for the gills and bloodline to be removed. The other crucial step, as always, is to make sure that the fish is fully tempered before packing it in the salt. It doesn't spend much time in the oven, so it's important the heat can penetrate it quickly and evenly.

We also love to serve salt-baked fish with Aioli (page 22) and Confit Tomatoes (page 182) and basil leaves, Tomatoes Farci (page 187), Tian (page 185), and Wax Beans with Anchovy and Basil (page 190).

Serves 10

FOR THE FISH

One 4½-pound whole steelhead trout or salmon, cleaned but not scaled
Freshly ground black pepper
1 lemon, sliced into thin rounds
A small handful of thyme branches
A small handful of parsley stems (optional)
7 pounds culinary rock salt, plus more as needed
5 cups cooked lentils (see page 20), held in their cooking liquor

FOR THE CUCUMBER SALAD

1 cup crème fraîche
Finely grated zest of 1 lemon, lemon reserved
6 tablespoons finely chopped parsley or mint
Olive oil
Salt and freshly ground black pepper
2½ large English cucumbers
3 to 4 cups purslane, agretti, or watercress, tough stems discarded
Olive oil

Remove the fish from the fridge at least 30 minutes before cooking so it can come up to room temperature. Preheat the oven to 450 degrees.

Rinse the fish, inside and out, under cold running water and pat dry. Season the cavity with pepper and then stuff it with the lemon slices, thyme, and parsley stems, if using.

Line a baking sheet that's large enough to hold the whole fish on the diagonal with parchment paper. Add the rock salt to a large bowl and mix in about 2 cups cold water. When it resembles

(Continued)

wet sand (you may need to add a little more water), lay half the salt mixture onto the parchment, making a bed that runs diagonally across the baking sheet. Make a shallow well in the center of the bed center and lay the fish in it, setting its belly within the well. Pat the remaining salt mixture around the fish, cocooning all but its head in a ¾-inch-thick layer of damp salt. If any cracks appear, patch them with more of the salt mixture.

Bake in the oven until the salt crust sets, 25 to 30 minutes. The fish will not be fully cooked at this point, but it is ready to come out of the oven when a cake tester or long metal skewer inserted into the fish comes out hot: Insert it through the salt crust at the fish's collar and press straight through, hitting the tray below, hold it in place for about 10 seconds, and then pull it out. The tip should be piping hot and the part that was against the top of the collar should be as well, but the center should feel just warm. If this is the case, remove the fish from the oven and let it rest for 30 minutes to gently steam within the salt casing. If the fish needs more time, return it to the oven for 5 minutes or so and check again.

While the fish rests, reheat the lentils in their cooking liquor in a medium pot over low heat until they are warmed through; keep warm over low heat.

MEANWHILE, MAKE THE CUCUMBER SALAD: Add the crème fraîche to a small bowl and season it with the lemon zest. Halve the lemon and add the juice of one half to the crème fraîche (we always strain our lemon juice). Stir the parsley, along with ½ tablespoon olive oil, a pinch of salt, and some pepper.

Slice the cucumbers into irregular triangular shapes, about 1 inch across at the thickest point, and transfer to a large bowl. Toss the cucumber pieces with enough of the crème fraîche dressing to generously coat. Fold in the purslane and add a little more dressing if needed. Taste and add salt and/or lemon juice as needed.

To serve the fish, use a sharp knife to gently chisel the salt crust along the fish's backbone until it cracks. Lift off the crust in chunky pieces to reveal the fish below. Once you've cleared away the top of the salt crust, continue to excavate carefully to remove the crust all around the fish, then use a pastry brush to brush away any residual granules of salt. Peel away the skin from the cleared area. Using a fish spatula (and your hands as needed), gently slide portions of fish up off the bone and place them on a platter or individual plates. Once you've removed all of the top fillet, remove and discard the spine and any visible bones. Then use the spatula to gingerly lift up the lower fillet, leaving its skin behind in the remaining crust, and transfer portions of the bottom fillet onto the platter or individual plates.

Serve with the warm lentils dressed with some olive oil alongside the cucumber salad.

Provençal Fish Stew

Here's a much simpler take on traditional bouillabaisse, which requires a couple of days to prepare. And although the recipe can be made in a day, the classic's sun-drenched spirit lives on here. Bowls of it are suffused with saffron, tomatoes, and garlic, and saffron aioli is dolloped on golden croutons. If you're a traditionalist, make Rouille (page 84) instead of the aioli for a closer approximation to authentic bouillabaisse.

A lobster wouldn't be found in a Fisherman's stew—instead the pot would be full of any meaty white fish that was left unsold at the dock that day. A large monkfish tail (still on the bone, if possible) would be a more traditional substitute here.

With a very sharp and sturdy chef's knife, split the lobsters as quickly and as confidently as possible.

Serves 4

FOR THE STEW

Olive oil
3 garlic cloves, thinly sliced
2 teaspoons fennel seeds, lightly crushed
⅛ teaspoon ground chilies
Salt and freshly ground black pepper
2 pounds ripe tomatoes, cored and roughly chopped (about 5 cups), or substitute 1 cup Fresh or Preserved Tomato Sauce (page 27) made with canned tomatoes
3 cups Vermentino, or similar dry white wine
A generous pinch of saffron threads
One 1-pound red snapper fillet, skin on
2 lobsters (about 1¼ pounds each)
1 pound littleneck clams, scrubbed and rinsed
1 pound mussels, preferably from Prince Edward Island, cleaned and debearded

Four ¾-inch-thick slices crusty bread
Saffron Aioli (recipe follows)
Basil leaves for serving

(Continued)

To make the stew's base, set a very large Dutch oven over medium heat, add 2 tablespoons olive oil, the garlic, fennel seeds, chili flakes, some salt, and a pinch of black pepper, and stir well. Cook while stirring occasionally until the garlic sizzles but doesn't brown, 2 to 3 minutes. Stir in the tomatoes (or tomato sauce), wine, and saffron and bring to a simmer, then reduce the heat to medium-low. Cook, stirring occasionally, until the sauce reduces slightly, 12 to 15 minutes. Season with salt and pepper to taste and transfer to a large bowl, scraping the pot clean.

Remove the snapper from the fridge at least 20 minutes before cooking so it can come to room temperature. Meanwhile, prepare the lobsters; when butchering them, be steadfast! Place a damp kitchen towel on a work surface and set a sturdy cutting board on top. Place one lobster on the cutting board so its underbelly faces up. Straighten its tail, hold the tip of a sharp chef's knife over the lobster's head, and pierce the lobster's head, then cut straight down through the midline of the carapace (where the head connects to the body) until you reach the tail end and the lobster is split in half lengthwise.

Remove and discard the dark gray stomach sac, black intestinal thread, and the tomalley (basically clean out and discard the guts). Use the back of the chef's knife to crack the claws by smashing them to loosen the shells (this makes shelling the claws easier later); remove and discard the claws' rubber bands, if applicable. Repeat the process with the remaining lobster. Sprinkle all the lobsters' cut sides with salt and pepper.

Slice the snapper fillet into 8 equal portions and season on all sides with salt and pepper.

Clean the pot you used for the base, set it over medium heat, and add 1 to 2 tablespoons oil. Once it is warm, lay in 2 of the lobster halves, cut side down (make sure the claws are in contact with the bottom of the pot), and cook until the meat lightly browns, about 2 minutes. Flip the lobster halves and cook on the other side until the claws are bright red, 1 to 3 minutes. Transfer the seared lobster halves to a tray. Add more olive oil to the pot, 1 to 2 tablespoons, and repeat the searing process with the remaining lobster halves; transfer to the tray.

Add a tablespoon or so of oil to the pot, then add the snapper pieces, skin side down. Once they are sizzling, 30 seconds or so, return the lobster halves to the pot, cut side up; be careful not to damage the tender fish. Add the clams and mussels, scattering them around, and pour in the reserved base. Increase the heat to medium-high and bring the base to a simmer, then reduce the heat to medium-low. Cover with a lid and gently simmer until the clams and mussels have opened, the lobster claws are fully cooked, and the fish flakes when prodded, 10 to 12 minutes. Discard any unopened clams and mussels.

Meanwhile, as the stew finishes cooking, grill or toast each slice of bread until golden brown or charred on both sides.

Place half a lobster, 2 pieces of fish, and a scattering of mussels and clams in each bowl and add a ladleful or two of the broth. Perch the toasts, topped with some of the saffron aioli, on top, scatter over the basil leaves, and finish with plenty of juice. Alternatively, serve family-style from the pot at the table, along with cooked cocos blancs (see page 15), baguettes, and blanched rainbow chard or spinach (see page 12).

Saffron Aioli

This is our standard aioli recipe (see page 22), enhanced with saffron.

Serves 4 to 6

1 small garlic clove, peeled
A generous pinch of saffron threads
1 tablespoon lemon juice
Salt

1 large egg yolk
Olive oil
Salt

Using a mortar and pestle, smash together the garlic and saffron with the lemon juice and about ¼ teaspoon salt until a smooth mash forms. Transfer it to a medium bowl and whisk in the egg yolk. (Alternatively, if you don't have a mortar and pestle, use the flat side of a chef's knife to smash the garlic together with ¼ teaspoon on a cutting board to form a paste. Scrape the paste into a medium bowl and whisk in the lemon juice, saffron, and egg yolk.)

Set the bowl on a damp kitchen towel (this helps hold the bowl in place) and start whisking, without pause, ⅔ cup olive oil into the garlic-egg paste. Initially add the oil *very, very* slowly (drop by drop); once you've added half of it at this painfully slow rate and the aioli has thickened and lightened in color, continue whisking in the remaining oil in a thin, slow stream—only start down this road once you're confident the emulsion is stable! The aioli should be a lovely light yellow and have a lovely, silky texture. Whisk in a pinch of salt, or to taste.

Saffron aioli is best the day it is made and served at room temperature, but it can hold for a day, covered in the fridge; bring to room temperature before serving.

CHAPTER 11

Rabbit

OUR COOKBOOK WOULD NOT BE COMPLETE WITHOUT A CHAPTER DEDICATED TO THE joy of cooking rabbit. It is among our very favorite things.

Rabbit is prized in rural kitchens across France and Italy for being plentiful and easy to hunt; we love its subtle flavor and versatility. Although it isn't as popular on this side of the Atlantic, King regulars have cottoned on and now get as giddy as we do whenever rabbit appears on the menu. Yes, chicken can be swapped in for rabbit in almost all the recipes that follow, but once you give rabbit an honest chance, we expect you won't look back.

The rabbits that we get are responsibly farmed and have a delicate gamy flavor. They arrive gutted and whole at our back door, and we use the opportunity to teach the cooks some basic butchery (see page 257). Breaking down a rabbit is easy, far simpler than butchering a chicken, but if you prefer, a butcher can do the job for you in an instant. We use all the parts: the two hind legs, saddle, two forelegs, and rib cage. Each offers a slightly different texture. In our kitchen, the rib cage is a "cook's treat"—the thin ribs are perfect for nibbling.

Whether we grill or fry rabbit, we always salt it first and submerge the pieces in a bright, briny marinade. We do this both for flavor and because the acidity breaks down the protein and keeps the lean, hard-working cuts tender. When grilling, we'll use sprigs of the marinade's harder herbs as a brush, basting on more flavor as the pieces crackle over hot coals.

But what speaks to us most of all are braises, where rabbit stews "low and slow." This is an age-old technique that requires some care: controlling the temperature at the beginning, to carefully brown the meat; patiently softening the sofrito (the vegetable base that builds baseline flavor); and adding the right amount of liquid so the sauce thickens just so. While braises are forgiving, rabbit is lean and asks for some focus while cooking delicate parts for just the right amount of time so the meat softens without shredding.

There are always myriad options—French or Italian, rich or light—and in this chapter, we've gathered the choices we happily return to.

As for leftovers: Pull whatever meat remains from the rabbit's bones and toss with pasta, butter, and grated Parm. Or mix it into peppery leaves along with a spoonful of beans and a mustard dressing. Whatever the second act, once your rabbit bones are bare, add them to a stockpot for a broth.

Butchering a Rabbit

TO BREAK DOWN A RABBIT

Lay the rabbit on a work surface with its spine facing up.

Cut off the 2 hind legs by tracing around each upper thigh muscle with a sharp knife and then slicing through the bone.

Cut off the front legs by doing the same, and then slice through the respective joints of both.

Splay the legs and flip the rabbit over. Remove the kidneys and any excess fat from the cavity.

Separate the rib cage from the saddle by cutting through the backbone. You will have 4 legs, a rib cage, and the loin.

TO BUTTERFLY THE SADDLE

Set it down on your work surface.

Use a sharp knife to cut out the backbone by tracing the knife's tip down either side of the spine, without cutting through the meat.

Once the spine is loosened, carefully cut it out while keeping all the meat intact. Add the backbone to the stockpot.

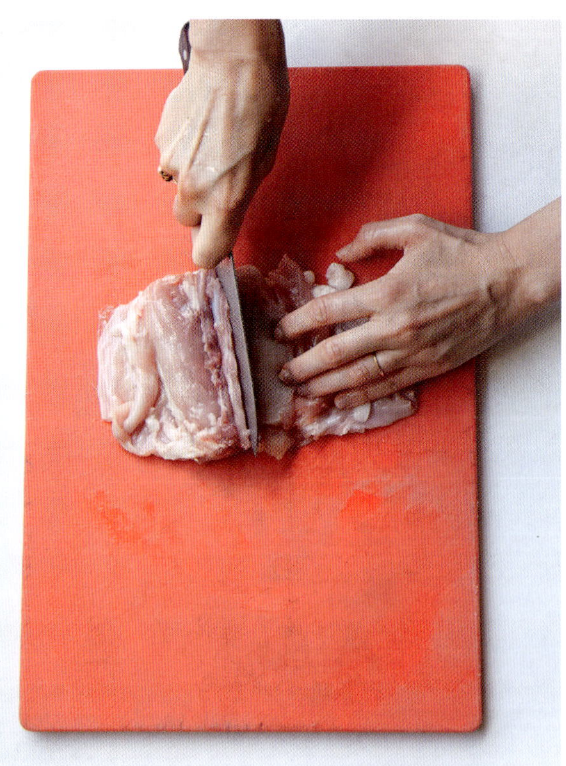

Braised Rabbit

This simply flavored braise can become a ragù tossed through pappardelle (see page 128), spooned onto soft polenta (see page 21), or a warm salad with lentils (see page 20) and a mustard vinaigrette.

Serves 4 to 6 on its own,
or 10 when served as a ragù with pappardelle

1 whole rabbit (about 2½ to 3 pounds), broken down into 6 parts (see page 257)
Salt and freshly ground black pepper
Olive oil
1 large carrot, peeled and cut into ½-inch dice
1 small red onion, cut into ½-inch dice
1 celery heart, cut into ½-inch dice
10 thyme branches
4 sprigs of parsley
2 bay leaves
6 sage leaves
2 garlic cloves, thinly sliced
3 cups Soave or similar dry white wine
1 cup chicken stock, homemade (see page 35) or store-bought

SPECIAL EQUIPMENT: Kitchen twine

Remove the rabbit from the fridge at least 40 minutes before cooking so it can come to room temperature. Season it generously on all sides with salt and pepper. Preheat the oven to 375 degrees.

Set a large heavy pot over high heat and pour in ¼ cup olive oil. When it is hot, add the rabbit, meaty side down. (If necessary, brown the pieces in batches to prevent overcrowding.) Lower the heat to medium and sear until the pieces are an even chestnut brown on the first side, about 5 minutes. Flip the pieces and sear the other side, about 5 minutes. If the pan looks dry at any point, add more oil. As each piece is browned on all sides, transfer it to a rimmed baking sheet. Turn off the heat.

Using paper towels, blot up any burnt bits from the bottom of the pot, leaving the nice golden "fond" in place! Set the pot back over medium heat and add a glug of olive oil, about 2 tablespoons. Stir in the carrots, onion, celery, and a pinch of salt and cook until the vegetables have softened but not browned, about 10 minutes.

MEANWHILE, WHILE THE SOFRITO COOKS, MAKE A BOUQUET GARNI: Gather the thyme branches, parsley stems, bay, and sage and tie together with with kitchen twine, making two tight loops around the bundle, and knotting the string firmly.

When the vegetables have softened, add the bouquet garni, along with the garlic. Add the seared rabbit pieces, meaty side up, arranging them in a single layer, and pour in all the accumulated juices from the baking pan.

Turn the heat up to high and pour in the white wine and chicken stock. Bring to a simmer and simmer for a few minutes, then before turn off the heat. Cover the braise with a cartouche (see page 15) and then the lid.

Move the pot to the oven and braise until the meat easily slides off the bone, 1 to 1½ hours. Remove from the oven and remove the lid and cartouche. Let the rabbit rest in its juices for at least 10 minutes before serving.

If you are not serving this as a stand-alone braise, let it cool fully, pick all the rabbit meat off its bones (save them for stock), shred the meat, then stir back through the braising juices. From there, toss through noodles or salad, or spoon onto polenta.

The braise can be made 3 days in advance and stored, covered, in the fridge.

Tina's Rabbit Pie

This is our head chef, Tina's, recipe.

This pastry is buttery, forgiving, and rather resilient—perfect for a hefty pie like this! The recipe will yield more pastry than is required, but we like to use the extra bits to decorate the top.

Once the pie is assembled, take your time with the bake. It truly needs hours in the oven plus plenty of standing time before slicing. The final rest will test your willpower, but slicing too soon will result in shambles. You must wait.

If you like, you can prepare the filling up to 3 days in advance and line the pan with dough up to 2 days ahead.

Fill this pie with any leftover braised meat: chicken, beef, pork, pheasant. . . . But it's usually rabbit for us. Serve the pie with a green salad on the side.

Serves 8

FOR THE HOT-WATER CRUST

3 cups (600 grams) all-purpose flour
Kosher salt
¾ pound (350 grams) unsalted butter, roughly diced
¾ cup water (170 grams), at room temperature

FOR THE FILLING

1 batch Braised Rabbit (page 260), rabbit cooled in the braising liquid
5 tablespoons unsalted butter
3 tablespoons all-purpose flour
Salt

FOR THE EGG WASH

1 egg
Splash of milk

SPECIAL EQUIPMENT:

A 3-inch-deep 8-inch round springform pan; a pastry brush

To make the pastry, combine the flour with a generous teaspoon of salt in a large bowl. Combine the butter and water in a small pot and heat over low heat just until the butter melts, about 2 minutes; don't let too much of the water evaporate. Stir to combine and remove the heat.

Pour the butter mixture into the flour and stir with a wooden spoon until the dough comes together (if it looks a bit greasy, don't worry!). Then knead it in the bowl for just a few seconds, until a smooth ball forms.

Turn the dough out and divide it into 2 portions, one twice as large as the other. The larger piece is for the bottom crust, the smaller piece for the top crust. Set aside to cool completely.

(Continued)

To make the filling, remove the rabbit pieces from the braising liquid (set the pot aside) and pull all the rabbit meat from the bones, shredding it into large bite-sized pieces. Discard the bones (some of these are very small, so make sure that none have been left behind) and stir the meat back into the pot. Remove and discard the bouquet garni.

To make a roux, melt 3 tablespoons of the butter in a small pot over low heat. Stir in the flour and, stirring constantly, cook the mixture together until the roux takes on a light honey color tone and smells nutty, about 3 minutes. Gradually add about a cup of the rabbit braising liquid to the roux, stirring constantly, and then cook, stirring often, until the sauce thickens enough to coat the back of a spoon, about 5 minutes.

Meanwhile, warm the braise over medium-low heat, stirring occasionally. Once it is just warm, add the roux, stirring constantly until well combined. Simmer for a couple of minutes, until the sauce thickens to the consistency of custard. Taste and season with more salt, if necessary, so the sauce is very flavorful. Remove from the heat and let the filling cool to room temperature. The filling can also be refrigerated until ready to use; covered, it holds for up to 3 days.

When ready to assemble the pie, preheat the oven to 400 degrees. Using your fingertips, press the large piece of cooled dough evenly over the bottom and two-thirds of the way up the sides of a 3-inch-deep, 8-inch round cake pan. Press on the dough on the sides of the pan so it rises up above the rim by at least ½ inch—the dough will shrink a little as it bakes. Refrigerate the pie shell until thoroughly chilled, at least 30 minutes. It will keep, covered with plastic wrap, for up to 2 days in the fridge.

Next, roll out the top crust. Lightly flour a large piece of parchment paper, and set the remaining dough on top, and roll it out into a ⅓-inch thick round at least 9 inches in diameter. Chill in the fridge, on the sheet of parchment, for 30 minutes.

Fill the lined cake pan with the cooled filling, scraping all the sauce and rabbit into the pan. Cover with the top crust, flipping it gently onto the pie so the floured side faces up. If any cracks appear, patch the dough back together. Pinch the edges of the top and bottom crusts together to seal. Cut three or four 1- to 2-inch-long slits into the top crust for steam vents. If you have extra dough, now is the time to cut out shapes and decorate the pie's lid.

To make the egg wash, mix the egg and milk together in a small cup and blend with a fork. Brush this over the top of the pie and refrigerate until the pastry feels cold to the touch, about 10 minutes.

Bake the pie in the oven for 1 hour. Reduce the oven temperature to 350 degrees and continue baking until the crust is golden brown and the filling is hot, 1½ to 2 hours. If the top starts to brown too quickly, loosely cover it with aluminum foil. To test that the pie is ready, insert the tip of a knife into the pie's center for 5 seconds: It should emerge hot. The pastry should also be pulling away from the pan's sides.

Remove the pie from the oven and let stand for at least 20 minutes. Release the sides of the pan and remove them. Slide the pie onto a warm serving plate and slice into 8 wedges.

Tuscan Fried Rabbit

It's as good as it sounds. The herbs and the acid in the crème fraîche tenderize and flavor the meat, so allow the rabbit to marinate for 2 days before cooking to take full effect.

Serve TFR like a Tuscan: simply with salt and lemon wedges.

Serves 4 to 6

4 sprigs of sage
4 sprigs of rosemary
2 garlic cloves
2 tablespoons fennel seeds
6 rabbit legs and/or saddles (about 3 pounds total) or 6 skinless chicken thighs
2 cups crème fraîche
Kosher salt and freshly ground black pepper
2 cups semolina flour
1 cup all-purpose flour, plus more for dusting
2 cups whole milk
2 quarts sunflower oil for deep-frying, plus more as needed
2 lemons, 1 thinly sliced into thin rounds, seeds removed

SPECIAL EQUIPMENT:
A deep-fry or candy thermometer

Remove the leaves from half the sage sprigs and the needles from half the rosemary branches. Using a mortar and pestle, bruise them to release the natural oils. Add the garlic to the mortar and bash once to split open the cloves. Add the fennel seeds, leaving these whole for pop. Alternatively, smash everything together on your cutting board, pressing down on the aromatics with the flat side of a chef's knife.

Pat the rabbit dry and add it to a large bowl. Toss in the garlic-fennel mash, the crème fraîche, 2 tablespoons salt, and 1 tablespoon pepper. Mix well to thoroughly coat all the rabbit pieces. Cover and refrigerate for at least 48 hours, and up to 4 days.

Remove the rabbit from the fridge at least 40 minutes before frying so it can come to room temperature.

To make the coating, mix the semolina and all-purpose flour in a large wide bowl until evenly combined. (This doesn't get seasoned because the marinade already has enough personality.) Add the milk to another large wide dish.

Sprinkle some flour on a baking sheet. Dredge the rabbit one piece at a time: Scrape off its excess marinade (herbs are welcome, gloppy crème fraîche isn't) and dunk it in the milk, submerging it fully, then lift it up, allow the excess liquid to run off, and add it to the flour, turning to coat the rabbit completely. Transfer to the baking sheet and repeat with the remaining rabbit pieces.

(Continued)

Choose a large, deep, heavy pot to fry the rabbit and secure a candy or deep-fry thermometer to its side. Add 3 inches of oil to the pot and slowly warm over low to medium-low heat until the temperature reaches 330 degrees. If you don't have a thermometer, plop in a stray rosemary needle: It should sizzle and turn golden in moments. If it blackens instantly, your oil is too hot—turn off the heat, let the oil cool slightly, and go again.

When ready to fry, tap off the excess flour from a piece of rabbit and slowly lower it into the hot oil. Repeat with another few pieces, but do not overcrowd the pot. Fry, adjusting the heat as necessary so the bubbling stays active but under control, until the rabbit is golden and crisp, about 5 minutes. Using tongs, flip the rabbit and fry on the other side, another 5 minutes or so. The actual timing will depend on each piece's size, but if a cake tester or pointy knife inserted into the rabbit's thickest part emerges warm at the tip, it is done. Remove the crisped pieces from the pot with a slotted spoon or tongs, allowing the excess oil to run off, and set the rabbit on the lined baking sheet. Blot dry and season generously with salt, then continue cooking the remaining rabbit pieces, adding more oil to the pot as necessary. If the oil looks dirty at all, skim it with a fine-mesh strainer between batches; add more oil if needed and let it heat to 330 degrees before continuing on with the fry.

Once your last pieces of rabbit go into the oil, dredge the lemon rounds and what remains of the rosemary and sage sprigs, first passing each through the milk and then the flour. After the last piece of rabbit exits the oil, turn off the heat and add the dredged herbs and lemon rounds to the pot. Gently fry the aromatics in the oil's residual heat until they crisp and turn golden brown, 1 to 2 minutes. Scoop them out with a slotted spoon, allowing the excess oil to run off, and transfer to the tray with the fried rabbit. Blot everything dry and season with salt.

Serve the TFR piled high, with the crispy herbs and the fried lemon rounds scattered about, with lemon wedges on the side.

Rabbit Marinated in Red Wine Vinegar
with Walnut Aillade

Our RWV-grilled rabbit tastes of the wild. Its mystery comes from the red wine vinegar, smoke, and char. Your vinegar's quality (and how it is aged) will make all the difference. We use a Tuscan vinegar.

We serve this with walnut aillade, a vinegary sauce from the Languedoc, and a salad of chicories or arugula, dressed in nothing more than the rabbit's resting juices.

The rabbit must marinate for 8 to 12 hours before grilling. If you like, the sauce can be made in advance.

Serves 4 to 6

½ cup red wine vinegar
½ teaspoon whole black peppercorns
Kosher salt
4 garlic cloves, smashed open
A small handful of sage sprigs
A handful of rosemary sprigs
1 whole rabbit (about 2½ pounds), broken down into 6 parts (see page 257)
2 cups Walnut Aillade (recipe follows)

Marinate the rabbit the night before you want to grill it. To make the marinade, pour the red wine vinegar into a container that's deep enough to hold the marinade and rabbit pieces comfortably. Toss in the peppercorns, about a tablespoon of salt, the garlic cloves, sage, and rosemary and stir to combine. Add the rabbit and mix well, turning to coat the pieces evenly. Cover and refrigerate for 8 to 12 hours; if possible, turn the rabbit now and again to distribute the marinade evenly.

An hour before you start cooking, pull the rabbit from the fridge so it can come to room temperature.

Set up a medium fire in the grill. Meanwhile, transfer the rabbit to a tray and pick off the sage, rosemary, and garlic bits. Keep the container with the marinade and herbs nearby.

Lay the rabbit pieces on the grill grate (since it's heavily seasoned, there's no need for additional salt). When solid grill marks form on the first side, after about 5 minutes, flip the rabbit. While searing it on the second side, use the reserved herb branches to brush some of marinade onto the rabbit as it sizzles; the vinegar baste will cook out and caramelize as the meat cooks through. Continue grilling while brushing on marinade and flip-flopping the rabbit occasionally until the meat is cooked through and the exterior looks lacquered, about 15 minutes total; do not flip the rabbit if it offers any resistance. Once the meat is two-thirds cooked, after about 10 minutes, stop basting with the marinade and simply grill to finish charring the pieces and cooking off any raw marinade.

To check for doneness, make a small slit by a joint in a medium piece of rabbit, pry it open, and peek: If things look juicy and cooked through, remove the piece from the grill and place it on a tray. If some pieces are larger, give them an extra minute or two and then check for doneness.

Let the rabbit rest for at least 5 minutes before serving it warm, with dollops of the walnut aillade. To accompany, toss a few handfuls of salad greens (torn radicchio is also nice here) with the rabbit's resting juices. Taste the greens and maybe add a pinch of salt plus a squeeze of lemon if needed.

Walnut Aillade

Rich, tangy, and herbal, this is an excellent condiment with grilled poultry as well as rabbit. We make our aillade with a mortar and pestle so the walnuts stay textured and don't turn to nut butter.

Makes 2 cups

1 garlic clove
3 tablespoons roughly chopped rosemary needles
Salt
2½ cups walnuts, roughly chopped
2 tablespoons red wine vinegar
Olive oil
Freshly ground black pepper

Using a mortar and pestle, crush the garlic and rosemary with a teaspoon of salt. Once a fine paste forms, add the walnuts and bash to a lumpy texture; the nuts should still be pebbly and uneven. Transfer to a larger bowl.

Stir in the vinegar and about ⅓ cup olive oil. Let the sauce stand for a few minutes. Once the nuts break down a bit—some nuts should be crumbly and others should retain their bite—and the oil thickens slightly, season with salt and pepper.

Rabbit Rolled in Speck
with Vinegar and Sage

Deboning a rabbit saddle is not simple, but if the prospect excites, this recipe is for you! Here the saddle is stuffed with olives and sage, rolled up into a little log, and wrapped in a sheet of speck (the thin slices are layered together to make it work). The speck's smokiness complements the flavors of the stuffing and the vinegar that is added to the pan after the rabbit is seared. The splash makes an easy, punchy pan sauce.

Rabbit saddles consist of two loins held together by a thin flap of lean meat. If you can't find rabbit, boneless, skinless chicken thighs will work as a substitute, but they will be a little more tricky to wrap and roll. Since they're smaller than a rabbit saddle, line a few up to form a gap-free bed and then roll and tie the log with a few extra loops of twine to keep it secure. In either case, if the speck tears, patch it with scraps.

Serve this with Smashed Pumpkin (page 191) and French Tapenade (page 25); Tian (page 185); Braised Endive (page 198); Smashed Celeriac (page 161); and/or crushed cooked cocos blancs (see page 15) with watercress and Mustard Vinaigrette (page 29).

Serves 4 to 6

A 1½- to 2-pound boneless rabbit saddle (see page 257) or 1½ to 2 pounds boneless, skinless chicken thighs
12 thin slices speck (about 4 ounces)
Salt and freshly ground black pepper
20 sage leaves
½ cup roughly chopped Taggiasca olives or other rich dark olives
Olive oil
2 tablespoon capers, rinsed
½ cup red wine vinegar

SPECIAL EQUIPMENT:
Kitchen twine

Remove the rabbit from the fridge to take off the chill while you arrange the speck on a work surface, overlapping the thin slices by about 1 inch, to form a rectangle. Season the rabbit all over with salt and pepper.

Place the saddle on the speck so its smooth side faces down and it runs the length of the bed. Lay fifteen of the sage leaves down the saddle's centerline. Or, if using chicken, lay the thighs on the work surface, shingling them by about an inch, to form a single piece of meat. Arrange the sage down the middle of the thighs. Spoon the olives over the sage on the rabbit.

To roll up the saddle, fold the left flap of meat over the olives then repeat with the right flap. Roll the speck over the rabbit so that you have a speck-covered cylinder. Set the roll seam side down on the work surface. Tie it in four or more places with kitchen twine. Season it all over with pepper.

(Continued)

Preheat the oven to 450 degrees. Add 3 tablespoons olive oil to a roasting pan, and set it over medium heat. Once it is hot, lay in the saddle and sear on the first side until nicely browned, 2 to 3 minutes. Carefully turn it, taking care not to break the speck wrapping, and brown the remaining sides (a roll has many sides, so try to color everything evenly and gently!). When the roll is seared all over, carefully sear the ends, about 2 minutes per end.

Lay the seared saddle in the pan and throw in the remaining sage leaves and capers. Once the leaves crisp, about 2 minutes, deglaze the pan with the vinegar. Let it simmer for a few seconds, then move the pan to the oven. Roast until the saddle is cooked through, about 30 minutes (chicken thighs will cook for the same time). To check the doneness, insert a cake tester or a metal skewer into the roll's center for 5 seconds, then remove it and place the tip against your bottom lip: It should feel warm.

Remove the pan from the oven and let the rabbit rest in the pan for at least 10 minutes. Then untie it, and while it's still warm, slice into 1-inch-thick rounds. Place on a warm plate and spoon over the vinegary pan juices. Scatter over the crisped sage leaves and capers and finish with a drizzle of olive oil.

Lapin a Pastis

Fennel and pastis go arm in arm in this braise. The pastis (the French liquor that tastes of anise) and fennel (literal anise) both mellow as they braise, so neither overpowers the rabbit. That said, to make this dish, you must like the taste of sweet, herbal anise, as it's as present here as the rabbit itself.

Serves 4 to 6

1 whole rabbit (about 2½ pounds), broken down into 6 parts (see page 257)
Salt and freshly ground black pepper
4 or 5 medium fennel bulbs, stalks and fronds still attached
1 pound small waxy potatoes, such as Butterball, or new potatoes, peeled
Olive oil
A pinch of fennel seeds, crushed
1 celery heart, finely chopped
2 garlic cloves, finely chopped
1½ cups pastis or Pernod
1 cup chicken stock, homemade (see page 35) or store-bought
1 to 2 tablespoons unsalted butter, cut into small pieces

Remove the rabbit from the refrigerator at least 40 minutes before cooking so it can come to room temperature. Season it generously all over with salt and pepper.

Trim off the stalks from the fennel bulbs and reserve. Remove and discard the outer layers of the bulbs (or save them for future stock) and halve the bulbs tip to root. Slice each half into 1¼-inch-wide wedges. Cut the potatoes into wedges or cubes approximately the size of the fennel wedges.

Preheat the oven to 400 degrees. Set a wide heavy pot over medium heat and add ⅓ cup olive oil. Once it is warm, add the rabbit (if necessary, brown in batches to avoid overcrowding) and sear it on both sides until golden, about 4 to 6 minutes per side; adjust the heat if necessary so the rabbit colors evenly and doesn't scorch. As each piece browns (some will cook more quickly than others), transfer it to a tray. When all the pieces are nut brown, remove the pot from the heat and pour off the oil.

Return the pot to low heat. Add 2 tablespoons olive oil, the fennel seeds, a pinch of salt, and the celery and cook gently for about 5 minutes, until the celery is translucent. Add the potatoes, increase the heat to medium, and cook, stirring frequently, for a couple of minutes. Stir in the fennel wedges and garlic and season with salt. When the garlic's scent blooms but before it browns, increase the heat to high and deglaze the pot with the pastis and chicken stock. Simmer for a moment, then nestle the browned rabbit, meaty side up, in the vegetables. Add any accumulated juices from the tray and taste the liquid—it should be fragrant and flavorful, and a little boozy, but that will mellow as it cooks.

Arrange the reserved fennel stalks on top of the braise and dot with the butter. Cover with a cartouche (see page 15) and then the lid.

Move the pot to the oven and cook until the meat is falling off the bones, about 1½ hours. Remove from the oven and lelt the rabbit rest, in the pot, for at least 20 minutes before serving.

Rabbit au Riesling
with Buttered Noodles

It was snowing in New York City the day we first made this—apt, since it is such a warming Alpine dish. Crème fraîche and mustard round out the flavors of the braising liquid, which celebrates the bright and floral qualities of the wine.

This is a regular fixture on King's winter menus. And no one, it seems, can resist the buttered noodles that accompany it.

Serves 6

1 whole rabbit (about 2½ pounds), broken down into 6 parts (see page 257)
Salt and freshly ground black pepper
Olive oil
1 large shallot, thinly sliced
¼ cup roughly chopped thyme leaves
1 garlic clove, finely chopped
1½ cups dry Riesling (our favorite is from Alsace)
1½ tablespoons crème fraîche
1 tablespoon Dijon mustard
1 cup chicken stock, homemade (see page 35) or store-bought, or water

FOR THE NOODLES

21 ounces (1 batch homemade) Fresh Tagliatelle (page 128) or other long noodles
8 tablespoons (1 stick) unsalted butter
¼ cup roughly chopped parsley (optional)
Salt

Remove the rabbit from the refrigerator at least 40 minutes before cooking so it can come to room temperature. Pat it dry and season all over with salt and pepper. Preheat the oven to 375 degrees.

Set a wide heavy pot over medium heat and add ⅓ cup olive oil. When the oil is hot and shimmery, add the rabbit, meaty side down (if necessary, work in batches to prevent overcrowding), and brown on both sides, about 7 minutes per side; adjust the heat as necessary so the rabbit colors evenly and does not scorch. If the pot looks dry, add a little more oil. As each piece browns (some will cook more quickly than others), transfer it to a tray. Once all the rabbit is browned, remove the pot from the heat and pour off all but 1 tablespoon of the oil.

Stir the shallot and thyme into the pot and let them sizzle in the residual heat for a minute or so. Add the garlic and season with salt and pepper. Return the pot to low heat and gently cook until the garlic's scent blooms, about 3 minutes. Add the Riesling, increase the heat to medium, and simmer to cook off the alcohol, about 3 minutes. Dollop in the crème fraîche and mustard, stirring to marble the sauce. Taste and season with salt as needed, but keep in mind that this shouldn't taste too punchy.

Add the browned rabbit, meaty side up, to the pot in a single layer (if necessary, turn some of the pieces on their side), and pour in any accumulated juices. Pour in the stock and add a bit more olive oil, 2 to 3 tablespoons. Cover the braise with a cartouche (see page 15) then the lid.

Move the braise to the oven and cook until the meat is falling off the bones, about 1½ hours; as the rabbit cooks, remove the lid and cartouche to baste the pieces every 30 minutes or so. Remove the pot from the oven and let the braise rest in the pot while you cook the noodles.

Bring a large pot of well-salted water to a boil. Once it is rumbling, set a large pan over medium heat and add the butter. Immediately add the pasta to the boiling water and boil until the noodles are a minute shy of al dente, about 3 more minutes.

As soon as the butter foams, splash about 2 tablespoons of the hot pasta water (scoop it directly from the pot) into the pan and swirl everything together to form an emulsion. If the pasta needs another minute to cook, turn off the heat under the butter sauce. Once it is done, transfer the pasta to the pan and add a few more splashes of pasta water, about 2 tablespoons. Toss vigorously until the pasta and sauce become one, about 1 minute more. Turn off the heat and finish the pasta with chopped parsley, if you like.

Divide the pasta among individual plates and spoon the rabbit over the buttery noodles; make sure to include plenty of juices and gubbins in each portion. Alternatively, put the rabbit and pasta in two large bowls and serve family-style.

Lapin à la Richard Olney

Richard Olney's writing on French country cooking always had a keen sense of place. In deference to him and the many brilliant works he left behind, we wait until late summer, when tomatoes are about to burst, to make this recipe, a bright rabbit braise charged with saffron and basil. The tomatoes are added at the end, along with cucumber and herbs—neither cooks, they are simply warmed through in the pot's residual heat so that their delicacy is preserved.

Whether it is served warm or at just above room temperature, this recipe never fails to transport us to Olliès-Toucas in southeastern France, where Olney lived.

Serve it with cooked lentils or cocos blancs (see page 15), drained and dressed with olive oil, along with blanched spinach (see page 12) and/or white rice.

Serves 6

1 whole rabbit (about 2½ pounds), broken down into 6 parts (see page 257)
Salt and freshly ground black pepper
Olive oil
1 medium red onion, thinly sliced
6 bay leaves
3 garlic cloves, thinly sliced
2 good pinches of saffron threads
4½ cups dry rosé (Bandol or similar would be luxurious)
1 pound heirloom tomatoes, cored and halved across their equator
2 medium cucumbers, peeled and halved lengthwise
½ cup basil leaves, plus (optional) more to garnish

Remove the rabbit from the fridge at least 40 minutes before cooking so it can come to room temperature. Pat it dry and season all over with salt and pepper. Preheat the oven to 375 degrees.

Set a wide heavy pot over medium heat and add ⅓ cup olive oil. When it is hot, add the rabbit, meaty side down (work in batches if necessary to avoid overcrowding), and sear until chestnut brown on the first side, about 6 minutes, then flip the pieces and sear on the other side for the same amount of time; adjust the temperature as necessary so the rabbit browns evenly and does not scorch. If the pot looks dry, add a little more oil. As each piece browns (some will cook more quickly than others), transfer it to a tray. Once all the rabbit is browned, remove the pot from the heat and pour off the oil.

Return the pot to medium-low heat and stir in 2 tablespoons fresh oil and the sliced onions. Season with salt and pepper and cook until the onions soften but do not color, about 4 minutes. Add the bay leaves, garlic, and saffron and sizzle until their aromas bloom but do not brown, 2 to 3 minutes. Add the rosé and 1 cup cold water, bring to a simmer, and simmer until the alcohol cooks off, about 5 minutes.

(Continued)

Nestle the rabbit pieces, meaty side up, into the onions in a single layer, turning some of the pieces on their side if necessary. Cover with a cartouche (see page 15) and then the lid. Move the pot to the oven and cook until the meat is falling from the bone, about 1 hour and 40 minutes.

MEANWHILE, PREPARE THE TOMATOES: Scoop out their seeds and pulp with a little spoon and then, while the tomatoes over a large bowl, tear them into chunky 2-inch wedges and drop into the bowl. Toss with salt to taste and about 1 tablespoon olive oil.

Cut the cucumber halves on the bias into 2-inch spears with a pointy tip. Add these to the bowl with the tomatoes. Roughly chop or tear in the basil leaves, then toss well. Check for seasoning and add salt as needed; the juices should taste light and bright.

When the rabbit is cooked, remove the pot from the oven and baste the pieces with the scented juices. Allow everything to settle for a few minutes, then stir in the tomatoes and cucumbers, scraping in all their juices and the basil. Let the pot's heat soften the fresh vegetables for a few minutes and toss again. Finish with a pour of olive oil, salt if needed, and, if you like, more torn fresh basil.

CHAPTER 12

Birds

IN TUSCAN VINEYARDS, WILD BIRDS ARE OFTEN SHOT TO PROTECT THE GRAPE CROP AS IT ripens. They are then cleaned and cooked in oversized hearths. At their simplest, they are eaten with their giblets and plenty of Sangiovese. That is the spirit that inspires us whenever birds pass through our kitchen.

While we have limited access to wild fowl in America, we have found guinea hens and quail rich in flavor. They both possess a coat of yellow fat, the sign of a life well lived. Of course, chickens will work in lieu of any other bird in this chapter's recipes—and we do include a recipe for chicken on page 291—but we urge you to branch out and discover the delights that guinea hens, quail, pheasant, teal, woodcock, and squab can offer. Their flavor is rich and gamy, and gnawing on their little bones is a delight.

We season all game heavily. If we're cooking a whole bird, we give the seasoning time to sink in; exactly how long depends on its size. Hard herbs and garlic are constants.

The grill is our favorite method for cooking game, whatever it may be. Small quail require very little time on a scorchingly hot grate, and off the heat, they don't require much of a rest. But larger birds, like guinea hens and pheasant, require lower, gentler heat as well as a slower cook; a steady medium fire is frequently best. Similarly, these require a longer rest after they've been pulled off the grate. Whatever the bird or its size, when it's time to head to the table, we pour over all its resting juices and, of course, some olive oil. Grilled spatchcocked birds benefit from the richness of soft (or grilled) polenta and beans. Many of our sauces—such as Aioli (page 22) or Bagna Cauda (page 24), as well as Anchovy Butter (page 177), Salsa Verde (page 33), and Ligurian Olive Sauce (page 30)—lend the following recipes additional stature. But often a simple lemon wedge is just perfect.

Some good supermarkets sell spatchcocked birds, and any good butcher will happily remove the backbone. Still, knowing how to do it oneself is gratifying (see page 281), and it's not difficult. Our hope is that with this chapter's recipes, along with the tips woven in, the appeal of game birds will become clear.

Grilled Spatchcocked Quail

Grilled quail need little adornment. They're ideal as starters, to get a barbeque going, or as a meal's centerpiece. For the latter, you'll need to serve two per person.

Spatchcocking quail means there's no wrangling meat off tiny bones at the table. It's simple enough, but you'll need a pair of good kitchen shears to do the job efficiently.

Serves 4 as a starter, 2 as a main

4 whole quails (about 3½ ounces each)
Salt and freshly ground black pepper

To spatchcock the quail, lay the bird breast side down on your work surface. Using kitchen shears, carefully cut down along either side of the backbone and remove it. Discard the backbone.

Splay open the quail, like a book, so it lies flat on a cutting board, and press down lightly on it with your palm to flatten it further. Flip it over and press on its arch, again using the palm of your hand, to flatten it. While it won't lie as flat as a penny, it should be fairly flat. Repeat with the remaining quail.

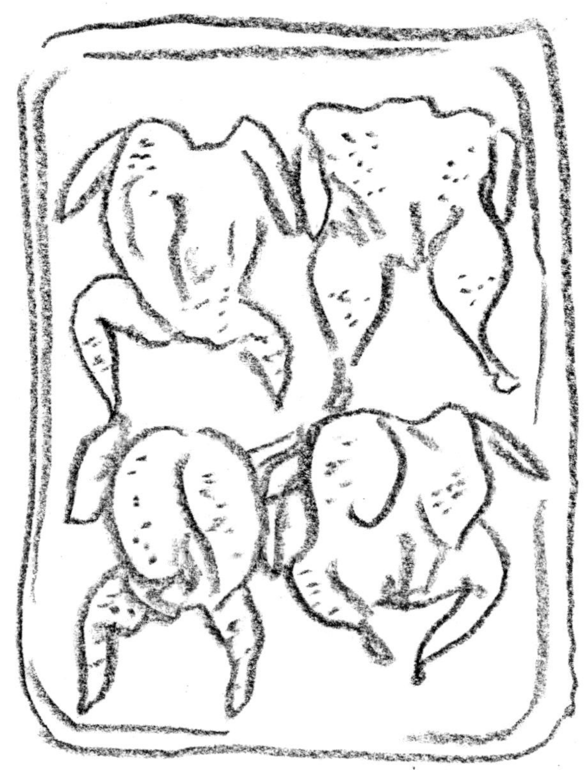

Set up a medium-hot fire in a grill and season all over with salt and pepper. As it heats, flatten each quail again and season with a bit more salt. When the grill is ready, lay the quail breast side down on the grate and leave undisturbed until grill marks appear and the meat closest to the flame turns opaque, about 7 minutes. Flip and grill on the other side until grill marks appear and the meat is cooked through, about 7 minutes more. To check for doneness, poke a knife into a thigh, near the bone, and peek: It should be slightly blush at the center but far from bloody.

Transfer the quail to a platter and let rest for a few minutes before serving. Finish with olive oil.

Grilled Quail, mustard frills, and Walnut Aillade (page 269)

Grilled Quail with Wax Beans with Anchovy and Basil (page 190)

Grilled Quail, Polenta (page 21), and Confit Chanterelles (page 192)

Grilled Quail, grilled Polenta (page 21), and Ligurian Olive Sauce (page 30)

Grilled Quail with
Favas Braised in Milk (page 179)

Grilled Quail, Lentils (page 20),
and Whipped Lardo (page 215)

Roasted Quail with a crostini and
Quince Preserves (page 38)

Roasted Quail with
Tortino di Indivia e Alici (page 202)

Spatchcocked Guinea Hen

with Crushed Potatoes, Olives, and Crème Fraîche

Find a plump, juicy guinea hen that looks as if she's enjoyed life. Her thick layer of fat will add flavor and protect the tender meat. It will render out in the pan as the hen cooks and leave you with the crispiest of skins.

Ask your butcher to spatchcock the guinea hen, or do it yourself (with a good pair of kitchen shears) by laying the bird breast side down on your work surface, cutting along either side of its backbone, and removing it (see page 281). Then squash the bird flat with a relative amount of force. Spatchocking a guinea hen is a bit more challenging than quail because it is bigger, but the same principles apply.

Serves 4

One 3- to 5-pound guinea hen, poussin, or chicken, spatchcocked (see headnote)
1½ pounds small potatoes, such as fingerling or Butterball, or new potatoes
Salt
3 garlic cloves
3 bay leaves
Freshly ground black pepper
Olive oil
¼ cup thyme leaves
½ cup Taggiasca olives, drained
¾ cup dry white wine
3 tablespoons crème fraîche

Remove the bird from the fridge at least 30 minutes before cooking so it can come to room temperature. Preheat the oven to 450 degrees.

Put the potatoes in a medium pot, along with a good pinch of salt, the garlic cloves, and bay leaves, add enough cold water to cover, and bring to a boil over medium-high heat. Reduce the heat slightly and simmer until the largest potato is easily pierced with a sharp knife, 8 to 10 minutes. Drain the potatoes, discard the garlic and bay leaves, and arrange the potatoes on a baking sheet in a single layer. With the heel of your palm, gently squash each one by applying enough pressure so the skins burst but the potato remains whole. This gives the potatoes a knobby surface that results in more crispy bits (the best bits!) when they are roasted. Season the potatoes with salt.

Generously season the guinea hen all over with salt and pepper. Choose a heavy ovenproof skillet that is large enough to comfortably hold the bird, set it over medium heat, and add 2½ tablespoons olive oil. Once the oil is hot, lay the bird skin side down in the pan and apply a weight, like a small frying pan, to help render the fat for the crispiest of skins. Whatever you choose, be sure it is heat-resistant. Lower the heat to medium-low and sear, without moving the bird, until the skin turns a deep golden brown, about 10 minutes. Be patient!

Turn off the heat, remove the weight, and flip the guinea hen over so its flesh sits in the rendered fat. Move the pan to the oven and roast until the juices run clear when the thickest part of the thigh is pierced but the meat remains a bit rosy at the center, about 40 minutes.

Meanwhile, heat another large ovenproof skillet, ideally one wide enough to hold the potatoes in a single layer, over medium heat. Spoon in some fat from the guinea hen's pan, about 2 or 3 tablespoons (duck fat or olive oil will work too). Add the potatoes to the hot skillet and cook until they brown and crisp. Turn them over and sprinkle over half the thyme and a tablespoon of olive oil. Move the pan to the oven's lowest rack and roast until the potatoes are deliciously crunchy, about 20 to 25 minutes; every 5 minutes or so, give the pan a hard shake to prevent sticking and ensure even cooking. Remove from the oven.

RETURN YOUR ATTENTION TO THE GUINEA HEN ONCE IT'S FINISHED ROASTING: Set the pan back on the stove and sprinkle over the olives and the remaining thyme. Drizzle on some olive oil, about a tablespoon, and turn the heat to medium. Once it is hot, add the wine to the pan (don't pour it over the bird) and simmer until the alcohol burns off, about 2 minutes. Dollop in the crème fraîche and stir it into the sauce. Spoon the olives and pan drippings over the bird's crisp skin, lacquering it, and heat for a minute.

Remove the pan from the heat and let the bird rest in the pan for at least 10 minutes, basting the skin with the pan sauce every now and again.

To serve, transfer the bird to a cutting board and carve it by separating the legs and slicing the breast much as you would for a chicken. Arrange the individual pieces on a platter and spoon the pan sauce and olives all around. Pile the crisp potatoes into a warm bowl and bring everything to the table.

Guinea Hen in Barolo

with Porcini and Radicchio

This recipe is prepared *alla cacciatore*, or "in the hunter's style." Woody herbs, red wine, and porcini mushrooms guarantee that this roast is robust and warming.

Nothing else is really needed here, but if you like, add some cooked lentils (see page 20) or blanched spinach (see page 12) to the table.

Serves 4

2 guinea hens (about 2 pounds each)
Salt and freshly ground black pepper
10 bay leaves
8 rosemary branches
⅔ cup dried porcini mushrooms
2 heads garlic, halved across their equators
1 large head radicchio, cut into 6 wedges
2 cups whole canned tomatoes, drained
2 cups Barolo or similar tannic red wine
Mild red wine vinegar for seasoning if needed
Olive oil

Remove the guinea hens from the fridge at least 40 minutes before cooking so they can come to room temperature. Peheat the oven to 500 degrees.

Season the guinea hens inside and out with salt and pepper. Stuff the cavities with 6 bay leaves and half the rosemary branches.

Choose a large pot that will hold the guinea hens with their accessories (wine, mushrooms, radicchio) comfortably. Once it is hot, add the birds, positioning them so one side of the breasts faces down. Lower the heat to medium-high and sear until golden brown, 3 or so minutes. Turn the hens so the other side of the breasts faces down and brown on that side, about 3 minutes. Lastly, turn the hens breast side up and brown the undersides, 3 to 5 minutes.

Transfer the pot to the oven and roast for 20 minutes.

Meanwhile, place the porcini mushrooms in a small bowl and pour over just enough boiling water to submerge them. Let soak until plump and spongy, 5 to 10 minutes.

Remove the porcini, squeezing the excess liquid back into the bowl, and set them aside. Strain the soaking liquid through a sieve lined with cheesecloth (or use a tea strainer!) and discard the grit.

Pull the pot with the half-cooked hens from the oven (leave the oven on) and set it back on the stovetop over medium heat. Nestle in the split garlic heads, placing them cut side down. Scatter the porcini mushrooms around. Add the remaining bay and rosemary and then add the radicchio wedges, scooching them in cut sides down. Cook until the porcini and the radicchio wedges brown on the first side, about 5 minutes, then stir in the tomatoes, red wine, and reserved porcini liquor. Season with salt and generously drizzle over olive oil, 2 to 3 tablepoons.

Return the pot to the oven and braise until the guinea hens are cooked through, 20 to 25 minutes more. Check for doneness by poking around a leg joint with a knife: A little pinkness is good; blood is not. The joints should feel nimble and wiggle easily when jostled. Remove the pot from the oven and let the birds rest for at least 10 minutes.

Transfer the birds to a cutting board and carve them like chicken. Lay the parts on a warm platter, and set the carcass aside for a stockpot down the road or discard.

Taste the pan sauce and adjust the seasoning with salt and/or acid as needed—we like to use a mild red wine vinegar here. Spoon the roasted vegetables and pan sauce all around the platter of guinea hen. Pour over all the juices from the cutting board. Season with olive oil and serve immediately.

Salt-Baked Figgy Quail
Stuffed with Rice

Figgy quail are otherworldly. The fig leaves used to wrap the quail infuse them with their sweet, coconut-y perfume. Stuffed with rice and bundled, the quail roast under a salt crust so none of the aroma escapes and the meat cooks through evenly. As an accompaniment, there are roasted figs.

You will need a lot of fig leaves for this dish. We suggest finding someone with a tree and asking for some of their trimmings. If you can't find fig leaves (available in the fall at peak season), fresh grape leaves will do nicely as a wrapping for the quail, but they won't work as a substitute elsewhere in this dish.

Serves 4

FOR THE RICE STUFFING

2 cups basmati rice
Salt
4 large fig leaves
4 sprigs of thyme
4 garlic cloves

FOR THE QUAIL

4 quail (a bit more than a pound each), cleaned and gutted
Salt and freshly ground black pepper
10 tablespoons (1¼ sticks) unsalted butter, at room temperature
3 tablespoons thyme leaves
12 large fig leaves, soaked in cold water
6 cups culinary rock salt

FOR THE FIGS

4 tablespoons unsalted butter, at room temperature
8 large fig leaves
4 cups figs, stems removed and torn in half
Maldon salt and freshly ground black pepper
1 cup Beaujolais or similar juicy red wine
3 tablespoons thyme leaves

SPECIAL EQUIPMENT: Kitchen twine

Preheat the oven to 375 degrees. To make the stuffing, put the rice in a sieve and rinse it under cold water until the water runs clear. Drain and set aside.

Set a medium pot filled with 3 quarts water over high heat, add 1 tablespoon salt, the fig leaves, thyme, and garlic, and bring to a boil. Add the rice, reduce the heat, and simmer for 5 minutes (set a timer!). Drain the parcooked rice and spread it out on a tray so it quickly cools to room temperature.

To prepare the quail, season their cavities with salt and pepper. Stuff each with some of the cooled rice, filling the cavity by just over three-quarters. Truss the legs with kitchen twine, tying them firmly together to seal the cavity. Rub some of the softened butter all over the quail, coating the skin generously. Sprinkle the butter coating with salt, pepper, and the thyme leaves.

(Continued)

Lay a fig leaf on a work surface. Place a quail in its center and lay another fig leaf on top. Wrap the lower leaf up and around the bird, pressing it into the butter coating. Wrap the top leaf over the first leaf and use more of the softened butter to seal the leaves together and set the wrapping in place. Wrap the remaining quail in the same fashion.

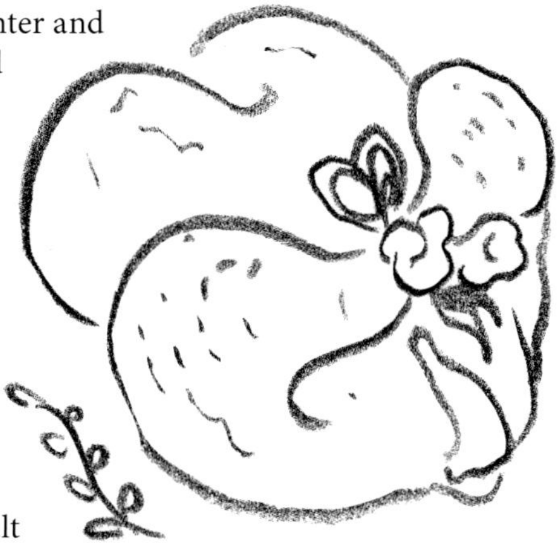

Preheat the oven to 450 degrees. To prepare the figs, grease a 10-inch cast iron skillet large enough to fit the quail snugly with half of the softened butter. Dip the fig leaves in cool water to soften them and prevent them from singeing, pat them dry, and lay them over the bottom of the pan. Toss the figs with salt and pepper, the wine, and thyme in a large bowl. Arrange the figs on the leaves and dot the fruit with the remaining butter. Set aside.

To bake the quail, add the rock salt to a medium bowl and add ½ cup cold water. Mix together until the consistency resembles wet sand; you may need to add more water. Line the bottom of a skillet with one-quarter of the salt mixture. Nestle the fig-leaf wrapped quail in the salt bed and then completely cover each one with the remaining salt mix, forming a snowy mound.

Bake the figs and quail in the oven for 15 minutes—the kitchen will smell incredible! Pull both pans from the oven and let them rest for at least 15 minutes to allow the residual heat to gently finish cooking the figs and birds.

To serve, crack open the salt crusts with the back of a knife and remove and discard the top crusts, then sweep away as much of the remaing salt as possible, with increasing care as you near the fig wrapping. Remove the quail from their salt bed and brush off all salty granules with a pastry brush.

Carefully arrange the bundled birds on a serving platter or on individual plates and serve with the baked figs and plenty of their juices.

Tunisian Chicken

This egg-enriched soup was inspired by the Tunisian tharíd soup in Clifford A. Wright's book *A Mediterranean Feast*. Wright asserts that a version of this was one of Prophet Muhammad's favorites.

The original calls for bread and chickpeas. Instead, we use fregola, and we add lots of fresh parsley. The broth is tinged with cinnamon and sweetened with tender carrots.

Chicken's mild flavor makes it ideal for this dish because it won't overshadow the slightly creamy spiced broth.

Serves 4

One 4-pound chicken
2 quarts chicken stock, homemade (see page 35)
1 yellow onion, quartered
6 thin celery stalks from the inside of a bunch, roughly chopped
3 medium carrots, peeled and roughly chopped
2 bay leaves
4 whole black peppercorns
A small handful of thyme sprigs
A small handful of sage sprigs
A small handful of parsley stems (optional)

FOR THE STEW

Salt and freshly ground black pepper
3 cinnamon sticks
2 cups fregola
4 medium carrots, peeled and sliced into 2-inch batons
2 large eggs
Juice of 1 lemon
Olive oil
½ cup chopped parsley to garnish

Plop the chicken into a large tall pot. Add the chicken stock, onion, celery, carrots, bay leaves, peppercorns, thyme, sage, and parsley stems, if you have them, then add enough cold water to cover everything by 1 to 2 inches and bring to a simmer over medium heat.

While the chicken poaches, skim off any foam that rises to the surface so the broth remains clear. After the broth has simmered for an hour, check that the meat is cooked by wiggling the legs: They should feel relaxed. Pierce the joint where the leg meets the breast with a sharp knife: The juices should run clear. If they do not, continue simmering for 5 to 10 minutes more. Remove the pot from the heat and let the chicken relax in the broth for 30 minutes.

Transfer the chicken to a large bowl and let it cool to room temperature. Strain the broth through a sieve into a clean pot; press on the captured vegetables and aromatics to release all the liquid, then dispose of them. Pour any juices in the chicken's bowl into the strained broth. Set aside.

(Continued)

To make the stew, remove and discard the chicken's skin. Carve the meat into gnawable pieces: Remove the legs and separate the drumsticks from the thighs, cut the breasts in half (leave them bone-in or not, your choice), and cut off the wings; set aside. Resolve to use the carcass for another broth later in the week, if you like; or, if that is too optimistic, freeze it for another time or discard.

Season the chicken pieces generously on all sides with salt and freshly grated cinnamon (simply run one stick over a Microplane)—the chicken should be covered in a blanket of cinnamon, 2 to 3 teaspoons.

Add 2 quarts of the broth (reserve any remaining broth for another use) and the remaining 2 cinnamon sticks to a large pot and bring to a boil over medium-high heat. Taste and season with enough salt so the broth is very flavorful. Stir in the fregola and carrots and cook until both are tender but retain some bite, about 10 to 15 minutes. Turn off the heat.

Warm a large skillet over medium heat and add 2 tablespoons olive oil. When it is hot but not scorching, reduce the heat to low and add the chicken "skin side" down (yes, there is no skin now, but there once was) and sear until evenly browned on the first side, 3 to 4 minutes. (Work in batches if necessary to avoid overcrowding.) Flip the chicken pieces and brown on the other side, 3 or so minutes more. Remove from the heat and set aside.

Now, begin the egg liaison—this may feel cheffy, but be brave!

Beat the eggs together with the lemon juice in a medium bowl. Whisking constantly to avoid scrambling the eggs, slowly dribble in a ladleful of the hot chicken stock (try to leave the carrots and fregola behind), pouring it down the side of the bowl to temper the heat. Once the first ladleful is safely incorporated, add another just as carefully, and continue adding ladlefuls until you have a deliciously rich, silky sauce. Let it cool slightly if necessary, so it feels just warm to the touch, then pour it into the pot of broth and stir to combine.

Quickly bring the pot to the table and dole out servings into bowls, making sure there is plenty of eggy broth as well as chicken, carrots, and fregola in each serving. Finish with an olive oil drizzle and plenty of chopped parsley sprinkled over.

Duck Legs Braised in Beaujolais

with Prunes and Thyme

This meal epitomizes fall in France's Rhône Valley. A fruity Beaujolais gives a dose of acid, balancing the richness of the prune, duck, and lardons.

We serve this with cooked white beans, cocos blancs, or flageolets (see page 15).

Serves 4

4 whole duck legs (3½ to 4 pounds total)
Salt and freshly ground black pepper
1 cup diced (a bit over ½-inch) well-marbled bacon
2 medium shallots, finely diced
½ cup finely chopped thyme leaves
3 garlic cloves, thinly sliced
2 cups Beaujolais or other light young red wine
1 cup chicken stock, homemade (see page 35) or store-bought, plus more if needed
1 cup pitted prunes

Preheat the oven to 400 degrees. Remove the duck legs from the refrigerator and season all over with salt and pepper. Let them come to room temperature.

Set a heavy large pot over medium-low heat and add the duck legs, skin side down. Cook to gently render the fat and brown the skin, going slow and low to prevent scorching, about 30 minutes. Then increase the heat to medium or medium-high to give the skin a rich brown color if necessary. Flip the legs and sear the flesh side until chestnut brown, about 3 minutes more. Transfer the ducks to a tray.

Reduce the heat under the pot to medium-low and stir in the diced bacon. Cook gently, stirring to render out the fat without browning the bacon. With a slotted spoon, transfer the bacon to the tray with the legs and pour off all but a thin layer of fat from the pot.

Stir the shallots into the pot and cook, stirring occasionally, until they soften but do not color, about 5 minutes. Add the thyme and garlic and cook until the aromatics bloom, 2 to 3 minutes. Return the duck legs and bacon to the pot, along with any accumulated juices, turn the heat up to high, and add the Beaujolais and chicken stock; there should be enough liquid to submerge the legs by three-quarters so the skin remains just above the fray. Bring the liquid to a simmer, then turn off the heat and cover the legs with a cartouche (see page 15) and then the lid.

Slide the pot into the oven and braise until the legs have cooked through but the meat isn't so tender it is falling off the bones, about 45 minutes. Remove from the oven and transfer the duck to a tray, leaving the braising liquid and bacon behind in the pot.

Add the prunes and then return the legs, along with all their puddled juices, to the pot. Cover again with the cartouche and lid, return the pot to the oven, and continue cooking until the meat is spoon-soft, about 1 hour longer. Remove from the oven and let it rest for at least 15 minutes.

Just before serving, spoon off the excess fat that has risen to the surface. Taste the juices for seasoning.

Cassoulet Toulousain

We first served cassoulet at King for New Year's Eve in 2020. Days were spent preparing all the meal's components: brining the duck legs, soaking the beans, making and hanging the sausages. . . . If you take the same approach, this Toulousain classic will feel more manageable.

You can brine the duck legs up to a week out. Confit them in fat and let them cool in their fat until needed (they will last almost indefinitely in the fridge like this). A couple of days before you will be serving the cassoulet, soak and cook the beans and braise the pork belly. You can cook the belly and duck legs at the same time and store them both for a day or two.

On the day of your party, all that should remain is searing the sausages and baking the cassoulet. Serve warm bread and a huge bowl of lightly dressed mustard leaves.

Serves 10 to 14

FOR THE DUCK CONFIT

10 bone-in, skin-on duck legs
Kosher salt
12 whole black peppercorns
A handful of thyme branches
A handful of sage branches
2 quarts duck fat, available at specialty butcher shops or online
5 fresh Toulouse sausages

FOR THE PORK BELLY

2 pieces of nutmeg
9 garlic cloves
Kosher salt and freshly ground black pepper
Olive oil
One 2- to 3-pound slab pork belly, skin removed and cut into 8 equal pieces
2 shallots, diced
4 thin celery stalks from the inside of a bunch
2 medium carrots, peeled and thinly sliced
¼ cup chopped thyme leaves
½ cup sage leaves, thinly sliced
4 canned whole tomatoes, drained
3 garlic cloves, thinly sliced
1 cup dry white wine
4 cups chicken stock, homemade (see page 35) or store-bought, plus more if needed

FOR THE BEANS

3¼ cups small white beans, preferably Tarbais (or cocos blanc, navy beans, or flageolet beans)
1 large red onion
8 to 10 whole cloves
1 smoked ham hock or pork knuckle (about 1 pound)
1 head of garlic, split across the equator
A small handful of sage branches
A small handful of thyme branches
2 to 3 large celery stalks from the outside of a bunch
1 large carrot
A few parsley stems (optional)
1 fresh Holland chili or a medium mild dried chili
Kosher salt

FOR THE SAUSAGES

6 fresh Toulouse sausages, available at specialty butchers or online (or any herby, garlicky sausage)
Olive oil or duck fat

6 tablespoons roughly chopped thyme leaves

Begin by seasoning the duck legs: Lay them in a deep roasting pan that's large enough to hold them in a snug single layer. Sprinkle over ½ cup kosher salt and the peppercorns. Scatter the thyme and sage branches over and around them. Massage the seasonings into the legs, coating them evenly. Cover with plastic wrap and refrigerate for at least 24 hours (or up to 4 days).

TO PREPARE THE PORK BELLY, START BY MAKING A RUB: Finely grate the nutmeg into a mortar. Add 6 of the garlic cloves and bash them a few times with the pestle. Add a good pinch of kosher salt, some pepper, and about a tablespoon of olive oil and keep bashing until a smooth paste forms. (Alternatively, if you don't have a mortar and pestle, smash the garlic and salt to a paste on your cutting board using the flat side of a chef's knife. Transfer the paste to a bowl, grate over the nutmeg, and stir in the olive oil and pepper.) Massage the rub into the belly, coating each piece evenly. Place the pork belly on a tray, cover with plastic wrap, and refrigerate for up to 24 hours.

MEANWHILE, SOAK THE BEANS: Add them to a large bowl and cover with plenty of cold water. Let soak overnight on the kitchen counter or hold in the fridge for up to 48 hours.

BACK TO THE DUCK CONFIT: Remove the legs from the fridge at least 40 minutes before cooking so they can come to room temperature. Preheat the oven to 225 degrees.

Put the (likely solidified) duck fat in a large pot set over very low heat and warm it gently so it liquefies but does not come to a simmer, 5 to 10 minutes; do not let it bubble! Alternatively, let it come to room temperature over several hours in a warm kitchen. Either way, pour the duck fat over the duck legs in the roasting pan, adding enough to mostly submerge them. Lay a cartouche (see page 15) over the top and then carefully move the pan to the oven. Let confit until the legs wiggle easily at their joints and the meat slides off the bone, 5 to 6½ hours; while you want the legs tender, they shouldn't cook to the point of shredding.

Remove the legs from the oven and let them cool in their fat. If necessary, you can use the legs as soon as they've cooled to room temperature (at least 1 to 2 hours), but they will taste far, far better if they rest, in their fat bath, for at least 24 hours in the refrigerator.

For the pork belly, remove it from the fridge at least 40 minutes before cooking so it too can come to room temperature. Then season it on all sides with more salt and pepper.

Set a large wide pot over medium heat and add 2 tablespoons olive oil (or, if you like, use some of the duck fat). When the oil is hot, working in batches so as not to overcrowd the pot, add the belly, and brown each piece on all sides, adjusting the temperature if necessary to prevent scorching, 5 to 6 minutes per side; do not turn the pieces of belly until golden. Then remove the seared pieces from the pot and transfer to a tray. Turn off the heat and allow the fat to cool slightly, then pour off all but 2 to 3 tablespoons of it.

Place the pot back on the stove and stir in the shallots, celery, carrots, chopped thyme, and sliced sage. Cook over low heat, stirring occasionally, until the shallots are translucent but have not colored, 5 to 7 minutes. Season this sofrito with salt and pepper, then add the canned tomatoes and sliced garlic and cook until the garlic has lost its bite but not colored, about 5 minutes. Splash in the white wine and let it bubble until the alcohol cooks off, about 2 minutes.

(Continued)

Return the browned belly to the pot, nestling it into a single layer (it's fine if the pieces are snugly packed), and add enough chicken stock to cover the pieces by three-quarters. Cover the braise with a cartouche (see page 15) and then the lid.

Transfer the pot to the oven and braise the belly at 225 degrees until the pieces turn soft, about 2 hours.

Remove the belly from the oven, taste a piece of it, and take a sip of the braising liquid. Season both with salt as necessary.

As with the legs, it's best to hold the belly in its cooking liquid for a day or so before assembling the cassoulet. Once cooled, remove and discard any excess fat that rises to the top.

NOW FOR THE BEANS: Drain them in a colander and rinse under cold running water. Halve the red onion, slicing it through its equator, and stud the cut sides with the cloves. Add the beans and onion to a large wide pot along with the ham hock, split garlic, sage, thyme, celery, carrot, parsley, if using, and chili. Cover with enough cold water to submerge everything by 2 inches and then cover with another cartouche. Bring to a simmer over medium heat and simmer until the beans are tender but still retain their shape, about 2 hours; remove the cartouche every now and then and skim off any foam and impurities that have risen to the surface. If the water runs low at any point, top it up, adding enough water to keep the beans submerged by at least ½ inch. To check that they've cooked nicely, taste 5 beans from different parts of the pot—each should be soft throughout.

Remove the pot from the heat and discard the garlic and herbs; season the beans with salt to taste. Once it is cool enough to handle, transfer the ham hock to a cutting board. Using a fork, or your hands, shred the meat off the bone. Stir the meaty shreds back into the pot and discard the bone. Let the beans cool completely in their liquid, at least 1 hour; they can be held in the fridge, covered, for a day.

When you're ready to assemble the cassoulet, prick the sausages all over with a fork. Set a wide heavy skillet over medium heat and add 2 tablespoons olive oil (or duck fat). Add the sausages (cook them in two batches if necessary to avoid overcrowding) and cook, turning occasionally until browned on all sides, about 5 minutes (you do not want these fully cooked, just nicely colored). Turn off the heat.

Increase the oven temperature to 400 degrees and choose a large deep baking dish or casserole that that will hold everything snugly (if necessary, use two dishes). Use some of the fat from the duck confit to generously grease the dish.

With a slotted spoon, transfer enough of the beans to the baking dish to line the bottom with a 1-inch-thick layer. Leaving most of the pan drippings behind, transfer the belly, sausages, and duck legs to the dish, distributing them evenly. Lift the remaining beans from their pot and scatter them around the meats.

Add a couple of spoonfuls of cooked vegetables from the pork belly to the baking dish. Dot the top of the cassoulet with 2 tablespoons of the duck fat. Sprinkle half the thyme leaves over the cassoulet.

Bake the cassoulet on the oven's upper rack until a golden crust has formed, about 40 minutes. Scatter over the remaining thyme, and allow the cassoulet to settle before serving.

CHAPTER 13

Desserts

If even a morsel of effort has gone into preparing a meal, it would be a shame to waste the opportunity of serving a dessert. Or a pud, as we Brits call it.

No matter what form the meal takes—simple, lazy, indulgent—dessert is your final hoorah. And it should arrive at the table with an element of cheer, although it needn't be extravagant. Even a bowl of ripe cherries plonked down for grazing will do nicely. But there are times for something a little more. . . .

While the savory menu at King is small, our list of puds is mighty! And while most of our cooking leans French and Italian, when it comes to the last course, we return to England just as often.

Fiona Thomas heads up our dessert department, tracking each season with scoops, slices, and dollops. The first of any season's haul, especially in the warmer months, often goes straight from the punnet to the plate, needing little more than a spoonful of softly whipped cream. As summer dwindles, we add the more mature fruits to cakes and tarts: time in the oven enhances the natural sugars and masks any textural imperfections. At the very end of their run, we turn fruit into jams and compotes, pots bubbling away on the stove. It's a bid to enjoy the fruits for a little longer than nature intended. Once jarred, these ripple through ice creams and glaze tarts, and fill galettes.

In fall, there are apples and pears. A little later, by the time quinces and citrus arrive, we've fully embraced winter and its hearty desserts, serving sweets straight from the oven and doused in cream. These warm, sticky puds rely heavily on our pantry's nuts and dried fruits. Often they ask for a good hit of booze to keep things toasty.

And there is chocolate! We serve just one chocolate dessert: the King Chocolate Cake. Originally it started off as a tart, which we now serve at home and have included here, but over the years, it evolved into a flourless cake. Simple, very beloved, very rich and very indulgent, it ticks all chocolate boxes.

Olive Oil Cake

A much-loved classic, nutty and not too sweet. While this cake feels quintessentially Italian, our recipe is actually adapted from a recipe from the great British food writer Diana Henry.

Make sure to use stale bread, which you must turn into fine crumbs before using. Do not use store-bought panko! Also, know that the quality of your olive oil will define this cake's flavor.

This cake keeps for days—but it won't last that long.

Serves 10

A few tablespoons of softened butter for greasing the pan
1¾ cups (210 grams) blanched almonds, ground
Leaves from 3 sprigs of rosemary, very finely chopped
1½ cups (120 grams) white bread crumbs, made by removing crusts and blitzed in a food processor
½ cup (75 grams) coarse polenta
1 tablespoon baking powder
1¾ cups (375 grams) granulated sugar
Finely grated zest of 3 lemons, lemons reserved for juicing
6 large eggs
1½ cups (300 grams) olive oil

SPECIAL EQUIPMENT: A 3-inch-deep, 8- to 9-inch round cake pan

Preheat the oven to 350 degrees. Generously butter the cake pan. Line the bottom with a round of parchment paper cut to fit. Now cut 2 strips of parchment to line the pan's sides; these should overlap and form a collar that stands 2 inches above the rim.

Combine the ground almonds, rosemary, breadcrumbs, polenta, and baking powder in a large bowl. Set aside.

Place the sugar in a medium bowl and rub the lemon zest into it with your fingertips, distributing it evenly; stop mixing once your sugar resembles wet sand. Use a whisk and elbow grease to beat the eggs into the lemon sugar so everything comes together, 2 to 3 minutes. (Whisking by hand guards against overmixing.)

Juice 2 of the lemons, to yield ½ cup juice (you might need the third lemon); we always strain our lemon juice and suggest you do the same. Stream the olive oil and lemon juice into the bowl with the beaten eggs, stirring until uniformly combined. Pour the wet ingredients into the dry ingredients and stir until just combined.

Scrape the batter into the prepared pan. Bake in the oven until the cake is golden and the sides pull away from the parchment lining, about 60 minutes. Halfway through, rotate the pan 180 degrees. To test for doneness, poke the cake's center with a cake tester or toothpick: It should emerge batter-free but a little oily. If a few fine crumbs are attached, no problem.

Remove from the oven and let the cake rest for at least 15 minutes before unmolding it and slicing.

Ricotta and Pine Nut Cake

Another recipe from Tina, King's head chef. But this time, it's actually her husband, Chuck, who deserves the credit.

After she told him about the challenges in finding a ricotta cake that has the structure of a cheesecake but not the dense texture, he suggested modifying a simple pound cake recipe. That did it!

It's perfectly delicious for breakfast or tea on its own; we also serve slices with baked fruit.

Serves 10

8 ounces (2 sticks/340 grams) unsalted butter, plus more for greasing the cake pan
¾ cup (120 grams) pine nuts
2¼ cups (350 grams) all-purpose flour
4 teaspoons (14 grams) baking powder
Kosher salt
3 cups (600 grams) granulated sugar
Finely grated zest of 1 orange
Finely grated zest of 2 lemons
6 medium eggs
1 pound 9 ounces (730 grams) ricotta
¼ cup (40 grams) lemon or orange juice, or a combination

SPECIAL EQUIPMENT:
A 3-inch-deep, 8- to 9-inch round cake pan

Preheat the oven to 350 degrees. Generously butter the cake pan. Line the bottom with a round of parchment paper cut to fit. Cut 2 strips of parchment to line the sides; these should overlap and form a collar that stands 2 inches above the rim.

Place the pine nuts in a medium bowl and pour over just enough hot water to cover. Let soak until the nuts are thoroughly moistened, about 10 minutes.

Meanwhile, combine the flour, baking powder, and 2 teaspoons salt in a medium bowl. Set aside.

In the bowl of a stand mixer fitted with the paddle attachment, or in a large bowl using a handheld mixer, cream the butter and sugar with the orange and lemon zests on medium speed. When the butter is pale and has doubled in volume, about 5 minutes, crack in the eggs one at a time, beating until each one is incorporated before adding the next. Pause to scrape down the sides as necessary.

Add half the dry ingredients to the creamed butter, mixing just until combined. Add the ricotta and the citrus juice, mixing until combined. Add the remaining dry ingredients, mixing until just uniform. Overmixing will aerate the batter, and we want this cake dense.

Spread the batter evenly in the lined cake pan. Remove the pine nuts from their bath and pat them dry. Sprinkle them over the cake's top, lightly pressing them into the batter (they should remain exposed but stay put).

Bake the cake in the oven, rotating the cake pan 180 degrees every 30 minutes, until it is golden and pulls away from the pan's sides, about 90 minutes. It should feel springy when pressed at its center, and a cake tester inserted into the cake's center should emerge clean.

Remove the cake from the oven and let rest for at least 15 minutes before unmolding and slicing.

Peach and Polenta Cake

Stone fruit makes the best bottoms—or tops—for cakes: plums, apricots, or nectarines, or a mixture of all the above. But figs and apples also give us a good excuse to make this deliciously moist cake, a fixture at King throughout the year.

Don't be tempted to use a springform pan, as it will leak. This makes a large cake, but it keeps for almost a week and is also delicious for breakfast.

Serves 10 to 12

Butter for greasing the cake pan
8 to 10 (approximately 2¼ pounds/1,000 grams) peaches, nectarines, or plums, or a mix, halved and pitted

FOR THE CARAMEL

2 cups (400 grams) sugar
4 tablespoons (60 grams) unsalted butter

FOR THE CAKE BATTER

2 cups (225 grams) blanched whole or slivered almonds
1⅓ cups (210 grams) coarse polenta
1⅓ cups (190 grams) all-purpose flour
Kosher salt
2¼ teaspoons baking powder
14 ounces (3 sticks plus 4 tablespoons/395 grams) unsalted butter, at room temperature
2 cups plus 1 tablespoon (415 grams) granulated sugar
Finely grated zest of 2 lemons, plus juice from 1 of the lemons, strained
6 large eggs

Crème fraîche for serving

SPECIAL EQUIPMENT: A 2-inch-deep, 12-inch round cake pan

Preheat the oven to 350 degrees. Generously butter the cake pan. Line the bottom with a round of parchment paper cut to fit. Now cut 2 strips of parchment to line the pan's sides; these should overlap and form a collar that stands 2 inches above the rim.

To make the caramel, combine the sugar and water in a small heavy pot and heat over high heat, swirling the pan often but not stirring, until the sugar dissolves, then continue cooking until an amber-colored caramel forms, 12 to 14 minutes.

Remove the pan from the heat and add 2 tablespoons of the butter to the caramel, swirling to combine. Immediately pour the hot caramel into the prepared cake pan and carefully shimmy it around to coat the bottom evenly. Arrange the fruit cut sides down evenly over the caramel. Tear up and squish in any extra pieces of fruit as needed to fill up all the nooks and crannies (no gaps should remain!); keep in mind that the fruit will shrink as it bakes. Set the pan aside.

To make the batter, add the almonds and polenta to a food processor and pulse until the mixture has the texture of fine cornmeal, 2 to 3 minutes. Pour the mixture into a large bowl and stir in the flour, ½ teaspoon salt, and the baking powder.

(Continued)

In the bowl of a stand mixer fitted with the paddle attachment, or in a large bowl using a handheld mixer, beat the butter and sugar together at medium speed, until the butter is whipped and pale, about 5 minutes. Crack in the eggs, beating them in one at a time and making sure each is incorporated before adding the next.

Remove the bowl from the mixer stand, if using, and scrape in the dry ingredients. Add the lemon zest and lemon juice and fold everything together until smooth and uniform. Pour the batter into the cake pan, spreading it evenly.

Bake the cake in the oven, rotating the pan 180 degrees every 30 minutes or so for even browning, until it is golden and the center feels firm to the poke, 1 hour and 40 minutes to 2 hours. A cake tester inserted into the center should come out clean. Remove the cake from the oven and let cool completely on a rack.

To unmold the cake, first loosen and then remove the parchment paper from the pan's sides. Run a paring knife around the inside of the pan to ensure complete separation. Set a serving platter that is larger than the pan over the top and, holding the platter firmly, flip the cake over and onto the plate. Shimmy the pan for encouragement and ease it up and off, then carefully peel away the parchment paper from the bottom of the cake. If any caramelized fruit sticks, peel it off the paper and set it back into place on the cake.

Serve slices with dollops of crème fraîche.

King's Christmas Cake

Traditional British Christmas cakes are layered with marzipan and finished with royal icing. That tradition was abandoned at our home thirty years ago, when my mother found me and my siblings nibbling off the icing from the cake she had prepared weeks prior. Our punishment was a bare cake—and we've not seen an iced one since.

King's recipe has been slightly adapted, but it is still served without the finishing touches of the icing. We prefer the simplicity of a plain fruitcake. You'll need to soak the dried fruit for at least 3 days before making this—the dried fruit must fully swell to keep the cake's dense crumb moist for months.

—Jess

Serves 8

¾ cup (200 grams) currants
¾ cup (200 grams) sultanas (golden raisins)
¾ cup (100 grams) raisins
¾ cup (200 grams) dried figs, roughly chopped
2 cups (400 grams) whiskey
1 tablespoon apricot jam or marmalade
9 tablespoons (125 grams) unsalted butter, at room temperature, plus more for greasing the cake pan
½ cup plus 1 tablespoon (125 grams) packed dark brown sugar
4 large eggs
¾ cup plus 2 tablespoons (130 grams) all-purpose flour, sifted
½ teaspoon baking powder
½ teaspoon ground cinnamon
¼ teaspoon ground cloves
¼ teaspoon freshly grated nutmeg
1¾ cups (200 grams) walnuts, half finely chopped and the other half roughly chopped
Kosher salt
Finely grated zest of 1 orange
Finely grated zest of 1 lemon

SPECIAL EQUIPMENT: An 8- to 9-inch springform cake pan

Place all the dried fruit in a large sealable container, add the whiskey and marmalade, and mix well. Seal the container and let the fruit macerate for at least 3 days in the fridge. Now and again, as the fruit soaks, stir it to distribute the liquor.

Before baking, remove the fruit from the fridge. Preheat the oven to 350 degrees. Generously butter the cake pan. Line the bottom with a round of parchment paper cut to fit. Now cut 2 strips of parchment to line the pan's sides; these should overlap and form a collar that stands 2 inches above the rim.

In the bowl of a stand mixer fitted with the paddle attachment, or using a large bowl and a handheld mixer, beat the butter and sugar together at medium speed until pale yellow

(Continued)

and creamy, about 5 minutes. Beat in the eggs one by one, making sure each one is fully incorporated before adding the next.

Reduce the speed to low, add the dry ingredients, and mix until incorporated. Scrape in all the nuts, the boozy fruit plus all the soaking juices, and the orange and lemon zests and beat just until everything is evenly dispersed.

Pour the batter into the prepared cake pan and smooth the top. Make a shallow well into the center to prevent a bloated dome from developing as the cake bakes. Bake in the oven until the top is cracked and dark golden brown and a cake tester inserted into the cake's center comes out clean, about 2 hours. Remove the cake from the oven and let cool completely in the pan on a rack.

Remove the cake from the pan and peel off the parchment from the bottom of it. Wrap the cake in parchment paper, put it in an airtight container, and let it age for at least a week at cool room temperature. It will hold for up to 3 months.

Eton Mess

In our opinion, British desserts are some of the world's best: unassuming, comforting, very forgiving. Eton Mess is all of these things: it combines meringue, berries, and whipped cream, stirred up in a bowl—the "mess."

Rhubarb, blackberries, elderberries, and raspberries all make delicious variations, but nothing beats the classic, and so in this recipe we call for only strawberries. If your fruit needs additional sweetness, add a little powdered sugar to the cream before whipping.

Serves 6

FOR THE MERINGUE

1 cup (200 grams) granulated sugar
⅓ cup (80 grams) egg whites (about 3 large egg whites)
Delicate pinch of cream of tartar
1 teaspoon cornstarch
1 teaspoon white vinegar

FOR THE FRUIT FILLING

1 quart heavy cream
1 pint fresh strawberries, hulled and halved, or quartered if large

To make the meringue, preheat the oven to 275 degrees. Blitz the sugar in a food processor until it resembles dust, about 1 minute.

In the bowl of a stand mixer fitted with the whisk attachment, or using a medium bowl and a handheld mixer, beat the egg whites and cream of tartar together at medium speed until foamy, about 3 minutes. Slowly beat in the blitzed sugar, adding it one large spoonful at a time, and then continue beating until the egg whites are glossy and hold soft peaks. Beat in the cornstarch and vinegar and continue beating until the meringue is brilliantly white and holds stiff peaks—a pointy tip at the end of a lifted whisk or, if you're feeling brave, the famed upturned-bowl-over-the-head trick.

Spoon the meringue onto a baking sheet lined with parchment paper and swirl it into a shallow mound that sits about 2 inches high (the shape itself doesn't matter much). Bake in the oven until a delicate crust forms but the meringue hasn't fully baked through, about 1 hour. Turn the oven temperature down to 150 degrees and continue baking until the meringue is snow-white and crisp but not chalky, about 1½ hours more. Don't be tempted to take a peek until toward the end of the baking time—opening the door frequently will lower the oven temperature.

When the meringue is done, turn off the oven and leave the meringue in the oven for 30 minutes longer so it dries out further. Remove from the oven and let cool completely. The baked meringue holds in an airtight container at room temperature for 2 days.

To assemble the mess, whip the cream in a clean bowl until it holds soft peaks, 4 to 6 minutes.

Crumble the meringue into a large bowl, breaking it into knobbly pieces about the size of a walnut.

Gently fold the whipped cream and strawberries into the meringue, marbling everything together. Serve immediately.

Tiramisu

The word *tiramisù* means "pick me up" in Italian. But ours rather bowls you over, as it is doused in equal parts booze and espresso. Best not to plan on getting much done after eating it.

For the uninitiated, tiramisu layers together soaked sponge cake (or ladyfingers) with mascarpone cream and cocoa powder. We prefer to make our own savoiardi sponge rather than buy dry ladyfingers from the store. Plan to make this delicious classic a day in advance so it has time to properly rest and set.

Serves 6

FOR THE SAVOIARDI

Unsalted butter for greasing the baking sheet
5 large eggs, separated
⅔ cup (130 grams) granulated sugar
⅔ cup (150 grams) all-purpose flour, sifted
Powdered sugar for dusting

FOR THE SOAKING LIQUID

⅔ cup (140 grams) freshly brewed strong coffee
⅔ cup (160 grams) brandy
⅓ cup (65 grams) granulated sugar

FOR THE MASCARPONE CREAM

6 large eggs, separated
¾ cup (180 grams) granulated sugar
3 cups (720 grams) mascarpone, lightly whipped

1 to 2 tablespoons unsweetened cocoa powder for dusting

SPECIAL EQUIPMENT:
An 8-by-12-inch baking dish that's at least 2 inches deep

To make the savoiardi, preheat the oven to 350 degrees. Butter an 18-by-13-inch baking sheet and line it with a sheet of parchment paper cut to fit.

In a large bowl, using a handheld mixer, beat the egg yolks with half the granulated sugar at high speed until the yolks double in volume and turn pale yellow, about 10 minutes.

In the bowl of a stand mixer fitted with the whisk attachment, or in another large bowl, whip the egg whites with the remaining sugar at high speed until stiff peaks form, about 5 minutes. Don't overwhip, or the whites will turn grainy.

Using a large metal spoon or spatula, gradually fold the sifted flour and beaten whites into the whipped yolks, incorporating them one large spoonful at a time and alternating the flour and egg whites. When the batter is more or less uniform, pour it onto the lined baking sheet and carefully spread it out in the pan, taking care not to deflate it. Dust the top with a thin coating of powdered sugar.

Bake in the oven until the sponge cake bakes through but doesn't brown, about 20 minutes. A cake tester inserted into the center should come out clean. Transfer the baking sheet to a rack and let the cake cool completely.

WHILE THE SAVOIARDI BAKES, PREPARE THE SOAKING LIQUID: Pour the hot coffee into a small bowl, add the brandy and sugar, and stir until the sugar dissolves.

PREPARE THE MASCARPONE CREAM: In the bowl of a stand mixer fitted with the whisk attachment, beat the egg yolks with half the sugar at medium speed until pale yellow and voluminous, about 10 minutes. In a medium bowl, using a hand mixer, beat the egg whites with the remaining sugar at medium speed until stiff, glossy peaks form.

With a large metal spoon or a spatula, gently fold the whipped mascarpone and beaten egg whites into the egg yolk mixture a spoonful at a time, alternating the mascarpone and whites, until *just* incorporated. Overmixing could break the mascarpone, so err on the side of caution.

To assemble the tiramisu, cut the sponge cake in half. Lay one half in an 8-by-12-inch baking dish, trimming away any excess cake if necessary so it fits snugly. Brush one-quarter of the soaking liquid evenly over the cake and let stand until fully absorbed. If the sponge can take more, add a few extra splashes so the cake is drenched but not caving in. Pour the remaining soaking liquid into a 9-by-13-inch baking pan.

Spread half the mascarpone cream over the top of the soaked cake, smoothing it out evenly. Using a fine-mesh sieve, lightly and evenly dust the top with cocoa powder.

Place the remaining sponge cake into the pan of soaking liquid. Once the soak has been fully absorbed, use two thin spatulas to lift the cake out of the liquid and onto the tiramisu. If it breaks, just piece it back together. Drizzle whatever soaking liquid remains evenly over the top of the cake. Top it off with the remaining mascarpone cream, spreading it evenly.

Cover the tiramisu and refrigerate until it sets and the flavors meld, at least 12 hours. Tiramisu can be held, covered in the fridge, for up to 3 days.

Just before serving, remove the tiramisu from the fridge. Top it off with a thin dusting of cocoa powder (or add the cocoa once helpings have been doled out). With your largest spoon, scoop out portions and drop them into shallow bowls, making sure all the liquor at the dish's bottom also makes its way into the bowls.

Fig and Almond Tart

Serves 8 to 10

FOR THE FRANGIPANE

1½ cups (200 grams) blanched (skinless) whole almonds
½ pound (2 sticks/200 grams) unsalted butter, at room temperature
1 cup (200 grams) granulated sugar
3 large eggs

FOR THE TART

One 10-inch tart shell prepared with Short-Crust Pastry (page 40) and chilled
12 to 15 large ripe figs (about 1 pound)
2 tablespoons Banyuls wine
1 tablespoon granulated sugar
Salt

Powdered sugar for finishing
Crème fraîche for serving

To prepare the frangipane, pulse the almonds in a food processor until fine crumbs form, about 3 minutes. Transfer the crumbs to a medium bowl and set aside.

Add the butter and sugar to the processor bowl and mix until the butter is very soft and looks a little "whipped," about 5 minutes. With the blade running, add the eggs one at a time, adding another one only once the previous one has been incorporated. Transfer to a large bowl and fold in the blitzed almonds until thoroughly combined. Cover and refrigerate until the frangipane no longer looks shiny and loose, at least 10 minutes.

To make the tart, preheat the oven to 350 degrees. Slide the shell onto a baking sheet and bake in the oven until the tart looks blonde, about 20 minutes. Remove from the oven and let cool completely on a rack.

MEANWHILE, MACERATE THE FIGS: Working over a medium bowl, tear each one in half (or into quarters if they're very large), dropping them into the bowl. Add the Banyuls, sugar, and a pinch of salt and toss well.

Spoon the chilled frangipane over the bottom of the cooled tart shell but do not spread it out! If it's properly chilled, the spreading will tear your pastry—this will spread on its own in the oven. Scatter the macerated figs evenly over the bottom of the tart shell, pressing some into the frangipane.

Bake the tart in the oven, turning the pan 180 degrees halfway through, until the frangipane is golden and a finger pressed into its center meets some resistance, 60 to 70 minutes.

Remove from the oven and let the tart cool for at least 20 minutes, then remove the sides of the pan and transfer the tart to a serving plate. Serve the slices with a dusting of powdered sugar and dollops of crème fraîche.

Huckleberry Galette

The parents of one of our summer pastry interns were keen foragers. One August, they shipped us a haul of huckleberries that arrived just as we were rolling out galettes. So we put them on top of our frangipane, and this was the result.

Ever since, we've sought out huckleberries every year. If none are available, we use wild blueberries instead. While not as tart, they're a good alternative. If you're using blueberries, wild or cultivated, reduce the sugar to about 80 grams.

Serves 6 to 8

FOR THE FRANGIPANE

½ cup plus 1 tablespoon (100 grams) blanched (skinless) whole almonds
8 tablespoons (1 stick/100 grams) unsalted butter, at room temperature
½ cup (100 grams) granulated sugar
Salt
1 large egg

FOR THE PASTRY

3½ cups (450 grams) all-purpose flour, plus more for dusting
2 tablespoons granulated sugar, plus more for sprinkling
Salt
½ pound (2 sticks/220 grams) chilled unsalted butter, cut into 1-inch cubes
1½ cups (345 grams) heavy cream, plus extra as needed

FOR THE FILLING

6 cups (850 grams) huckleberries
Scant ½ cup (100 grams) granulated sugar, plus more for sprinkling
2 tablespoons cornstarch
1 tablespoon lemon juice, or to taste

FOR THE EGG WASH

1 egg
1 tablespoon whole milk or cream

Cold cream for serving

To make the frangipane, preheat the oven to 425 degrees. Spread the almonds on a baking sheet and toast in the oven until uniformly golden, about 12 minutes. Remove from the oven and let cool completely.

Transfer the almonds to a food processor and pulse until they break down to a coarse flour, 1 to 2 minutes. Transfer to a medium bowl and set aside.

(Continued)

Add the butter, sugar, and a pinch of salt to the processing bowl. Whiz until the butter becomes smooth and doubles in volume, about 5 minutes. Add the egg and blitz to combine. Gradually pulse in the almond flour until fully incorporated, about 2 minutes.

Transfer the frangipane to a bowl and refrigerate until it is chilled but still spreadable, about 15 minutes. Covered in the fridge, the frangipane holds for 3 days; let it stand until spreadable before using.

To make the pastry, place the flour, sugar, and a pinch of salt in the clean processor bowl and pulse a few times to combine. Add the chilled butter and blitz until it breaks down to pea-sized bits, about 30 seconds. Pour in the cream and blitz a few more times, until a ragged dough forms. If the dough doesn't come together after the cream is incorporated, add another tablespoon of cream and pulse 3 or 4 more times, until a rough ball forms.

Lay a large sheet of plastic wrap on a work surface and turn the dough out onto its center. Knead the dough lightly, until the ball comes together, then pat it into a flat disk. Wrap tightly in plastic wrap and refrigerate until firm to the poke, at least 15 minutes. Wrapped and held in the fridge, the pastry keeps for 2 days.

Preheat the oven to 425 degrees. Take the pastry out of the fridge and let it stand until it is soft enough to be rolled out but still cool to the touch. Lightly dust your work surface and the pastry with flour. Roll the dough into a 16-inch round that is about ¼ inch thick. Transfer the round to a baking sheet lined with parchment and chill once more until cold to the touch, at least 15 minutes.

As the dough chills, remove the frangipane from the fridge and let it stand at room temperature until it is *just* spreadable. Meanwhile, make the filling: Combine the huckleberries and sugar in a small bowl and toss well. Add the cornstarch and lemon juice and toss again. Let stand for at least 10 minutes, but no longer than 30 minutes, or the berries will lose too much juice.

Dollop the frangipane over the round of dough and spread it out evenly, leaving a 2-inch border all around. Pile the fruit and its juices over the frangipane. Lift and fold the edges up and over the filling, pinching the folds into pleats that ripple around the edges of the galette. Do not worry if it looks rustic—it is as it should be.

To make the egg wash, beat the egg together with the milk in a small bowl. Brush the egg wash over the pleated pastry and then sprinkle the crust lightly with sugar.

Bake the galette in the oven until the pastry is golden, about 20 minutes. Lower the oven temperature to 350 degrees, rotate the pan 180 degrees, and bake until the fruit is jammy and the pastry is crisp and golden brown, 25 to 35 minutes more. Remove the galette from the oven and let sit for at least an hour before slicing so the fruit firms up.

Serve slightly warm, cut into slices, with cold cream poured over top.

Treacle Tart

Wholeheartedly British, this tart is made with stale bread and treacle (Lyle's Golden Syrup). It became a post-war favorite due to its humble cupboard-friendly ingredients.

Lyle's Golden Syrup is iconic back home. Every household has a sticky tin in the back of the cupboard—one lasts a generation because other than making this tart (or adding a spoonful to porridge), we're not quite sure what else it is good for. There's no exact American substitute, but thankfully there's the internet and plenty of specialty stores, where you can find a tin of your own.

Serves 8 to 10

One 10-inch tart shell prepared with Short-Crust Pastry (page 40) and chilled

FOR THE FILLING

10 tablespoons (1¼ sticks/145 grams) unsalted butter
2½ cups (900 grams) Lyle's Golden Syrup
7 tablespoons (100 grams) heavy cream
Salt
2 lemons
3 large eggs
1¼ cup cups (150 grams) fine breadcrumbs

Fior di Latte Ice Cream (page 342) for serving
Cold cream for serving

SPECIAL EQUIPMENT:
Fluted tart ring with removable bottom

Preheat the oven to 350 degrees. Prick the tart shell all over the bottom with a fork. Set the pan on a baking sheet and bake in the oven until the shell is golden brown, about 25 minutes. Remove from the oven and let cool completely, at least 35 minutes.

To make the filling, brown the butter by heating it in a medium pot over medium-low heat until it smells nutty and is a rich golden brown, 8 minutes. Do not let the butter burn! Turn off the heat.

Stir in the golden syrup, heavy cream, and 2 teaspoons salt into the browned butter and warm over medium heat, whisking, until the mixture emulsifies, 2 to 3 minutes. Remove from the heat and allow to cool slightly, about 4 minutes, then finely zest the lemons directly into the pot. Stir to combine and cool the syrup until just warm to the touch, about 30 minutes.

Meanwhile, juice the zested lemons, strain the juice, and set aside.

When the syrup has partially cooled, whisk the eggs together in a large bowl. Whisk in a small amount of the warm syrup to temper the mixture so the eggs don't curdle, then add the remaining syrup a little bit at a time. Whisk in the lemon juice and breadcrumbs.

Pour the filling into the cooled tart shell and bake in the oven until golden brown, about 45 minutes. As the tart bakes, rotate the tin every 15 minutes so it cooks evenly.

Remove the tart from the oven and allow it to cool on a rack. Once cool enough to handle, but still warm enough that any leaked treacle is pliable, gently pop the tart out of the tin's ring.

Slice the tart and serve with Fior di Latte Ice Cream (page 342) and cold cream.

Tarte Tatin

Tarte Tatin is hard to get right: the best ones have dark caramel, tender apples, and a crisp puff. Our recipe removes a lot of the guesswork from the process because we cook the caramel and apples separately and then assemble the tart before baking it to order. It's a hack that works well for service.

Generally we use Honeycrisp apples, but Granny Smith or Pink Ladies also work well. Basically, seek out an apple that holds its shape when cooked. Feel free to use store-bought puff pastry.

Serve warm slices of the tart with Honey Lavender Ice Cream (page 348) or cold cream for drizzling and Fior di Latte Ice Cream (page 342).

Serves 8

FOR THE CARAMEL APPLES

1 cup granulated sugar
4 tablespoons (60 grams) chilled butter, diced
6 Honeycrisp apples (about 2 pounds/900 grams), peeled, cored, and each cut into 6 wedges

FOR THE PASTRY

All-purpose flour for dusting
14 ounces Rough Puff Pastry (page 39) or store-bought puff pastry, chilled
1 egg
Splash of milk or cream

SPECIAL EQUIPMENT:

A 10-inch cast-iron frying pan or other heavy ovenproof frying pan

Begin by making a very dark caramel for the apples in a saucepan: Add the sugar to the saucepan and shimmy the pan around to evenly coat the bottom with the sugar, then place it over medium heat. Warm until the sugar melts; resist the urge to stir. Once you have a golden brown caramel, shake the pan to encourage even coloring. When the caramel is chestnut brown, after about 11 minutes or less (always err on the safe side with caramel to avoid burning it), turn off the heat and swirl in the cold butter. The caramel will hiss and smoke furiously. Keep swirling, and once the caramel is uniformly golden, add the apples, stirring to coat all the pieces. Remove from the heat.

Place a cartouche (see page 15) over the fruit and return the pan to medium heat. Stew until the wedges soften and offer only *slight* resistance at their centers when poked, about 15 minutes. Overcooking will cause the apples to lose their shape. Remove the pan when the apples are ready.

(Continued)

Once the apples are cool enough to handle, arrange the pieces in a 10-inch cast-iron pan, core side up. Pack the apple in snugly into concentric circles. (The apples will shrink as they cook.) Pour over some of the caramel from the saucepan so that the bottom is covered with a ¼-inch-thick layer. Let the apples cool completely.

Preheat the oven to 425 degrees. Roll out pastry on a lightly floured surface to an 11-inch round that's about ½ inch thick all the way across; the round should comfortably flop over the tart with at least an inch of overhang.

Lay the puff pastry over the cooled apples and tuck the overhanging puff into the pan. Poke the top with a fork to provide a steam vent and bake in the oven until the pastry is golden brown, about 50 minutes. Remove from the oven.

Let the tart cool slightly, at least 10 minutes, before turning it out. You want to do whis while the tart is still warm but not scalding hot: Lay a large plate over the pan, completely covering it, and slide a large pot holder or folded dish towel under the pan. With conviction, flip the pan and plate—beware of hot caramel—and set on the counter. Remove the pan.

Serve warm slices with ice cream and cold cream.

King's Summer Pudding

In Britain, where summer sometimes lasts a matter of days, there is a narrow window when all the berries are juicy and ripe. To celebrate the moment, we make this age-old pud. It was added to our dessert menu in 2021, the same year our first bottle of King rosé arrived from Domaine de Fontsainte in the Languedoc. It seemed only right to slosh some into the berries for good measure.

While a full assortment of mixed berries is preferred, any colorful combination (red, black, and/or blue) will work nicely here. That said, your mix and its ripeness will directly affect the final color and flavor, so choose a combo that gives the pud a saturated red-purple tint.

It's important that the bread be sliced as thin as possible to create a delicate lattice. At King, we use the meat slicer. But at home, we just freeze the loaf, for an hour or so, to make the job easier.

Make this at least a day before serving so that the pudding has time to firm in the fridge.

Serves 10

½ large loaf (about 350 grams) day-old brioche or Pullman bread, crust removed
2½ pounds (1,200 grams) mixed, very ripe berries (red and black currants, blackberries, blueberries, strawberries, and/or raspberries)
1¼ cups (250 grams) granulated sugar
2¾ cups (375 grams) King rosé or other dry rosé
1 vanilla bean, halved lengthwise, seeds scraped out and reserved
Crème fraîche for serving

SPECIAL EQUIPMENT: A 6-cup bowl about 9 inches in diameter

Wrap the bread in plastic wrap, place it in the freezer, and freeze for about an hour.

To prepare the berries, hull the strawberries, if using, and pluck the currants off their branches. Add all the berries to a large heatproof bowl.

Add the sugar to a small pot and warm it slowly over medium-low heat to dissolve the sugar and make an amber caramel; do not stir as the caramel forms, but swirl the pot to encourage even melting, When you have a dark caramel, after 3 to 5 minutes, reduce the heat to low and carefully pour in the wine (stand back, it will sputter). Add the vanilla seeds, swirl to combine, and increase the heat to medium. Simmer to boil off the alcohol, about 3 minutes.

Remove the caramel from the heat and pour it over the berries. Allow the berries to cool to room temperature, about 20 minutes.

(Continued)

Line a 6-cup bowl about 9 inches in diameter with plastic wrap, using two crisscrossed sheets so there are no gaps, leaving a 3-inch overhang all around. Press the plastic wrap into place and line the bowl with a second layer of plastic wrap.

Slice the semifrozen loaf of bread lengthwise into ¼-inch-thick slices. Start lining the bowl with the bread, laying the first piece across the center of the bowl's bottom. Lay another slice next to the first, overlapping it by about ½ inch. Continue adding slice after slice of bread, over the bottom and up the sides of the bowl, in this fashion until it is completely covered with bread. (Overlapping the bread guards against gaps and leaks.)

Carefully ladle the berries and all their juices into the bowl, leaving a ¼- inch of space free at the top. Cover the berries with a final layer of bread, folding over the edges as necessary, to form a lid. Pull the overhanging plastic wrap up over the top of the pudding's center, adding more pieces of plastic if needed to completely seal the top.

Set a small plate over the pudding; it should just fit inside the bowl. Then set a small jam jar (or something similar) over the plate to weight the pudding down slightly. Transfer the bowl to the fridge and let rest until the pudding sets and the bread has absorbed the berries' juices, 12 to 24 hours.

When you're ready to serve, remove the bowl from the fridge and remove the weights and plate. Pull back the plastic at the top, exposing the bread lid. Place a wide platter over the pudding and, holding both the plate and the bowl firmly, flip the pudding over and onto the plate (see page 321). Set the pudding on the counter, carefully lift off the bowl, and remove the plastic wrap. Ta-da!

Serve the pudding at the table and scoop portions onto plates, along with dollops of crème fraîche.

Far Breton

A dessert that always feels strangely nostalgic. Strange because none of us come from Brittany, where this dish originated. Sade thinks we're drawn to it because the custard tastes of mother's milk. . . .

The recipe is low-maintenance and scales brilliantly, and the batter only gets better with age. Tradition calls for prunes, but feel free to use (almost) any dried fruit. That said, we always return to this classic.

The prunes like an overnight soak, and the batter needs a few hours (or days) to rest as well. The longer it chills in the fridge, the better the flavor.

Serve this warm, with ice cream, if you like. It's also perfect cold at breakfast the following day.

Serves 10 to 12

24 pitted prunes
⅔ cup (140 grams) Armagnac or other brandy or rum
4 cups (950 grams) whole milk
4 large eggs
4 large egg yolks
1⅓ cups (185 grams) all-purpose flour, plus more for dusting
Salt
1 cup (200 grams) granulated sugar
8 tablespoons (1 stick/113 grams) unsalted butter, melted, plus more for greasing the pan
Cold heavy cream for serving

Place the prunes in a medium bowl and pour in enough Armagnac to cover. Cover and refrigerate overnight. Or, if you're like us and happen to need this on a moment's notice, fast-track the soak by adding the prunes and liquor to a small saucepan and warm everything gently over very low heat. Once at a simmer, cook until the prunes soften and soak up the booze, 1 to 2 minutes. Turn off the heat and let cool completely.

Add the milk, whole eggs, yolks, flour, ⅛ teaspoon salt, and the sugar to a blender or food processor and blitz to combine (you can also use a large bowl and a handheld mixer or a whisk). With the blade running, stream in the warm melted butter and whiz until the batter looks smooth and lump-free. Transfer to a bowl, cover, and chill the batter in the fridge for at least 3 hours. If possible, go for longer, as this flavor only improves with age, up to 3 days.

Preheat the oven to 425 degrees. Generously grease a large baking dish with butter (ours is approximately 15 by 11 inches and 3 inches deep). Dust the inside of the dish with flour, tapping out excess.

(Continued)

Remove the prunes from the booze (save the residual liquor for another use, such as in cocktails or to soak more prunes), and scatter them over the bottom of the dish, making sure to cover it well. If necessary, tear any oversized prunes in half so each half makes for a polite bite.

Remove the batter from the fridge and whiz it up again in the blender to mix in any sediment on the bottom. It will foam, and that is fine.

Pour the batter over the prunes and bake in the oven until the Far looks golden and puffed but its center retains a gentle wobble, about 30 minutes. Remove from the oven and allow the dish to settle a few minutes.

Serve warm, with a pour of heavy cream over each serving.

Lavender Crème Caramel

A perfect crème caramel relies on the strength of the caramel and the gentleness of the cook. Be brave enough to let the caramel turn a deep, rich brown—too pale, and it's insipid; too dark, and its bitterness overwhelms. Secondly, the delicate custard should be cooked until it is *just* set, or it loses its mouth-melting raison d'être.

We get dried lavender from a local tea shop. Make sure whatever you use is similarly safe for cooking.

Serves 10 to 12

Unsalted butter for greasing the cake pan

FOR THE CUSTARD

2 cups (500 grams) whole milk
2 cups (500 grams) heavy cream
2 tablespoons (10 grams) organic dried lavender
4 large eggs
4 large egg yolks
1 cup (200 grams) granulated sugar

FOR THE CARAMEL

2 cups (400 grams) granulated sugar

SPECIAL EQUIPMENT: 12-inch round cake pan

To make the custard, bring the milk and cream to a simmer in a medium heavy pot over medium heat, 3 to 5 minutes. Add the lavender and turn off the heat. Let the lavender infuse the cream until it has cooled to room temperature and is perfumed, about 1 hour and 20 minutes.

Strain the dairy through a fine-mesh sieve set over a medium bowl. Press on the trapped lavender to extract all its flavor and then discard.

In the bowl of a stand mixer fitted with the whisk attachment, beat the eggs, yolks, and sugar on high speed until pale and fluffy, about 3 minutes. Reduce the speed to low and slowly whisk in the lavender-infused cream.

Preheat the oven to 300 degrees. Grease a 12-inch cake pan with butter. Place it on a folded tea towel set in a large deep roasting pan (the towel will hold the cake pan in place). Pour enough water into the roasting pan to come halfway up the sides of the cake pan.

To make the caramel, sprinkle the sugar evenly over the bottom of a large heavy pan. Set the pan over medium-low heat and don't disturb the sugar as it melts. Once it has mostly melted, about 4 minutes, swirl the pan to encourage even coloring. Continue cooking the caramel, swirling often, until it is chestnut brown and smells almost burnt, 2 to 3 minutes.

Pour the hot caramel into the prepared pan, evenly coating the bottom. Let it cool completely.

(Continued)

Pour the custard into the caramel-lined pan and cover the pan with aluminum foil (this prevents a film from forming). Carefully move the roasting pan to the oven, taking care that the water doesn't splash into the crème, and bake until the custard is just set and a cake tester inserted into the center comes out clean, about 1½ hours. Carefully remove the pan from the oven and let the crème caramel cool in its water bath for 20 to 30 minutes.

Remove the pan from the water bath and wipe it completely dry. Place a large rimmed plate that fully covers the pan over the top and, while holding the two firmly together, flip and listen for a gentle flop. Set the plate on the counter and carefully lift off the pan. If there's too big a pool of caramel (the puddle should be thin and proportional), pour some of it off by gently tilting the plate over a bowl.

Slice the crème caramel and serve. Kept in its pan and covered, the crème caramel keeps well in the fridge for a day.

Clafoutis

King's small kitchen allows for only ten of these a night. Served straight from the oven and sent to the table in its cast-iron pan, the clafoutis is always well received by the lucky few. Scoops of our Fior di Latte Ice Cream (page 342) alongside, or right on top, is standard practice.

As spring fades, fresh cherries replace the rhubarb.

Serves 6

FOR THE ROASTED RHUBARB

1 pound (453 grams) rhubarb, rinsed
⅓ cup (67 grams) granulated sugar
2 or 3 strips of orange peel removed with a vegetable peeler

FOR THE BATTER

Unsalted butter for greasing the pan
1½ cups (290 grams) granulated sugar, plus more for dusting
6 large eggs
½ vanilla bean, split lengthwise, seeds scraped out and reserved
Finely grated zest of ½ orange
1½ cups (300 grams) whole milk
1⅓ cups (300 grams) heavy cream
⅓ cup plus 1 tablespoon (40 grams) almond flour
¾ cup (100 grams) all-purpose or 00 flour
Powdered sugar for finishing

SPECIAL EQUIPMENT:
A heavy ovenproof skillet about 10½ inches in diameter

To make the roasted rhubarb, preheat the oven to 350 degrees. Top and tail the rhubarb, cutting away any fibrous end bits. Slice the stalks into 2-inch lengths. Spread them out in a medium roasting dish that holds them in a single uncrowded layer. (If necessary, use two dishes.)

Sprinkle over the sugar and orange zest. Toss to coat the rhubarb and then allow it to macerate at room temperature until things get a bit juicy, 15 to 20 minutes.

Splash over 2 tablespoons of water and spread the fruit out once more. Cover the dish with aluminum foil and bake in the oven until the rhubarb is soft but not falling apart, 10 to 15 minutes. Rhubarb has an uncanny way of suddenly overcooking, so keep a watchful eye and check frequently. When it is cooked, remove the dish from the oven and let cool completely. Increase the oven temperature to 400 degrees.

To make the clafoutis, grease a large, heavy skillet, about 10½ inches in diameter, with softened butter. Dust the inside of the pan with sugar, tapping out excess. Add the just-cooked rhubarb to the pan, taking care to leave all its pretty juices behind in the roasting dish (these will go into the custard soon enough).

(Continued)

Place the eggs, sugar, vanilla seeds, and orange zest in a large bowl. Whisk to combine and then stream in the milk and cream, whisking all the while. Stir in the almond flour, all-purpose flour, and reserved rhubarb juices until completely smooth; feel free to use an immersion blender.

Pour the batter into the prepared pan and bake in the oven until the clafoutis looks puffed and golden, 30 to 35 minutes. When prodded, the custard should feel firm at the edges but a little wobbly in the center. Remove from the oven and let cool for 5 minutes.

While it's still warm, dust the top of the clafoutis with powdered sugar and march the pan to the table.

Baked Apples in Parchment
with Prunes and Amaretto

We use Honeycrisp apples for their honey flavor and relatively firm texture, which stands up to this recipe's slow bake.

Serves 4

1 cup (160 grams) blanched whole almonds
1 tablespoon granulated sugar
8½ tablespoons (120 grams) unsalted butter, plus more for dotting the tops of the apples
⅔ cup (125 grams) pitted prunes, roughly chopped
4½ tablespoons (52 grams) packed light brown sugar, plus more for sprinkling
Salt
3 tablespoons (36 grams) Amaretto, plus more for finishing
4 Honeycrisp or other good baking apples (about 2 pounds/900 grams)
½ cup (120 grams) heavy cream

SPECIAL EQUIPMENT:
An apple corer; kitchen twine

Preheat the oven to 325 degrees. Cut eight 12-by-18-inch rectangles of parchment paper. Cut four 12-inch lengths of kitchen twine. Toss the almonds together with the sugar and spread out in a single layer on a small baking sheet. Dot ½ tablespoon butter over the nuts.

Bake the almonds in the oven until a rich golden brown, about 30 minutes. After the first 10 minutes, toss to distribute the sugar and encourage even coloring. Toss once or twice more as the almonds toast. Remove from the oven and let cool completely.

To make the apple filling, blitz half the toasted almonds in a food processor to form fine crumbs that resemble wet sand (the remaining almonds will be used as a garnish). Add the prunes, the remaining 8 tablespoons butter, 2 tablespoons of the brown sugar, and a pinch of salt to the chopped almonds. Pulse until a slightly chunky paste forms, about 1 minute. With the blade running, stream in the Amaretto, stopping once the filling turns buttery and light in texture, about 1 minute. Taste and add more salt and/or brown sugar as needed; this should be sweet, but nothing should obscure the pruney flavor.

Use the filling right away, or cover and store it in the fridge for up to 3 days. If it's been chilled, bring it to room temperature before using.

With a paring knife, score a line around the equator of each apple, taking care not to cut too far into its flesh (slitting just the skin prevents apples from bursting). With an apple corer, remove the apples' centers, removing the seeds and stems but not pushing down through the base (you don't want leaks!). A small spoon helps get at any stubborn bits in need of extracting.

Preheat the oven to 350 degrees. Lay two squares of the parchment paper in a small bowl and place an apple in the center. Season the apple's cavity with a pinch of brown sugar and a pinch of salt, then spoon (or pipe) some of the prune-almond filling into its tummy, filling it to the brim. Dot the top with a bit of butter, about a teaspoon, and finish with another generous pinch of brown sugar. Gather the parchment up and around the apple, encasing it in an open pouch. With your free hand, pour a glug of Amaretto, about ½ tablespoon, into the pouch, and gather, cinch, and twist the paper shut before knotting it firmly with kitchen twine. Repeat with the remaining parchment, filling, apples, booze, and twine.

Arrange the parcels in a medium baking dish and roast in the oven until a large apple feels very soft when squeezed through the paper, 2 to 2½ hours. If the apples are buxom, they may need more time. Remove from the oven and let the apples rest in their parcels for a few moments while roughly chopping the remaining nuts.

Serve the parcels piping hot in individual bowls. At the table, remove the ties, pour over a dash of cold cream, and finish by scattering over the reserved chopped almonds.

King's Chocolate Cake

This is the only cake that's remained on our menu from the early days.

We like a crackled crust and gooey center. To get the best, lightest texture, treat the yolks and whites with great care, whipping both so they fully expand and hold their shape. And when melting the chocolate, do not overheat it, or it will seize.

Eat this straight from the pan with a spoon while it's warm (as we often do), or let it cool, slice, and serve with exaggerated dollops of crème fraîche.

Serves 10 to 12

14 ounces (3½ sticks; 375 grams) unsalted butter, plus more for greasing the cake pan
1¼ pounds (600 grams) semisweet chocolate (600 grams), chopped into postage stamp–sized pieces
Salt
12 large eggs, separated
2¼ cups (450 grams) granulated sugar
Whipped crème fraîche for serving

SPECIAL EQUIPMENT:
A 12-inch springform pan

Preheat the oven to 350 degrees. Generously grease the cake pan with butter. Line the bottom with a round of parchment paper cut to fit. Now cut 2 strips of parchment to line the pan's sides; these should overlap and form a collar that stands 3 inches above the rim.

Pour an inch or so of water into a medium pot and set it over low heat. Combine the butter, chocolate, and a generous pinch of salt in a large heatproof bowl and set it over the pot; take care that the bottom of the bowl does not touch the water. Heat the butter and chocolate, stirring occasionally and scraping down the sides of bowl, until almost melted, about 10 minutes. Just as the last chunks of chocolate melt, remove the bowl from over the pot and stir everything together until glossy. Allow to cool completely.

Beat the yolks and sugar together on high speed until the yolks triple in size and turn a soft, pale yellow. Gently fold the cooled chocolate into the whipped yolks. Avoid overmixing, or you'll lose all the lightness; some streaks are okay.

In the bowl of a stand mixer fitted with the whisk attachment, or in a large bowl using a handheld mixer, beat the egg whites on high speed until they hold stiff peaks, 3 minutes.

Gently fold the beaten whites into the chocolate base with a large metal spoon or spatula until just combined, being careful not to deflate the whites. Pour the batter into the lined cake pan.

(Continued)

Bake in the oven until a crust forms on the top of the cake but the center is still soft, 45 to 60 minutes. A cake tester inserted into the center should emerge with some streaks and wet crumbs. If you're unsure about doneness, err on the side of underbaking, as the cake will continue to firm as it cools. Remove from the oven and cool in the pan on a rack.

Remove the sides of the pan and transfer the cake to a plate. To serve, cut into thin wedges, with large dollops of crème fraîche.

Chocolate Tart

This was the inaugural chocolate dessert at King, served to much fanfare. But it also proved to be one of our downfalls early on. Having to slice this delicate tart during our bare-bones services didn't end well!

Years later, my husband, Sean, requested a copy of the recipe and started baking it at home. It was his first attempt at baking and, after a few tries, he mastered it. Which means you can too!

The light, buttery tart shell and airy chocolate sabayon filling never miss. I insisted this be included in our book since none of our dinner parties feel complete without it.

—*Annie*

Serves 8

An 11-inch tart shelled prepared with Short-Crust Pastry (page 40), chilled
1¼ cups (300 grams) heavy cream
1¼ cups plus 2 tablespoons (240 grams) dark chocolate, preferably 65% cacao, broken into chunks
3 large eggs
6 large egg yolks
½ cup plus 1 tablespoon (125 grams) granulated sugar
Whipped crème fraîche for serving

Preheat the oven to 350 degrees. Prick the bottom of the chilled tart shell all over with a fork. Bake in the oven until golden brown, 25 minutes.

Remove from the oven and let the tart shell cool completely, at least 35 minutes. The pastry holds at room temperature for about 6 hours.

To make the filling, pour the cream into a medium pot set over medium heat. Meanwhile, put the chocolate in a medium heatproof bowl. As soon as the cream comes to a simmer (do not let it boil), pour it over the chocolate and stir until it is melted and looks shiny and smooth. Set aside.

Preheat the oven to 350 degrees. Set a medium pot filled with an inch or two of water over low heat. Meanwhile, in the bowl of a stand mixer fitted with the whisk attachment, or in a large heatproof bowl using a handheld mixer, whip the eggs and egg yolks with the sugar on medium speed until pale and fluffy, 7 to 10 minutes.

When the water in the pot is at a simmer, set the bowl of whipped eggs over the pot. Start gently folding and using a large whisk, whisk the eggs, moving without pause, until they are just heated through and a thick sabayon has formed, 5 to 7 minutes. From time to time, use a spatula to scrape down the sides and scrape the bottom (you don't want any scorching). If

(Continued)

necessary, lower the heat to make sure the water never heats to a boil. The sabayon is ready when the lifted whisk can dribble a Figure 8 over the surface sabayon that holds its shape for a few seconds before fading away. Remove from the heat.

Gently pour the cooled chocolate ganache into the sabayon, adding about a quarter of it at a time and using a wide spatula or large metal spoon to fold in each addition until mostly incorporated—some streaks are okay (the goal is to stir as little as possible and guard against deflating). When the filling looks uniform, pour it into the prepared tart shell and shimmy the tin to spread it out evenly.

Place the pan on a baking sheet and move to the oven. Bake until a toothpick inserted into the tart's center comes out with just a few fudgy crumbs but isn't wet, about 30 minutes. Remove from the oven and let the tart cool completely on a rack before pressing it out of the tin.

Remove the sides of the pan and serve slices of the tart with dollops of crème fraîche.

CHAPTER 14

Ice cream & other frozen desserts

WE LIKE OUR ICE CREAM RICH WITH EGG YOLKS AND CREAM: MORE FRENCH IN STYLE than Italy's gelato. However, we still take our flavor cues from our favorite gelaterias.

Our Fior di Latte Ice Cream (page 342), a plain custard-based version, focuses on capturing and amplifying the qualities of excellent dairy. It is our base recipe, the frozen canvas for all sorts of stir-ins, fruit purees, and ripples.

With ice cream, we begin every recipe by warming milk and cream to just-before-a-simmer, turning off the heat as soon as the pot trembles. Anything more, and the cream's delicacy is lost.

Most important: Don't let the possibility of scrambling a custard or investing in a small tabletop ice cream spinner put you off trying the recipes that follow. Making frozen desserts at home is a treat, and developing a feel for cooking custard comes quickly. If you like, use a thermometer, and remove the custard base from the heat as soon as it reaches the right temperature (180 degrees). This is something anyone can master. But to get you started, we've also included a semifreddo—no machine needed. With ice cream, you want to chill it as quickly as possible to develop the best texture—that's why a metal storage container is best for freezing (these chill quickly). You can hold any of these bases in the fridge for up to 3 days before churning.

Our sorbets, light and bright, celebrate fruit at its seasonal peak. In their simplest form, these are just fruit juices combined with simple syrups and churned until they thicken. The trick is getting the flavor balance right. Taste and adjust according to your palate. Still, it helps to remember: you can always add more simple syrup, but you can't take it away. Also keep in mind that freezing dulls flavors slightly, so it's best to make the base a smidge sweeter than you might want for an ideal result. Practice makes this simple process very easy indeed. If you're without a machine, there are other options. Simply freeze the sorbet's base, and, after it sets, scrape the top with the tines of a fork to make a granita. We like to pour Prosecco over coupes filled with these lashings.

Pernod Semifreddo

It took three years of savings for us to afford a proper ice cream machine at King. In the interim, we relied on this semifreddo. It does require more than a few bowls and a lot of whipping.

The alcohol in the Pernod stops this semifreddo from setting up too firmly, allowing for scoops rather than the more traditional slices. Today, with our ice cream machine constantly churning, we still serve this dessert, by request, to our old-school regulars.

To accelerate freezing, let it set in a wide pan.

Serves 6

FOR THE SEMIFREDDO BASE

8 large egg yolks
2 cups (480 grams) chilled heavy cream
6 tablespoons (90 grams) Pernod or pastis, or more to taste

FOR THE SIMPLE SYRUP

1 cup (228 grams) water
1 cup (200 grams) granulated sugar

Langues de Chat (page 341) for serving

To make the semifreddo base, in the bowl of a stand mixer fitted with the whisk attachment, beat the yolks at high speed until they double in volume and turn pale yellow, about 6 to 8 minutes. (This stage sets the semifreddo's structure.)

MEANWHILE, MAKE THE SIMPLE SYRUP: Combine the water and sugar in a small pot and heat over medium heat, stirring, until the sugar dissolves. Then continue simmering until the syrup thickens slightly, 2 to 3 minutes. If you have a thermometer, it should read about 180 degrees. Remove from the heat.

With the mixer running, slowly pour in the hot syrup, very, very slowly trickling it down the side of the bowl. Going slowly prevents scrambled eggs! Once you've added all the syrup, continue to beat the base until it cools to room temperature, 2 to 3 minutes. If using a stand mixer, remove the bowl from the stand.

In a clean mixer bowl, or in a large bowl using a handheld mixer, whip the heavy cream at high speed until stiff peaks form, about 4 minutes. Using a large metal spoon or a rubber spatula, gently fold the airy base into the whipped cream, adding one-third of it at a time; fold gently so as not to deflate the cream, and do not overmix. If a few streaks remain, it's fine.

Pour the Pernod down the side of the bowl and gently fold it in until any remaining streaks have mostly disappeared. Taste and add a little more Pernod, if you fancy (remember that freezing mutes flavor, so additional splashes are likely welcome).

Pour the mixture into a baking pan approximately 12 by 9 inches (using a metal container speeds the freezing process). Smooth out the semifreddo and cover it with a rectangle of

(Continued)

parchment paper cut to fit over the top. Freeze until set, at least 3 hours. The semifreedo is ready when it can be scooped up like ice cream.

Serve this in coupes with langues de chats standing straight up in the semifreddo.

Langues de Chat

These vanilla wafers are as delicate as the cat's tongues they're named for. The recipe comes from JR Ryall, head pastry chef at Ballymaloe House in West Cork, Ireland. He serves these as part of his dessert trolley, topped with finely chopped pistachio. We sprinkle ground fennel into our batter and leave their faces bare.

Makes about 15 cookies

4 tablespoons (56 grams) unsalted butter, at room temperature
⅓ cup (66 grams) granulated sugar
2 large egg whites
½ cup (65 grams) all-purpose flour, sifted
Pinch of salt
½ teaspoon fennel seeds, finely ground
1 vanilla bean

SPECIAL EQUIPMENT: A small offset spatula

Combine the butter and sugar in a large bowl and beat together using a wooden spoon or handheld mixer until pale and fluffy, about 5 minutes. Slowly add in the egg whites, a little at a time, until a smooth batter forms. Fold in the flour, salt, and ground fennel.

Lay the vanilla bean on a cutting board and run the tip of a paring knife down its length, splitting the pod open to reveal the seeds within. Then run the knife's point down the length of the split halves, collecting all the tiny seeds as you go. Add the vanilla seeds to the batter and fold them in. Cover the batter and chill in the fridge for at least 1 hour. It holds for a couple of days in the fridge.

Preheat the oven to 400 degrees. Place a dab of batter in each corner of a baking sheet and then line the sheet with parchment paper, anchoring it with the dabs of batter. Drop a tablespoon-sized dollop of batter onto the parchment and, using a small offset spatula, smear it out into a petal shape or an elongated oval; we make these about 6 inches long, 4 inches wide, and ¼ inch thick. Repeat with the remaining batter, leaving at least 1 inch between the langues de chat (as these bake, the dough will spread).

Bake the cookies in the oven until golden brown and slightly darker at the edges, 7 to 8 minutes. Meanwhile, as the cookies bake, find a rolling pin(s) or a wine bottle.

Remove the langues de chat from the oven. Working quickly, use a thin spatula to peel each piping-hot cookie off the baking sheet and drape it over the rolling pin so its curve sets as it cools.

Once cooled, these can be stored in an airtight container for up 2 days.

Fior di Latte Ice Cream

Rather romantically, *fior di latte* literally means "the flower of milk." It's named for the bloom a pot of milk presents when it is *just* warmed. Unlike a classic Italian gelato, our fior recipe makes a rich, custardy ice cream.

This is the base on which we build endless variations: reducing the amount of sugar when adding sweet mix-ins or cutting back on the yolks when adding something fatty, like nuts. We serve this ice cream with our Tarte Tatin (page 317) and Far Breton (page 323).

Makes 1 quart

2 cups (456 grams) heavy cream
1 cup (226 grams) whole milk
5 large egg yolks
½ cup (100 grams) granulated sugar

SPECIAL EQUIPMENT: A candy or deep-fry thermometer

Attach a candy thermometer to a medium heavy pot. Warm the cream and milk together in the pot over high heat until the liquid quivers, about 5 minutes; it should be at 180 degrees, just below a simmer. A boil will scald the milk's flavor, so take care!

As the dairy warms, place the yolks and sugar in the bowl of a stand mixer fitted with the whisk attachment, or add them to a medium bowl and, using a handheld mixer, beat at high speed until the yolks turn pale yellow and double in volume, at least 5 minutes. Beating in air at this stage is vital to producing a stretchy ice cream.

With the mixer running, gingerly ladle in some of the warm dairy, pouring it down the side of the bowl, to avoid scrambling the eggs. Once the first ladleful is incorporated, add another one just as carefully, beating all the while. Continue adding the dairy and beating until the outside of the bowl feels warm to the touch. At this point, stop ladling and whisking and, using a wooden spoon, stir the warm whipped yolk mixture into the pot with the remaining dairy.

Begin to stir until a custard base with the consistency of paint forms, about 7 minutes; lower the heat as the custard thickens, which should start happening at about 160 degrees if you're using a thermometer. Slow and low is the best way to protect the eggs. If at any point the custard wafts smoke, remove it from the heat, whisk to cool it, and then return it to low heat again and proceed. The custard is done when a dipped spoon holds a lush coating and if you run a finger through the coating, a pronounced line remains (approximately 180 degrees). When it reaches this point, keep stirring but immediately remove the pot from the heat and pour the custard into a metal bowl; if it looks at all curdled, pass it through a fine-mesh sieve into the bowl.

Let the ice cream base cool completely, at least 30 minutes, then chill it in the fridge, covered, up to 2 days. When you're ready to make the ice cream, pour the cold custard into an ice cream maker and churn according to the manufacturer's instructions.

Freeze in a sealed container for at least 3 to 4 hours before scooping.

Pain Perdu Ice Cream

Jess and I went to Ballymaloe Cookery School, where both of us fell in love with the brown bread ice cream. So we eventually added leftover bread to King's own Fior di Latte, and this flavor was born.

Pain perdu's direct translation from the French is "lost bread." It's a bit of a misnomer, as that dish basically refers to French toast. For this recipe, we toast sourdough, toss it with melted sweet butter, and then toast it again to caramelize.

We also like to infuse the custard base with tonka beans, the seeds of a tree native to South America, for a warmth and spice that is more subtle than cinnamon, but you can use that if you can't get the beans.

—Clare

Makes about 1 quart

FOR THE ICE CREAM

2 cups (456 grams) heavy cream
1 cup (226 grams) whole milk
3 tonka beans or 1 small cinnamon stick
5 large egg yolks
½ cup (100 grams) granulated sugar

FOR THE PAIN PERDU

1 cup 1-inch pieces torn sourdough bread (crust removed)
5½ tablespoons (75 grams) unsalted butter
6 tablespoons (75 grams) granulated sugar

For the ice cream base, warm the cream and milk, along with the tonka beans (or cinnamon stick), in a heavy medium pot over high heat. Allow the milk to simmer but turn the heat off just before the milk boils, about 5 minutes. If using a cinnamon stick, pull it out so the flavor remains subtle. If using tonka beans, leave them in the pot (they'll come out later).

Then proceed with the eggs and sugar to make the ice cream base, following the instructions for our Fior di Latte Ice Cream (page 342).

WHILE THE BASE COOLS, MAKE THE PAIN PERDU: Preheat the oven to 350 degrees. Spread the bread out on a baking sheet and bake in the oven until golden brown, about 10 minutes.

Meanwhile, melt the butter in a small pot over low heat. Add the sugar and stir until it dissolves. Remove from the heat.

Remove the toasted bread from the oven and pour the melted butter over it. Toss to evenly coat, then return the pan to the oven and bake until the bread is crunchy and caramelized, about 15 minutes. Remove from the oven and let cool completely.

Place a loaf tin, or similar-sized container, in the freezer.

When you're ready to churn, remove the tonka beans from the custard, if you used them; pour the custard into an ice cream machine; and churn according to the manufacturer's instructions. Once it's at soft-serve consistency, scoop the ice cream into the chilled tin and swirl in the pain perdu until evenly dispersed. Freeze before scooping.

Strawberry Ripple Ice Cream

Skip Wimbledon and make this ice cream instead.

Makes about 1 quart

FOR THE STRAWBERRY RIPPLE

1½ cups strawberries (about 9 ounces/260 g), hulled and quartered
5 tablespoons (62 g) granulated sugar
Salt (optional)
½ lemon (optional)

FOR THE ICE CREAM

2 cups (456 grams) heavy cream
1 cup (226 grams) whole milk
5 large egg yolks
½ cup (100 grams) granulated sugar

To make the strawberry ripple, place the strawberries in a medium bowl, add the sugar, and toss to combine. Let the berries macerate in the fridge for about 12 hours, tossing now and again to distribute the sugar. (While it's best to leave the fruit overnight, if time is short, a few hours will do.)

Transfer the strawberries and all their puddled juices to a small heavy pot, bring to a simmer over medium heat, and cook, stirring to prevent scorching, until the fruit breaks down, about 20 minutes. In the end, this should have the texture of a loose jam. Taste and add a pinch of salt and/or squeeze of lemon juice if needed. Let the ripple cool completely. Covered, it holds for 5 days in the fridge.

Place a loaf tin, or similar-sized container, in the freezer. Make the ice cream base following the directions for our Fior di Latte Ice Cream (page 342).

Let the custard cool, then churn it or refrigerate until ready to use. When ready to churn it, pour the custard base into an ice cream maker and churn it according to the manufacturer's instructions. When it is at a soft-serve consistency, scoop it into the chilled baking pan, dollop the strawberry mixture over the ice cream, and, using the back of a spoon, ripple it through the base. Careful not to overmix! The streaks of strawberry should remain distinct. Cover the loaf tin with plastic wrap and place in the freezer to set. Allow at least 3 to 4 hours before scooping

Butterscotch Ice Cream

Dark and stormy—just how we like it. If you don't have bourbon, whiskey or rye will work.

Makes 1 quart

FOR THE ICE CREAM

¾ cup (280 grams) heavy cream
1½ cups (340 grams) whole milk
5 large egg yolks
Scant 2 tablespoons (20 grams) granulated sugar

FOR THE CARAMEL

½ cup plus 2 tablespoons (120 grams) packed dark brown sugar
2 tablespoons (30 grams) unsalted butter
¾ cup (180 grams) heavy cream
Several large pinches of flaky salt
2 tablespoons (20 grams) bourbon, or more to taste

Make the ice cream base following the directions for our Fior di Latte Ice Cream (page 342). While it cools, make the caramel.

Place the brown sugar in a small heavy pot and heat over very low heat to make a caramel; do not stir as the caramel forms, simply swirl the pan to encourage even dissolving and heating. After about 6 minutes, the syrup will smoke and puff like a volcano before turning a deep, dark brown. Watch carefully at this point: You don't want the caramel to burn, though you do want it dangerously close to the line. Immediately turn off the heat and add the butter, swirling to combine. Whisk in the cream and salt until thoroughly incorporated.

Whisk the butterscotch into the ice cream base until combined, then pour in the bourbon. Taste for potency and add more bourbon, if you like, bearing in mind that its flavor will be muted when frozen. Let the base cool completely, then churn or refrigerate until ready to use. When ready to churn the ice cream, pour the custard base into an ice cream maker and churn according to the manufacturer's instructions. Freeze the ice cream in a sealed container for at least 3 to 4 hours before scooping.

Honey Lavender Ice Cream

Lavender, used judiciously in this ice cream, brings a whiff of Provence to the end of a meal. You will know if you have used too much!

We purchase dried lavender from a local tea shop.

Makes 1 quart

2 cups (456 grams) heavy cream
1 cup (226 grams) whole milk
1 teaspoon organic dried lavender
5 large egg yolks
¼ cup (50 grams) granulated sugar
3 tablespoons honey (45 ml), plus more to taste

To make the ice cream base, warm the cream and milk together in a medium heavy pot over high heat until the liquid quivers, about 5 minutes; it should be at 180 degrees, just below a simmer. Quickly add the dried lavender and turn off the heat.

Let steep until the milk and cream are infused with the lavender's flavor, about 20 minutes. Strain through a fine-mesh sieve into another medium heavy pot; discard the lavender. Set the pot over medium heat and rewarm the dairy to just under a simmer, about 180 degrees.

As the dairy rewarms, place the yolks, sugar, and honey in the bowl of a stand mixer fitted with the whisk attachment, or add them to a medium bowl and use a handheld mixer, and beat on high speed until the yolks turn pale yellow and double in volume, at least 5 minutes. (Beating in air at this stage is vital to producing a stretchy ice cream.) Then continue making the custard base, following the instructions for our Fior di Latte Ice Cream (page 342). Taste the finished custard and add an additional tablespoon or so of honey if needed. Let the ice cream base cool completely, at least 30 minutes. This holds, covered in the fridge, for up to 2 days.

When you're ready to make the ice cream, pour the chilled base into your ice cream maker and churn according to the manufacturer's instructions.

Freeze in a sealed container for at least 3 to 4 hours before scooping.

Fig Leaf Ice Cream

I became obsessed with pale green ice creams after developing a mint stracciatella ice cream for Jess. Since we often get fig leaves from the market in the summertime—their unexpected coconut flavor is magical—I started to play around with this recipe. Extracting the leaves' color was a must!

To perfume each scoop with the flavor of fig leaves, I infused both the cream for the ice cream's custard base *and* the syrup that sweetens the base at the very end. It did the trick.

—Fiona Thomas, head pastry chef

Makes 1 quart

FOR THE FIG LEAF SYRUP

1 cup (200 grams) granulated sugar
¾ cup (180 grams) water
4 fig leaves, rinsed

FOR THE ICE CREAM

2 cups (456 grams) heavy cream
¾ cup (170 grams) whole milk
8 fig leaves, rinsed and dried
5 large egg yolks
¼ cup (50 grams) granulated sugar
Salt

To make the fig leaf syrup, combine the sugar and water in a small pot, bring to a simmer over very low heat, and simmer just until the sugar dissolves, 2 to 3 minutes. Remove from the heat and let cool to room temperature.

WHILE THE SYRUP COOLS, BEGIN TO MAKE THE ICE CREAM BASE: Warm the cream and milk in a medium heavy pot over high heat until the liquid starts to quiver, about 5 minutes; it should be at 180 degrees.

Take the pot off the heat and quickly add the 8 fig leaves. Press down on them to submerge them if they rise up to the surface. Let steep until the dairy is infused with the leaves' flavor, at least 1 hour.

Remove the fig leaves from the dairy, wringing out their liquid back into the pot before discarding them. Set the dairy aside until ready to use. This holds, covered in the fridge, for 1 to 2 days.

To finish the fig syrup, bring a small pot of water to a boil over high heat. Place an ice bath near the stove. Add the 4 fig leaves to the boiling water and blanch until bright green, 1 to 2 minutes. Drain and quickly plunge the leaves into the ice bath, setting their color. Once they are cool, remove the leaves, squeeze bone-dry, and blot off any remaining water with a kitchen towel.

(Continued)

Roughly chop the blanched leaves and add them to a blender or food processor. Add 1 cup of the cooled fig leaf syrup and blend until a sharp green color emerges, about 1 minute. Set a sieve over a small bowl and strain the syrup into the bowl. Using the back of a ladle, press down on the leafy bits to extract as much flavor as possible, then discard them. Set the syrup aside. It holds, covered in the fridge, for a few days. You will need 1 cup (240 ml) syrup for this recipe; the excess syrup, which can be stored indefinitely, is a great way to flavor soda water to work into cocktails.

To finish the ice cream base, set the pot of infused dairy over high heat and bring to just under a simmer, about 180 degrees.

Then continue making the custard base with the eggs and sugar, following the instructions for our Fior di Latte Ice Cream (page 342). Pour the cooked custard into a bowl and let it cool to room temperature, at least 30 minutes. As it cools, stir in 1 cup (240 ml) of the fig leaf syrup, mixing until uniformly green.

Then continue making the custard base, following the instructions for our Fior di Latte Ice Cream (page 342). Taste the finished custard and add an additional tablespoon or so of honey if needed. Let the ice cream base cool completely, at least 30 minutes. This holds, covered in the fridge, for up to 2 days.

When you're ready to make the ice cream, pour the chilled base into your ice cream maker and churn according to the manufacturer's instructions. Season the base with a pinch of salt and stir to combine. Let the base cool completely, at least 30 minutes. This holds, covered in the fridge, for up to 2 days.

Freeze in a sealed container for at least 3 to 4 hours before scooping.

Cassata Ice Cream

This is our take on Sicilian ricotta ice cream, with all the flavors of a cassata. It doesn't use the usual custard base and it is actually made more like a sorbet. We make our own candied peel at King, but at home, we're more likely to just buy it.

Makes 1 quart

FOR THE SYRUP

¾ cup (180 grams) water
¾ cup plus 2 tablespoons (175 grams) granulated sugar

FOR THE ICE CREAM

1 pound (453 grams) fresh, whole-milk ricotta
½ cup (114 ml) heavy cream
2 tablespoons honey
Finely grated zest of 1 orange
Salt
½ cup (60 grams) dark chocolate, shaved into thin shards (it's easiest to do this starting with a large block of chocolate)
½ cup (60 grams) candied orange peel, cut into chip-sized pieces
½ cup (60 grams) unsalted pistachios, toasted and chopped into chip-sized pieces

To make the simple syrup, combine the water and sugar in a small pot and heat over medium heat until the sugar dissolves, then continue simmering until the syrup thickens slightly, 2 to 3 minutes. (If you have a thermometer, it should read about 180 degrees.) Turn off the heat and let the syrup cool to room temperature.

To make the ice cream base, using a food processor or blender, whiz up to combine the ricotta, simple syrup, cream, honey, orange zest, and a pinch of salt and process until everything is thoroughly combined, about 2 minutes.

Place a loaf tin, or similar-sized container, in the freezer.

Spoon the base into your ice cream maker and churn according to the manufacturer's instructions. When it is at a soft-serve consistency, transfer the ice cream into the chilled container and stir in the chocolate, orange peel, and pistachios until evenly distributed.

Cover the ice cream and freeze until set, at least 3 to 4 hours, before scooping it.

Pear Sorbet

This sorbet can easily be made into a granita by freezing the base and, once set, scraping it with the tines of a fork. Although this is true of any sorbets, these flakes make an especially fluffy granita.

Makes 1 quart

FOR THE SYRUP

⅔ cup (133 grams) granuated sugar
½ cup (120 grams) water
¼ cup (80 grams) light corn syrup

FOR THE SORBET

6 ripe pears (2½ to 3 pounds), rinsed
½ cup (100 grams) granulated sugar
Zest of 2 lemons removed in strips with a vegetable peeler (reserve the lemons)
About 3 tablespoons (45 ml) brandy, preferably Poire Williams

To make the simple syrup, combine the sugar, water, and corn syrup in a small pot, bring to a simmer over medium heat, and simmer until the sugar dissolves, 2 to 3 minutes. Remove from the heat.

To make the sorbet base, while the syrup is still warm, peel and core the pears, then cut in half lengthwise. Add the pear skins, cores, and seeds into the warm syrup.

Transfer the halved pears to a large pot that is wide enough to hold them in a single layer. Toss in the sugar and lemon zest. Juice the lemons and add the juice to the pot. Turn the pears cut side down and splash over the brandy, adding enough to just moisten the fruit. Cover the pears with a cartouche (see page 15) and simmer over medium heat until they soften and yield to the poke of a knife, 15 to 20 minutes. Remove from the heat.

Remove and discard the lemon zest and add the cooked pears, with all the juices, to a blender or food processor. Whiz until a smooth puree forms; leave the puree in the blender or processor.

Strain the sugar syrup through a strainer set over a small bowl, pressing on the pear skins and seeds to extract all their flavor, then discard. Add 1 cup of the pear syrup to the pear puree and whiz to combine. Taste and add more syrup if needed. Refrigerate this base until it feels cold to the touch, about 1 hour.

Pour the sorbet base into an ice cream machine and churn according to the manufacturer's instructions. Once it is thick and creamy, transfer the sorbet to a sealable container and freeze until firmly set, 3 to 4 hours, before serving.

Persimmon Sorbet

This sorbet must be made with overripe persimmons. We've used a mix of both Fuyu and Hachiyas, making sure they're always fit to burst. For Hachiyas this is especially critical—if the flesh doesn't wobble like jelly, it's inedible.

So choose extra-ripe fruit, and this sorbet will be perfectly fluffy with a lush honey flavor.

Makes 1 quart

1½ pounds (680 grams) overripe Fuyu and/or Hachiya persimmons
1 cup (195 grams) packed light brown sugar
1 cup (240 ml) water
1 cinnamon stick
Juice of 1 lemon, plus more if needed

Remove the stems from the persimmons and halve them root to tip. Scoop out the flesh, removing any black seeds, and transfer the flesh to a food processor or blender. Whiz the persimmons until a smooth puree forms; leave the puree in the machine.

Combine the brown sugar, water, and cinnamon stick in a saucepan, bring to a gentle simmer over medium-low heat, and simmer until the sugar dissolves, 3 to 4 minutes. Remove from the heat and let cool completely; discard the cinnamon stick.

Add the brown sugar syrup to the puree and whiz until combined, then blend in the lemon juice. Taste—depending on the sweetness of your persimmons, more lemon juice may be necessary; in the end, this should taste bold.

Transfer this base to a container and chill in the fridge until the flavors meld, at least 2 hours. The base can be held for up to 3 days.

Pour the sorbet base into an ice cream machine and churn according to the manufacturer's instructions. Once it is thick and creamy, transfer the sorbet to a sealable container and freeze until firmly set, 3 to 4 hours, before serving.

Tangerine Sorbet

Any orange citrus works here: mandarins, clementines, tangerines, oranges. If possible, try to find fruit with the stems and leaves still attached, as that makes a pretty presentation.

Serves 10

FOR THE SYRUP

1⅓ cups (267 grams) granulated sugar
1 cup (240 grams) water
6 tablespoons (120 grams) light corn syrup

FOR THE SORBET

16 tangerines (5 to 6 pounds), preferably with leaves and stems still attached
2 to 3 tablespoons Grand Marnier, plus more for serving
1 to 2 lemons, halved

To make the syrup, combine the sugar, water, and corn syrup in a small pot, bring to a simmer over medium heat, and simmer until the sugar dissolves, about 2 minutes. Remove from the heat and let cool completely.

To prepare the fruit, slice off the top ½ to ¾ inch from 10 of the tangerines, creating lids. Place these lids on a baking sheet lined with parchment paper. With a sharp knife, run the blade's point between the peel and flesh of each fruit, *and* the lids. Loosen and scoop out the flesh from each with a small sharp spoon, taking care to keep the fruit's shape intact, and transfer the flesh to a medium bowl.

Arrange the hollowed-out tangerines on the baking sheet with the lids and freeze until rock-hard, at least 2 hours. These hold, sealed in a container, for about a week.

Squeeze all the juice from the flesh and strain it through a sieve set over a medium bowl; working in batches will make life easier. Press on the pulp to extract every last drop of juice and then discard.

Juice the remaining 6 tangerines, straining the juice through a sieve set over a bowl and pressing upon the pulp just as before. You will need 2½ cups strained tangerine juice. Stir 2½ cups of the cooled syrup into the juice, then add the Grand Marnier and enough lemon juice to taste.

Pour the base into an ice cream machine and churn according to the manufacturer's instructions. Once it is thick and creamy, scoop the sorbet into the bellies of the frozen tangerines, slightly overfilling them so some squidges over when they are topped with their lids. Freeze until firmly set, at least 2 hours. Kept covered in the freezer, these hold for a few days.

Just before serving, transfer the fruit to the refrigerator to soften the sorbet slightly, about 15 minutes. Splash a little Grand Marnier over the sorbet in each tangerine shell, if you like.

Papa Keith's Colonel

When life gives us lemons (this recipe needs a few), we—especially if you're my Papa Keith—make a French lemon sorbet and drench it with ice-cold vodka.

As my grandfather knew, this is a perfect end to a lazy lunch in the sun. Feel free to be light-handed with the booze . . . though I'm not sure why you would.

—Jess

Makes 1 quart

FOR THE LEMON SYRUP

Zest of 7 lemons peeled in strips with a vegetable peeler; reserve the lemons
1¼ cups (250 grams) granulated sugar
¾ cup (180 grams) water
¼ cup (80 grams) light corn syrup

FOR THE COLONEL

2 cups (480 ml) lemon juice (from about 12 lemons, including the 7 for the syrup), strained, or more if necessary
Ice-cold vodka, to finish

To make the syrup, drop the strips of zest into a small heatproof bowl.

Combine the sugar, water, and corn syrup in a small pot, bring to a simmer over medium heat, and simmer until the sugar just dissolves, about 3 minutes. Remove the pot from the heat and pour the hot syrup over the peel-in-waiting.

Let the syrup cool to room temperature, then cover and let steep in the fridge overnight.

When ready to make the sorbet, remove the lemon zest from the syrup and add 2 cups (480 ml) of the syrup to a pitcher. Whisk in the freshly squeezed lemon juice (you're basically making lemonade) and adjust with more juice or syrup to taste—we like a sweet pucker!

Pour the sorbet base into an ice cream machine and churn according to the manufacturer's instructions. Once it is thick and creamy, transfer the sorbet to a sealable container and freeze until firmly set, 3 to 4 hours, before serving.

Scoop the sorbet into coupes and top each with a shot of chilled vodka. Serve immediately.

CHAPTER 15

Celebrations

THERE IS NO GREATER JOY THAN A ROOM OF FRIENDS AND FAMILY, SITTING AROUND A table laden with delicious food and wine. When you dine at King with a group larger than six, we call this a celebration for that very reason. And there are dishes simply meant for these larger gatherings. A cassoulet or pot-au-feu is a labor of love. To serve it to any fewer would be a disservice.

Here you'll find a few menus showcasing the balance and joy of putting together some of our favorite celebration recipes. For us, the preparation is just as satisfying as the subsequent meal itself. Find time to make yourself a prep list and research the best butcher or local farmers' market in advance. Set the table with linens and fresh flowers and bring out your tallest tapered candles.

Some recipes are more involved and will require a full day of cooking at home—approach this with the meditative joy we hope it brings. Plan ahead and make whatever is possible in advance.

With much of the hard work done, invite plenty of people over to celebrate. Then ring some more friends and get them over! When it's time to party, there can never be too many people at the table.

WINE PAIRINGS

Wine is as important as food at King, and none is complete without a good glass. Our wine list at King mirrors the menu—short and curated, a reflection of our favorite producers in France and Italy. It is just two sides of a piece of paper. At first, its length was restricted more by our purse strings and cramped storage than by conscious choice. These days, I find joy and discipline in maintaining a curated list.

Luckily, there are more delicious things to drink in the world today than ever, and we keep our list changing daily, much like the food. We like to support thoughtful, low-intervention winemakers and conscientious farmers who let their work in the vines shine. If that is your starting point in choosing wine, it will only ever get better.

The following pairings are our ideal, meant to serve as inspiration rather than prescription. These are not your everyday wines, but we're here to dream big! If Suenen, for example, is not within easy grasp, and it isn't for most of us, any well-made Champagne will do well.

We have hosted many wine dinners at King and the quantity of bottles opened really depends on your guests. That said, it is safe to assume two to three glasses for each guest who is drinking and roughly five glasses in every bottle. Or, if the spirit moves you, do as we would at King and upgrade to a large format. Our beloved King rosé, made in partnership with our friends at Kermit Lynch and Domaine de Fontsainte in Corbières, only comes in magnums, and there is something particularly satisfying about plonking a few of those down on the table.

—Annie

WINTER

Roasted Chestnuts

Vin Chaud

~

Cassoulet Toulousain
Baguette
Salade Verte with Anchoïade

Syrah Côte-Rôtie Côteaux de Tupin, Jean-Michel Stephan

~

Tangerine Sorbet

Champagne La Cocluette, Suenen

SPRING

Leek and Chèvre Tart

Chenin Blanc La Perlée, La Porte Saint Jean

~

Asparagus with Anchovy Butter

~

Roast Leg of Lamb with Braised Lettuce and Peas

Rosé Champagne Creux d'Enfer, Roses de Jeanne

~

Lavender Crème Caramel

Banyuls Reserva, Domaine de la Tour Vieille

SUMMER

Petit Aioli

Champagne V.O. Grand Cru, Jacques Selosse

~

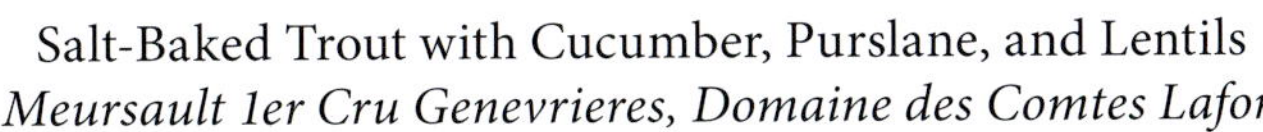

Salt-Baked Trout with Cucumber, Purslane, and Lentils

Meursault 1er Cru Genevrieres, Domaine des Comtes Lafon

~

King's Summer Pudding

Moscato d'Asti, Vietti

AUTUMN

Gruyère and Thyme Gougères

~

Mushroom Toasts

Beaujolais-Villages, Jean Foillard

~

Pot-au-Feu

Chambolle-Musigny 1er Cru Les Feusselottes, Cecile Tremblay

~

Fig and Almond Tart

Vin Santo, Fèlsina

ACKNOWLEDGMENTS

FIRST AND FOREMOST, WE WOULD LIKE TO THANK THE FOKS, THE FRIENDS OF KING—OUR guests—who have supported us from the jump. To the regulars who have returned time and time again, some three or four times a week (you know who you are) or those who have made special visits over the years, thank you for choosing us. We would not be where we are without you.

To the King Team past and present: Thank you for your brilliant spirit that pumps life through our restaurant each and every day. You are, and continue to be, the best teammates, full of passion, generosity, and fun. Thanks for inspiring us in our work (and pre-shift dancing) and for making King what it is. A special—and huge—thank you to the mighty kitchen team. Your tenacity and drive have no limits and your efforts in helping to pull the recipes together allowed us to get this book to the finish line (our kitchen now has recipes!). Huge thanks to Chef Angeles (affectionately Tina) for developing and leading such a merry band of cooks and for your recipe contributions. This book wouldn't be here without you. To Chef Fiona, our pastry whiz, for perfecting Day 1 recipes and creating the new. Thanks to Nathalie de la Fontaine, our brilliant general manager, for steering the ship, Laurel Delaney for the cocktails, Summer Fly our sous chef, Lucy Gibson, Auds Falk, Molly Morgan, and our OG Sade—thank you for every bite of deliciousness.

A huge thank you to our editorial team—we made it!

Thank you to our patient and scrupulous recipe testers: First, to Kitty and Savannah for leading this huge charge! Turning notes on parchment paper into real-life recipes is not easy; thank you for your patience! Our chefs at King and later Jupiter for helping us measure, weigh, and re-weigh ingredients. Sade, Nate, and Rex. Marcy, Sean Anderson, Maya Greenfeld, Michelle Fuerst, Matthew Thompson, Teasel Muir-Harmony, Catherine Wallace, Wally Anderson, Yossy Arefi, Victoria Conran, Pinkney Gould, Jordan Hepner, Hugh McIntosh, Zeke Emmanuel, Jake Platt, Marcy Pleener, Ivy Rogers, Suzanne and John Simon, Lily Soule, Bettina Stern, Natacha Stojanovic, Matthew Thompson, and Miles and Lauren Scissorhands.

Thank you to our purveyors who grow, raise, and catch the ingredients that have inspired so much in these pages.

And to our families.

Finally, to the nonnas and grand-mères who continue to keep these cooking traditions alive and to the women who went before us and who inspired us to give it a go: Darina, Alice, Ruthie, Sian, Vera, Skye, Belle, Margot. . . . We follow your lead.

INDEX

Page numbers in *italics* refer to photographs.

ABOUT THE AUTHORS

ANNIE SHI is the co-owner of the acclaimed restaurants King and Jupiter and owner of Lei in New York. Annie leads the beverage programs, translating the kitchens' seasonal and ingredient-driven philosophies into exceptional wine and cocktail offerings. She was selected as a *Forbes* 30 Under 30 and has written for and been featured in publications including the *New York Times*, *Food & Wine*, and *New York*. Prior to King, Annie started her career in finance and is a graduate of Yale University. She lives in New York City with her husband and two children.

JESS SHADBOLT shared her first stove with her mother, Lys. In 2008 she joined the River Café in London as the assistant to chefs Rose Gray and Ruthie Rogers, and after a stint at Ballymaloe Cookery School in Ireland, she returned to the restaurant as a chef. In 2016 she moved to New York City. She is the co-owner and chef of King—now her home away from home. When she is out of the kitchen, she can be found cooking for her friends and family either in Fort Greene, Brooklyn, or on Aldeburgh Beach on the Suffolk coast in the UK.

CLARE DE BOER is a five-time James Beard–nominated chef and a writer. She's the owner of Stissing House and co-owner of King, but is most often found in her home kitchen cooking for her husband and four sons. Clare writes about food for the *New York Times* and *Vogue* and has a bimonthly recipe newsletter, *The Best Bit*. She lives between Brooklyn and upstate New York.